The Joseph Communications:

# the Spaces Between

For the planet and every soul it so selflessly supports.

The Joseph Communications:

# the Spaces Between

Michael G. Reccia

First Paperback Printing March 2019

Published by Band of Light Media Limited © 2019

Band of Light Media Limited,
Briercliffe,
Burnley,
Lancashire,
United Kingdom

www.thejosephcommunications.co.uk

ISBN: 978-1-906625-16-0

Printed in the United Kingdom by Pioneer Print Solutions Ltd.

# CONTENTS

# Terminology: 'the Field', 'the Fall' – a brief explanation

You will find that Joseph sometimes refers to 'the Field' and 'the Fall' in this book. For readers new to the Communications, here is a brief explanation of these terms.

## The Field

When referring to 'the Field' Joseph is describing the conscious field of thought-energy we, as spirits on Earth, are surrounded by and live within. Every second of our lives we project our thoughts and beliefs as to the nature of reality into this energy field. The Field is actually created and maintained *by us*, but we have lost sight of this fact. As a result of us forgetting this, which is in itself as a result of 'the Fall' (see below), the Field is not operating as it was originally intended to. It was supposed to serve us, but at the moment we, in effect, serve it. It exhibits, and seeks to perpetuate in us, a negative charge and outlook, and, because of this and its disconnection with God-Light, is maintaining itself and us via a finite and dwindling amount of energy. The Field in its present state, and therefore also we as human beings existing within it, cannot last much longer. Joseph urges us to re-energise the Field with God-Light and, by doing so, to transform it and take control of it once again for the betterment and continuance of mankind and of the planet.

## The Fall

...is a term that Joseph applies to a complex decision and action taken by human souls millions of years ago which resulted in a cataclysmic change in vibration that plunged the Earth into a darkness we and the planet are still suffering from and feeling the effects of. This change in vibration separated us in conscious thought from our God-heritage and resulted in the negative, violent, power-hungry world and society we currently live in.

*'There are more things in heaven and earth, Horatio,*
*Than are dreamt of in your philosophy.'*
**Hamlet**

## An Introduction by Michael

'Reccia here came fifth in class …and he's as thick as my clog!'*

Thus quipped my traditionally tweed-jacketed, leather-elbow-patched physics teacher Mr Hamilton, addressing the thirty or so teenage boys present. Towering over me as he did so, he held my exam papers aloft in one hand and waved them above his head, expressing in equal measure his wonder and disgust that someone as stupid as myself could actually have gained a respectable fifth-in-class position in a college physics exam.

Considering my age now as I write this and the fact that I was in my early teens when the above sarcasm regarding my intelligence quotient was presented to a class in the mid sixties, Mr Hamilton, then seemingly in his fifties, must surely have long ago exited the college lab with its faint but slightly worrying aroma of leaking gas – and indeed this world – destined for a far more enlightened vibration where his faith in the absolute immutability of the laws of physics would have instantly been challenged by the amazing new surroundings he found himself in.

Also, I retrospectively beg to differ with his put-down statement. I was not, as it turns out, 'thick' at all – I was introverted, shy and latently mediumistic (unbeknownst to me at the time), and my ability to absorb knowledge was directly proportional to a teacher's ability to impart it. How adept we are at undermining a child's potential at a formative and impressionable age; how determined to chip away at any seedling ability a youngster might be subconsciously propagating before it has been given the opportunity to blossom and to achieve great things... Much wiser to adopt a spiritual approach when connecting with the next generation, carefully considering what a little encouragement and kindness and insight on our part can accomplish.

I digress.

The reason I begin the introduction to this book by bringing into focus my feeble grasp of the fundaments of physics as a student in the sixties is not in order to vent some long-held grudge against my former physics master. Indeed, no such grudge exists. Quite the opposite, in that I have Mr Hamilton to thank for one vivid, positive and very relevant memory of those times spent in bewilderment, surrounded by test tubes, Bunsen burners, bullies and chalked-on-the-board, complex, impenetrable equations proclaiming to the world in numbers, letters, symbols and mistaken 'absolutes' how things actually operate here, scientifically speaking ...that being of a lesson given by him which involved a prism.

As you will doubtless be aware, a prism is a (usually) glass object, commonly triangular in shape, with refracting surfaces set at an acute angle to each other, endowing it with the ability to split white light into the colours of the spectrum. To demonstrate this, 'Hamish' Hamilton (as we smirking little tykes liked to call him when we were quite sure he wasn't within earshot) proceeded to shine a beam of light through one face of said prism and, *lo and behold*, out from its opposite face spilled luminous bands of red, orange, yellow, green, blue, indigo and violet. Entering the object was a band of white light; exiting it was an orchestra of glorious colour.

...Which image is highly significant regarding the contents of this book, and has provided me with an appropriate opening metaphor for the intentions of the eighth *Joseph Communications* title.

First, however, and if you will indulge me, I must backtrack a little to comment on what, until the concluding chapter of this book, had been the ongoing process for well over a decade of Joseph and myself working symbiotically via a trance-state connection as a 'prism' for the viewpoint of a vast, spiritually enlightened group soul (a collective of millions of evolved spirits) that is deeply concerned for the welfare and future of humanity, for the animal kingdom and for planet Earth.

Successfully concluding – or 'bringing through' – Joseph's penultimate title *From Here To Infinity* had given me immense satisfaction. I was much relieved that the book was finally complete and safely in this world as eighteen chapters manifested via an equal number of trance sessions. The process, however, had left me completely exhausted and I had become pale of face, occasionally uncoordinated of limb and frequently disorientated. The demanding monthly sessions that, with my full consent, had allowed Joseph's ancient, discarnate spirit to repeatedly take control of my physical body and mind in order to speak to the world as directly as he could by gently shifting my personality to one side and taking centre stage for the duration of each session had wreaked increasing havoc with my health and life energies. A further contributor to this depletion was the fact that, as the meetings were drawing to a conclusion, I was concurrently dealing with several personal life challenges, not least of which had been the sudden death of my mother.

Physically and mentally I found myself at a very low ebb and as a result decided that *From Here To Infinity* would be the last book I could allow Joseph to bring through by using my body, physical mind and vocal chords whilst I was in a trance state. With regard to his spiritual 'mission' I felt confident that everything that had needed to be said by Joseph and his soul group in order to effect urgently needed personal and global change *had* in fact been said by this point, and that it was now my task and that of the other members of the *Band of Light* (Joseph's term for our little group) – my beloved Jane, and Tony and David – to focus our remaining time on this planet on the not inconsiderable task of making as many souls around the world as we possibly could aware of the existence of Joseph's vitally important message and warning for humanity.

As my mind, body and spirit began to slowly reintegrate and work in harmony once more on a physical and mental level, and my vampire-like pallor, evident, as mentioned, at the time of the book's final trance meetings (honestly ...ask Jane, who wryly christened me 'Dracoole' at the time) gradually replaced itself with more socially acceptable skin tones, our work on behalf of *the Communications* continued to move forwards at its usual hectic pace. Ongoing imperatives included a commitment to producing e-book and audiobook versions of the six Joseph titles published thus far, and to this end I subsequently found myself reading and recording chapters from the books each week, talking into a mic in the studio of our hard-working, meticulous sound (and video) maestro Avey. Spanish and Dutch websites were also in an evolving but at this stage embryonic state, each intended to promote the wonderful word-for-word translations of the books we had been so graciously provided with, courtesy of selfless souls Maria-Luisa and Professor Paul de Troyer; and advertising campaigns, interviews, radio shows and the expansion of a social media presence were also being addressed.

While all this was happening Joseph continued to be a linked presence, making me aware through our connection of his next urgent agenda. He soon made it repeatedly and increasingly clear that he had set his sights on a further volume of *the Communications* and that, with my permission, there was an eighth, vitally important book he urgently desired to present to the world, the title of which he temptingly gave as *the Spaces Between*. Those three words alone were sufficiently intriguing to pique my interest, and, through that permanent connection between us that instantly blossomed into a trance state whenever the *Band of Light* met to build energy on our side of the equation for this purpose, I could feel Joseph's fervent wish to once again add to the expansive spiritual information he had already imparted to those who were willing to listen to and consider his words through his books. Further, his intentions with this proposed new title, considering the current state of the planet and his imperative to encourage souls to reconnect with their spiritual core and ask them to transmit Light into the world while there is still time to effectively do so in this current cycle made for a persuasive and topical argument.

That having been said, committing to the two additional years of trance work a further book would likely involve me in was not a decision I took lightly. Indeed, as an analogy I speculate that my particular personal experience of trance mediumship is not dissimilar to the trials of childbirth in that you put yourself through unimaginable discomfort then, once this has passed, declare that never again will you place yourself in such a vulnerable situation (being male in this life I can only guess as to the accuracy of this statement, of course – although, in my defence, I do have memories of a long-ago existence spent as a female). However, once you see the fruits of your labour taking their first steps out into the world and interacting with people (in my case, each new book and the overwhelmingly positive, life-changing response each new title generates in a great many readers worldwide) you forget your former staunch resolution and prepare to immerse yourself in the self same experience once more in order to deliver more of the same.

The 'discomfort' (as in fatigue and disorientation) caused by previous trance sessions quickly forgotten, or at least committed to a cobwebbed, rarely visited 'records room' at the back of my memory, I therefore said yes to Joseph and the further undertaking, and the four members of the *Band of Light* began to meet monthly once more to allow Joseph to deliver a complete chapter for the book within the dimension-spanning energy bubble (with a life of around forty to fifty-minutes duration) generated by the soul group for each session.

Part way through the process of capturing his words for the new title, and necessitating a break from work on *the Spaces Between* of a few months in order that we might hit our proposed publication deadline, Jane and I also indulged in the mammoth task of compiling a seventh *Joseph Communications* volume, the double-sized **Many Voices, One Mission,** which would at long last (we had been planning this for a decade) chronicle how our lives had been shared with a great many spirit communicators, and make available the enlightening addresses the two of us had received night and day, at work and at rest, from Joseph and various other members of his soul group over a four-year period when we had first become a couple way back in 2006.

...Harking back to and refining my earlier statement, *the Spaces Between* – and indeed any one of Joseph's books following the initial title *Revelation* – can in no sense be described as 'more of the same'. As with each of his subsequent books, the new volume made it clear from its first words and earliest chapters that there was so much more he wished to reveal from a higher vibrational viewpoint; that there *are* literally 'more things in heaven and earth' than the majority of souls here have ever considered there to be in a world that has increasingly turned its back on its spiritual origins, and that the new title's contents would be particularly relevant to those men and women earnestly attempting to counter the views of a materialistic society that believes the acquisition of things and power to be the ultimate goal and the key to a fulfilling existence here.

On this subject, I think most readers of this title would agree that humanity as a whole is currently, as a result of its societal imperative to satisfy our supposed collective 'needs' and material appetites, plundering the planet, has little to no regard for other species or the environment, and has mind-locked itself into a tunnel vision perception of existence that blinkers us as to what actually co-exists (and has every right to do so) with us right under our noses on a *physical* level, let alone on a spiritual one.

Addressing this physicality-and-self-centred, head-in-the-sand attitude, Joseph in these pages invites readers to look at this world through the prism of his soul group's elevated perspective and to discover wonders and long-hidden truths that, if acknowledged by significant numbers of souls here, must surely cause society to re-evaluate its place in the scheme of things on Earth and in the cosmos, to question humanity's self-appointed status as the Alpha species on this planet, and to make us aware of the fact that, in spiritual reality, we *share* this glorious world not only with many other precious and equally important physical forms of life but also with older, wiser and more vibrationally advanced entities, superior to us in both spiritual capability and the capacity to create positively and in harmony with the planet and its ecosystem. Additionally, Joseph also seeks to remind us of our core heritage, expanding our knowledge of how we function as the spiritual beings we really are and helping us to better understand ourselves and the ways in which we operate as creators and essential parts of the Whole.

Preliminaries over, I now invite you to now seek out a quiet corner away from the noise and speed of this world and prepare yourself. You are about to re-examine your seeming individuality, your role, position and purpose in this world and also to reacquaint yourself with the many wondrous, awe-inspiring, unseen neighbours who inhabit this planet's 'spaces between' in this, Joseph's final *Communications* book given in trance.

'What's that?' I hear you cry. 'Surely not! Say it isn't so, Michael!' Well, yes, I'm afraid you *did* read the above statement correctly. After much soul-searching and consideration I've made the decision out of necessity to quietly shelve my trance facility, being sufficiently in touch with the promptings of my higher self to know psychically that a further volume of trance work at this stage in my life would at best result in serious illness and at worst might just remove me from this level of conscious altogether – and there is still a great deal of work that I, working as part of the *Band of Light,* am tasked with undertaking on behalf of the Joseph message.

Based on reaction to earlier books and an eagerness for additional titles, I can imagine a percentage of regular Joseph readers will at this point be of heavy heart as they contemplate that the book they are holding represents the final *Joseph Communications* title – but to those dear seekers I would say *rest assured, you have not heard the last of Joseph or his message,* as his concluding statements in chapter eighteen will testify. Indeed, and as I write this introduction just four short weeks after completing the final trance session for this book, I am rapidly finding myself becoming immersed in the next stage of my work on Joseph's behalf, which involves even greater demands as his 'spokesperson', still linked to his loving, selfless soul and able to draw on his wisdom and comments via clairvoyant and clairaudient links when being interviewed or writing articles should I require further input and an expansion of the knowledge he has already imparted in his books.

Joseph himself would tell you that it has always been his intention via the eight books in the series to provide you with all the spiritual knowledge and connection you need to make a lasting, effective, harmonious difference to your life, the lives of others and the state of the planet; that he has dictated them in order that they might act as a blueprint (and also an urgent call to action) for a better world and facilitate for all of us an escape from the effects of the Fall (*the Fall* – Joseph's fourth book, is recommended reading for every soul that has ever wondered why the Earth is as it is and why we can't seem to find lasting peace), and that they should be regarded as an aid to spiritual 're-membering' that can regularly be referred to and which *needs to be put into practice,* rather than serving as a fleeting 'entertainment' to be read but once then put aside in anticipation of the next spiritual 'fix'.

In conclusion, I'm sure Joseph would also say, 'I've done my initial work now in transmitting the information (once again!)** and I will, of course, continue to support you all. I can advise. I can encourage. However, if you truly desire spiritual change and are prepared to work for it, it's now very much up to you. You have at your fingertips all the tools you need to change things and put the world to spiritual rights...

'...Please use them.

'Time grows short.

'You can't afford to waste a single day...'

Michael G. Reccia
November, 2018

* For those of you unfamiliar with the word, a 'clog' is a type of shoe with a thick wooden sole, often studded, and iconically relevant as part of the history of the north-west of England, where the college I attended was based.

** This is not the first time Joseph has brought this information through, unfortunately. Please see the other books in the series.

## Chapter One
# Revealing the Secrets of the 'Spaces Between'

**Michael's observations:** This initial chapter was delivered by Joseph as a result of the first trance meeting that had been held by the Band of Light since the completion of his previous book, *From Here to Infinity*, in 2015. In his introductory address, Joseph reconnects with the four of us instantly and seamlessly and sets the scene for *the Spaces Between*. At the end of the chapter, he also invites and answers questions from Jane, Tony and David, commenting on the passage of time, from our point of view, that had transpired since our last interaction with him and acknowledging the major changes we had made to our work situations during that period in order to devote more of our time and energies to bringing through and promoting *the Communications*.

Instances where Joseph pauses to consider his words, or initially uses one word then corrects himself with what he feels to be a more appropriate one, remain in the text here and at other points in this book – offering, as they do, an insight into his thought processes as he endeavours to translate and shoehorn non-verbal, multi-dimensional concepts into physical speech.

In opening this initial chapter I took a breath, allowed Joseph to move in and take control, sidestepped my physical mind and body, and he simply began to speak – offering no title for his address. For each of the seventeen subsequent communications in this book, however, and in a change from his delivery pattern for previous books in the series, he provided us with a carefully considered (and often cryptic) heading, a number of which reveal his wry sense of humour.

**Joseph:** We begin with *majesty*. We begin with *spectacle*. We begin with *creation* – with a look at creation as it operates in the wider, spiritual spheres of existence. Join me, then, if you will, in *space*; join me in observing one aspect of angelic projection and witness, with your angelic eyes, the unfolding of *potential*, the unfolding of *adventure*, the unfolding of *experience* on and within billions of different spheres and worlds that have been created by the angelic host. This is a far cry from your normal, confined, everyday view of life. This, however, in the greater reality that awaits you, *is* your normal life. This was your start point before you came here, and this is your destination, via the refining process of moving through the cleansing spheres and returning to your angelic roots and inheritance.

I realise that you cannot see the spectacle unfolding around you as I am able to, but believe me, as you travel in imagination and in trust with me, *it is there*. Try to imagine, if you can, magnificent colours and sounds and constructs of energy that reflect the glory of and are in total harmony with the Divine that is within you, that *is* you. Try to imagine splendour upon splendour, bliss upon bliss, and the wonder of a hundred million different worlds that you can choose to visit and move through …in order to gain experience …in order to bring more joy and possibilities to yourself, to the angelic host and to the Divine … and in order to evolve and become more than you were before you set foot on these particular spheres and tasted the sweet fruits of experience that they have to offer you.

This book is called *the Spaces Between* for the reason I am about to reveal, but on an angelic level *there are no 'spaces between'*. For example, what you perceive as being an empty void between worlds when you look into the night sky is *alive…*

**…Alive, and not empty at all.**

Alive and filled with *potential*. Alive with the promise of that which 'not yet is' but *will* be, *could* be, *might* be …potential that is about to *become* …potential that is being examined and considered by the angelic host in order that greater splendour and beautiful new worlds and new experiences can be brought forth, can be created. And, so, the 'spaces' you perceive between the heavenly bodies and the 'spaces' between the planets are, in spiritual reality, areas of conception, areas of latent potential awaiting consolidation into form – and not actually spaces at all.

They are areas that are 'sleeping', that are 'considering', that are willing themselves *to be* through the volition of the angels who wish to create and to interface with new spheres of activity, new worlds of experience, new connections of matter … interweavings of matter that are formed into spheres by the wishes and the *intentions* of members of the angelic host so that other members of the host can enjoy moving through new vistas and new adventures – for the advancement of God, for the evolution of God and for the good and the evolution of the rest of the angelic host.

So, this is where we begin …with only a crude indication in words by me of your *true* life – *your original life*. And, having begun in this way, we must now leave that original life for a time, but with a promise that one day it will be yours again.

And, so, we now descend – literally – we *descend* through increasingly heavy vibrations towards the Earth. You will all have seen pictures of the Earth from space and will have noticed the cloud formations and the seas and the continents, and it is down towards these that we now descend …down through the cloud layers …down towards the continents …down towards the cities and towns or wherever it happens to be on Earth that you live (or *believe* that you live) at the moment …down towards your house …down through the roof of your house …down into your favourite room from which you regularly look out onto the world.

I would like you for a few moments to consider the two sides of the 'pair of scales' that I have given you. On the one side, there is the majesty and splendour of angelic creation …and there, on the other pan of the scales, is *you* – quite comfortable, perhaps; quite content, perhaps – sitting in your room, looking out of your window onto familiar surroundings. Those surroundings are only a *temporary* reality. Every aspect of them is a temporary reality, but for you at this moment that 'reality' on your side of the scales is, perhaps, all that you have ever considered up to this point. You fit into a society. You organise your work time and your free time according to that society. You work, eat, shop, sleep and, in doing so, you often do not find the time to appreciate or even consider the *physical* splendours of the world you are living on – let alone the spiritual ones.

From this viewpoint and this limited approach to life, not only can you not imagine the splendour of existing as part of the angelic host – you cannot even see, because you are so tied into societal programming, *the splendour and wonder of nature around you*. And, you concentrate instead on an individualised view governed by a collective, societal template of how your life 'should be'. And, as the years inevitably progress from birth to your exit from this world, **'how life should be'** is drummed into you and dictated by society.

So, the societal template becomes 'all'. Your societal filter of the world solidifies and consolidates and becomes 'all'. You may travel to different continents or simply journey no further than the corner shop, but those journeys – both the seemingly expansive adventure of travelling around the world and the modest journey of just walking down the street – encapsulate you further, reinforce your view that 'this is all there is' and often become the entire measure of your individual world.

How often do you look beyond that view …search for perspectives beyond that which is physical and familiar? You may watch the news on television in order to broaden your global view; but, again, that news and those viewpoints are coloured and biased by societal programming. They present life to you in a certain way and, although the news may be occurring half a world away, it still reinforces and entrenches your *localised* view of how society works and what to expect from it. And, so, you accept and fit into a life that is 'comfortable' ...even when it is *uncomfortable*. What I mean by that is, it is 'comfortable' because its template is *familiar* and because the alternatives are frightening, are unknown, and it is far easier to run along the 'rails' of society – accepting the world as it is presented to you – than to question your perspective and life view, to question your input from society and to seek to expand your vision.

With regard to certain stages in your life, society also conditions you as to how you should behave and how you should react on a mental level and physical level once you reach those stages but, unfortunately, never considering how you should approach them on a *spiritual* level – despite you having religions that purport to do that for you. Religion helps you to fit into society, and religion's view of Divinity and spiritual power is often one that is based on *control* and not one that is truly linked with the realities and truths of spiritual power and potential.

Society dictates that you must go to school. It is considered essential that you learn certain things, but those things are, for the most part, designed to fit you – slot you without questioning – into that society so that it can control you.

You are informed that the normal way of things is to produce a family, that you must provide a future generation so that that generation can also slot into society and reinforce... (and this is the first use of this word in this book, but you will have encountered it countless times in my others) ...*the Field* – the collective Field of human consciousness that controls you, feeds on the negative energetic emanations you emit as a spiritual being and keeps you running along that 'set of rails' as you head towards your exit from this world in a prescribed manner.

You are controlled by society so that you are informed, believe and absorb into your being the 'fact' – because it is presented to you as a fact – that as you grow older (which, in spiritual reality, doesn't happen, but we will examine this at a later date) your body begins to break down, your mental processes begin to break down, and you become more and more dependent on those around you, who then control you in a specific way as you age.

**...Again, societal programming.**

So, my first task in opening this book is to offer you a contrast to your present viewpoint, is to say: 'Here is the way that you are living at the moment; and here is the alternative – the splendour of creation that is, not only available to you but is yours by birthright!' And, by 'birthright' I mean by dint of you originally having been expelled ...[*laughing*] 'expelled' is the wrong word... *issued forth* in Love from the Divine as an angelic being in order to experience and bring that experience back to God.

Such a contrast of viewpoints! But, I realise I cannot talk about the wonders of angelic creation and hold those up against the way that your life is at the moment and expect you to instantly reject your established way of life to date, accept and embrace an angelic viewpoint and say: 'Yes, that is the way that reality *really* is.' That is not my intention in dictating this book. My task here is to say to you: 'You believe that your life is unfolding in a specific way, that it runs according to the clock and within the dictates and confines of society ...**AND IT DOES NOT!**'

What I am suggesting to you is that there are the 'spaces between' to consider and understand and that, if you were truly aware of your potential as an angelic being, you could at this very moment ...stand up in your home ...go over to a corner of your room ...take hold of the wall in that corner, knowing that *in spiritual reality* it is not solid at all ...lift it ...peel it back ... pull it towards yourself ...gaze through the hole you have created by doing so ...and witness with your *spiritual eyes* all manner of things that you would not have believed possible and that you would not have believed could exist from the restrictive physical, mental and spiritual viewpoints that have been imposed on you as a result of societal programming.

In this book we are going to examine what *actually* exists around you from a *spiritual* viewpoint ...the things that co-exist with you and can interact with you at any time during your physical life ...and the unseen influences that control, to an extent, what you are, what you achieve, how you feel and what you believe.

For example, there exist parasitical influences that can control and influence your health, and many of the illnesses and diseases that you contract have 'agendas'. There are also thought forms that make an unseen impression on your lives, and which we will examine as well as other sentient, unseen beings that interact with you subconsciously ...and sometimes negatively.

All this may sound a very dark prospect, but I will also counter the 'negative' aspects, because my mission is always to bring in *Light* to you, by revealing the *Light* influences that can help you to evolve and to grow and to re-examine your life and to rediscover and remember who and what you really are.

Additionally, this book will offer protection to you if you are seeking spiritually, because it will reveal exactly what is going on *behind the scenes* in those 'spaces between' I mentioned earlier. It will reveal the subtle, invisible interactions that take place between you all as human beings, and also the interactions that can take place between you as a human being and unseen influences that are spiritually based but not necessarily 'spiritual' in intent. This book will allow you to look at the Earth and your life on this planet in a different way ...to examine your place and role in the universe from an enhanced perspective ...to arm yourself, protect yourself and connect with the Light so that your life here will be of greater benefit to you and to your family

...and to become a channel for the Light for the other souls who are suffering around the globe, and also for the planet itself.

It will give you courage and knowledge to 're-member' – to reconnect yourself with who you really are.

**Joseph now addresses the Band of Light:** ...We have to start with an introduction to the book and, having done so, it might seem surprising to you that I did not also begin with a 're-introduction' between *us*. But, as Jane has quite rightly said in jest over the last few days: *Joseph will, no doubt, begin by saying that for him no time has passed and there has been no disconnection between 'now' and his last meeting with us.* I can condense what I wish to say into two words, and those are: *welcome back*! Welcome back into that connection with us that allows us to reinforce you; allows us to take charge, with your permission, of the direction in which the information is sent; and allows us to further the distribution of the information to souls around the globe.

I realise that for you 'time' *has* passed since we last communicated, according to the societal programming I have just been talking about. And, I have to begin by saying I am truly sorry (as I am truly sorry for *each* soul on Earth) that you have had challenges and situations around you that have seemed insurmountable. I am sorry that the Field has, as it does with *each* human being, tried to get in to influence and dampen down your ability to work as energetically as you did a couple of years ago (by your determining of time) and that it has attempted, at every twist and turn, to confine you and make you less able to bring out this information. But, having made the connection with me again, I – and others from the group soul – can invest in you the Light and correction in your energies that you need in order to live your lives and continue with your mission.

I have not been idle. I have, together with my colleagues 'behind the scenes', as it were, been reaching out to pinpoints of Light – to minds across the world, who have seen your advertising or seen the books mentioned on the internet or in reviews and in recordings, and we have gently suggested to them: 'Here is something that, if you listen to it or if you read it, will change your minds – *literally change your minds*!' So, behind the contacts you receive from people requesting the books, are members of the group soul who have been talking to those people, been gently having a subconscious, spiritual conversation with them, saying: 'This really is what you need. It's your choice, but we *recommend* that you pick up this information because you are ready for it. It will change your mind and your life.'

...We are at an early stage for questions because we have not yet begun to examine topics, but I would invite them now if there is anything you would like to ask on *any* matter.

**Jane:** Joseph, in the past Michael has suffered a lot after bringing the communications through. Is there anything you or the group could do to make it easier for him, or is there anything he should be doing to recover faster?

**Joseph:** As a disciplined soul he follows most of our directives. The problem comes, not from the communication with us (at the moment he is being held in Light and no harm can come to him) but the problem always comes from the Field that slows you down. When he is re-immersed in the Field, it pulls at him as a 'delicacy' ...as Light that can be absorbed ...as an energy source. And, there is always a gathering of negative beings around him who would use him, use his energies, for mischief and would deconstruct him if they could.

We try our very best not to let that happen but it is, unfortunately, the nature of the world you exist in that causes the problem and not our communication. It is the same Field that makes it impossible for me to communicate with you after a certain amount of time. It is a shutting down of that stream of Light-information by the darkness. We help as much as we can, and indeed Michael saw the Big Indian* last night, who was there to protect him as he was led back into this communication and who will be there for three more days to make sure he is as protected as possible.

The key is rest and order and an exclusion from the chaos of life until recovery has taken place. It would be ideal [*laughing*] if Michael were a monk in a monastery somewhere in medieval times where he could not be contacted or connected to for weeks on end. It is that type of quiet that is needed because the clamour of the world becomes overwhelming to his heightened senses. Do you see?

**Jane:** Yes.

**Joseph:** I am sorry that we cannot alleviate all the symptoms. Would that we could, but it is part of the task and part of what he has agreed to do.

**Tony:** Joseph, the books are gaining momentum and are selling well. We are translating them into other languages and are receiving wonderful testimonials from people around the world. People are asking about a 'next stage'. They want to form discussion groups. They want to go in greater depth into what they have read and their understanding of it with possible groups. Is that a way forward?

**Joseph:** You – and *we* – have an enormous task. We look at numbers …at numbers of souls that can be influenced whilst you still have the drive to influence them. What you have to ask at each stage is – *is this the most effective use of our time?*

As we see it, it is like having a three-dimensional globe in front of you (there are many more dimensions to it from our perspective, but from yours it is a three-dimensional globe) and all over that globe there are little pinpoints of Light …billions of little 'light bulbs', and billions of them are 'dark'. They are not illuminated. They are not 'black' or 'negative' – they are just not illuminated. Each time a book arrives with someone (And it is not that it simply has to *physically* arrive; it has to arrive *within*

25

*their soul.* They have to connect with it and say: 'I understand this. This is talking to me.') ...each time that happens one of those tiny 'bulbs' lights up. And, we stand around this globe – millions of us – and we wish for and want *every single* 'light bulb' to illuminate. So, we are concerned with the big picture and with getting the information to as many people as possible.

We applaud the decision, which we understand has been a difficult one, to drop the physical work that has taken up so much of your time. [*Michael: Joseph is here referencing David, myself and Jane's 'leap in the dark' decision, a couple of months prior to this communication, to end our hobby-magazine publishing business, which had provided the necessary finances to enable us to be able to bring through and promote the Joseph Communications.*] We applaud this because it creates a 'space' between us. That seeming void can now be filled with more opportunities to influence more souls and to switch on more 'light bulbs' – and we *will*, but we could not do so beforehand because there was so much for you to do. I understand completely the financial considerations from the viewpoint of societal programming that I have just been talking about. So, we again applaud your decision to push those to one side in order that more work can be done. And, more work *will* be done.

You do not have the time or energy to personally facilitate the organisation of study groups, and it must, therefore, be left to individuals to contact each other if they desire to examine *the Communications* further and to meet or join together for this purpose. Your task as the Band of Light is to create global awareness of *the Communications* and place the books in front of as many pairs of eyes as possible within your lifetimes.

The soul group will show you the way, and at all times, for all of you, you must acknowledge that there is a greater power that is in charge in expanding the information on an international level and that that power will flow through you.

I know it is a lot that we are asking at the moment (but we have asked a lot before and we are going to ask more in the future) that you have absolute faith in what you really are, which is part of God, and that God does not want his souls to suffer in the way that they are suffering on Earth because of the Fall, and that if you ask daily – hourly when necessary – the right path will be revealed.

Do you see that?

**Tony:** Thank you, Joseph, I do.

**Joseph:** Does that make sense?

**Tony:** It does indeed.

**Joseph:** David...

**David:** Joseph, just to take the theme full circle, would you like to reiterate the reasons why societal pressure can start to be 'countered', if you like, by just 'going away' for few minutes each day and connecting to the God-within and raising oneself above the Field?

**Joseph:** Yes. The purpose of this particular volume [*laughing*] is to 'raise eyebrows' ...is to initially shock people – but then to comfort and reassure them. We cannot dress things up. We have to show you a view of your world as it really is. I am not talking about the planet, but about the influences that surround people and about the way things really work. We have to give you that view of how things *really* work.

We have shown in the other books that you can connect to the God-within and that that will give you *power* for each day. And, of course, it will and is the most powerful thing to do, and you can also send out the Light once you are doing that. But, *knowledge is also power*, and I wish to give you knowledge as to how your life really is ...not your life according to the doctor, the government or the people who would sell you things under the pretence of saying that these things are 'good' for you ...not your life according to the view of society that you must grow older and become infirm, that you are only worth a certain number of years with regard to what you can contribute to society ...not your life with regard to you believing that you are insular, that you can lock your door and are 'safe' ...not your life with you regarding yourself as an individual that is in no way linked to or a part of what is going on in the rest of the world.

I intend to *disturb*, to *clear away* and then to re-establish the spiritual laws that apply to you so that I put you in control of your life ...*you*, the reader, in control of your life. What you then do with that knowledge is entirely up to you, according to your free will.

You can accept it or you can reject it, but at least you will have been given the knowledge. And that knowledge, in conjunction with the knowledge in the other books we have brought through, will provide a complete blueprint for spiritual ...not *existence* ... but spiritual *being* on this planet. And, those many souls who have already taken in the information from the other books will find this an essential manual explaining how to avoid some of the pitfalls of life, how to re-energise themselves, and how to protect and armour themselves against influences that, at this point, they probably do not realise exist.

So, to reiterate, yes, you have to become one with the God-within, and all the information I give you has to be viewed and considered from *that* viewpoint. But, in this book I also wish to enhance your knowledge of how life is being lived on this Earth at the moment. I wish to say: 'This is how you *think* your life is ...but this is how it *really* is. This is what you *think* you are capable of ...and this is what you are *truly* capable of. This is how you feel in a life that seems to become diminished as you grow older, and there is no need to feel this way – there is no need to feel useless, no need to feel old, no need to feel ill ...all these things can be effectively combatted by *you*.'

This is a book to disturb but also *enhance* your life by looking at what exists when you lift that 'corner of the room' and stare out into the hitherto unseen and unacknowledged spiritual reality here. Does that answer your question?

**David:** Yes, thank you.

---

* The 'Big Indian' (our nickname for a wonderful, wise, exalted spirit) is an active member of the group soul. He had appeared suddenly and stood silently and protectively by Michael's side the night before this trance session took place (you can read some of his addresses in *The Joseph Communications* book – *Many Voices, One Mission*).

## Chapter Two
## The Unseen Chorus

**Joseph:** Today's chapter is called 'The Unseen Chorus'. As you read this book, you are being made aware of communication from a communicator that you cannot see. Not only can you not see the trance medium who is transmitting this information, but *particularly* you cannot see the communicator from the spirit side of life ...and you accept that. You have bought the book that is in your hands because you accept that communication is coming from another sphere of influence from someone, who has passed on from your physical Earth and is able to return and talk to you.

If that is the case, then are you not also susceptible to the promptings of various other 'communicators'? And, I say 'communicators' in inverted commas because there is a variety of aspects of life that are communicated to you from beyond this actual physical sphere. I want you to consider *that* for a moment. You are reading *my* words ...but you are also often susceptible to the communications and promptings of *various other spirits*.

As we have explained in previous books, souls who pass on do not instantly become what they are at their angelic core. They do not instantly become that which they were before they came here but have to evolve through a number of cleansing and refining spheres in order to regain the perfection they once had. Therefore, spirits who pass from this Earth take with them their inherent and dominant vibrations – be they vibrations of harmony or disharmony.

What I am attempting to explain is that not everyone who passes to the spiritual side instantly becomes the angelic being that they were. *Quite the opposite*! Many hang on to the less desirable traits that they exhibited and bought into whilst they were on Earth. In fact, not every spirit passes on instantly to the first of the cleansing spheres. There are many spirits who are so drawn back to the effects of the Earth and to those things that they held to be so important during their earthly lives that they refuse *initially* to move on. There are also those spirits who refuse to move on simply because they will not acknowledge that there is anything beyond physical existence. Then there are those spirits who inhabit a sphere that is very close to the Earth (a sphere that has been explained in the book, **Your life After Death**), which is called the 'Lower Astral'. The Lower Astral is not a place that anyone would wish to go but, indeed, many souls find themselves in this sphere because of their actions whilst on Earth ...their inability to reach out in Love and harmony towards others and to reach inwards in Love and harmony towards themselves. And, so you have an *unseen* aspect of life on Earth that exists *despite* you not being able to tap into it.

**You have many spirits around you.**

You have people like myself who visit the Earth in order to restore harmony through information that can be absorbed or rejected. Then you have spirits who are close to you 'physically' because they have not yet escaped this sphere ...and *you send messages to those spirits*. You send messages to them via your moods. You send messages to them via your dominant beliefs, biases and prejudices. You send messages to them when you are feeling depressed, when you are feeling ill and when you are feeling angry. As I have said in a previous book [*reference to From Here To Infinity*], no thought that you are capable of thinking is thought in isolation. **Your thoughts are like magnets ...they attract more of the same thoughts towards you.** And, you are very often influenced *on a daily basis* by the wishes and intentions of spirits who have not yet left the Earth plane. Allow me to explain...

31

Imagine that you want a drink of alcohol. You started the day not wanting a drink, and then the image comes into your mind. Make no mistake – *you* have placed that image in your mind. It is one of many images that you are capable of accessing at any time. Once you have accessed that image, what begins as a simple wish for a drink suddenly takes on a severity and an intensity … *and becomes a drink that you must have*! You try to resist that need for a drink, and the more you resist it – the more the drink becomes attractive to you, to the point where you almost have to sit on your hands to prevent yourself from going to the drinks cabinet and taking that drink out. Then, there comes a point at which you can resist no longer and you go to the cabinet, you pour out the drink and you drink …and it feels fantastic! Then the whole process begins again. You sit there with an empty glass in your hand and you think: 'How could I have been so weak? Why can I not stop this habit that I *wish* to stop? Why am I not capable of it? Why do I tempt myself? Why does this thing become so attractive to me that I cannot resist it *despite* wanting to resist it?'

…And, the answer in this particular example (as in so many others) lies on the less corporeal side of life – in that someone, who has been roaming the Earth and is close to physicality and yet not physical and who had a problem with drink and still desires a drink, has seen your signal-thought that *you want a drink*. It flashes up there into the ether: 'I WANT A DRINK!' And, that person says: 'I want a drink, too.' That person homes in on your initial thought and says: 'Yes, you *do* want a drink and so *do* I.' And, in those times during the day when you feel you can resist the drink but it is still there as a temptation, that person is constantly whispering in your ear: 'Go and have the drink. *You* need the drink. *I* need the drink. Let *us* have a drink together.'

And, that tempting voice that you probably *until now* have thought was your own, actually comes from someone else and links to you. Not only that but, when you actually take the drink, the person who is non-corporeal allies themselves *so closely* with your aura that they practically have the sensation of having the drink as you drink. In a parasitical fashion, they share the experience with you. It is not a hundred-per-cent experience for them because they are not corporeal, but they can, by linking into your vibration, relive to a large extent the experience of having that drink they enjoyed so much whilst they were on Earth.

Let us say that it is the first time that this particular spirit has linked in to you – as a result of that, you become a 'meeting point' or target for them, and so your initial thought that you wanted the drink can now, on the morrow, be started up by that spirit. So, you could wake up in the morning not wanting that drink at all and being completely resistant to the idea of alcohol, but the spirit has made a link with you and is saying to you subtly through your aura: 'You want a drink! I want a drink! Let us drink!' And, so, this symbiotic relationship continues to allow that spirit to get what it wants in non-corporeal form by using you and stimulating your desires to accomplish that task.

**This happens in so many different ways.**

Look at the range of negative emotions (as you would see them) that you have. Look at the times that you get angry and then become angrier and angrier. Look at the times when you direct anger towards a particular situation, and that situation then becomes dominant so that you become angry towards it more frequently until it becomes a resentment and something that is *permanently* in your mind. Look at the times when you review your thoughts and think: 'How could I have thought that thought?' And, yet there is a temptation with it, even though that thought is not something that you, as a personality, would *ever* entertain initially …but there it is, and you think: 'I am shocked! How could I have had that thought?'

You leave yourselves open to temptation. You leave yourselves open to connection. You leave yourselves open to the 'unseen chorus' …and this is only 'Part One' regarding actual human spirits that have not yet moved on. This is only *one area* in which you can become affected. And, this is why this book is called *the Spaces Between*, because I wish to make you aware of the unseen world that actually operates twenty-four hours a day *every day* to influence you in ways that, if you knew about them, you would not wish to be influenced by.

I do not want you to go to bed this evening and say: 'I cannot sleep because there are unseen voices in my head and unseen connections trying to bend me to their will.' What I do want you to do is to *be aware* of certain trends within your thinking and aware that if your thinking becomes amplified in a negative way and – *this is crucial* – **if your thoughts are thoughts that you do not want, then those thoughts are not *totally* yours.** You have to think about this logically: if you have a thought that you do not want and you try to resist it and yet it is still there, then it is not totally generated by you, or you would not have it. If you truly don't want to think in a certain way, then you would not have that thought ...*except* if that thought is being amplified and generated from an outside source.

Initially, what I would ask you to do in times when you have such temptations is to realise that those thoughts do not originate from yourself and to make a *conscious decision* to stop them by saying: 'Because this is not something I want to do – I will not do it! It does not come from myself.' And, you defuse the situation. It will be difficult at first, but with practice you will be able to do it.

Secondly, there is a spiritual method. If you find yourself plagued by thoughts that you do not want, sit down and take yourself into a quiet, meditative state. Imagine, as you sit there, that you are building a wall ...a circular wall of golden bricks around yourself. First of all, in your imagination, you put in a foundation of bricks below your feet. Then you add beautiful, circular-shaped bricks, one at a time, around that foundation and build up that turret of golden, circular bricks around yourself until it rises above your head. Then, in your imagination, you place a further encircling roof of bricks on top of your wall so that you are completely isolated within this golden tube of protection that is around you.

Having done that, you then need to visualise your chakras as closing within this protective atmosphere that you have created for yourself. (Here you will need to refer to my earlier books or, alternatively, if you have some spiritual knowledge, you will know that you have energy points in your body – known as *the principal chakras* – that block or let in information and energies.) Then, if you need further evidence that you are being affected by outside influences, in meditation you can move from your head-mind to your heart-mind (and, again, this has been referenced in earlier books) and you can *ask* whether those thoughts that you have been having originate from yourself or from yourself *plus an outside source.*

Then, having closed your chakras, you can take down your 'wall of bricks' and continue with your day. But, at any time if you find yourself the subject of temptation and unwanted repetitive thoughts, you can repeat the exercise.

Bearing in mind the information given in my previous books about the Field of human consciousness that is set to negative and looking at what has been said today about the dangers of living in this physical arena, **you have to approach each day more spiritually.** You have to approach each day as though there will be points where connections will attempt to be made, and you have to understand that you do not live your life in isolation. You do not live your life as a separate entity. You are part of the Whole – you are part of the Divine. You are part of the angelic host and, on this level of consciousness, you still operate in that way. You are linked to everyone …to everyone that you can see physically and to everyone that you can't see who happens to be around you on a non-corporeal level.

Knowing that these influences are around, you also have to understand how the Field works and how it perpetuates itself by allowing communication with spirits who have not yet left this plane so that people can be held in thrall of certain substances and conditions, and how people in physical bodies then perpetuate those conditions and, therefore, perpetuate the Field in its negative state.

You have to look at your reactions to the world differently from now on. If you become angry – step back from that anger if you can, and then determine how much of that anger has been fuelled by anger outside of yourself.

If you have habits that you don't want (and this will help you in getting rid of them) realise that *a percentage* of that need comes from outside of yourself via the cravings of spirits who wish you to operate in a certain way to feed *their* habits that they have not yet moved on and evolved from. Realise that in a domestic row, for example, you are not only calling on your own viewpoint, but you are calling on the angers, bitterness and viewpoints of other spirits who have gone through similar circumstances and perversely wish to continue those circumstances because they have not yet learnt anything better.

This is not a communication to frighten you or to make you anxious. It is a communication designed to give you power in the right way. In understanding yourself better and in understanding that there are weaknesses (as you see them) in your personality that are also being affected by other spirits, you can then take control. You can take control of yourself and, in taking control of yourself, you can put positivity and harmony into your own life, into the lives of the people that connect to you and, ultimately, into the world. As an angelic being, you are a shaper of worlds ...and you are a shaper of this world *subconsciously* without you knowing it.

What this book intends to do is to give you the power to be *a conscious* shaper *of this world* – to shape this world for the good and to shape your own life for the good and to be free of the miseries and temptations that you have at the moment so that each day has a brighter purpose for you, each day is a brighter experience for you and each day is closer to the day that it should have been before the experiment that went wrong that we call 'the Fall' that has been examined in an earlier book.

What of those spirits that 'roam the Earth', as it were? And, it is not that they are walking down your highways and streets, but rather that they roam the Earth in *spiritual consciousness* seeking out points of recognition that they can continue their existence with, as they see it. They roam the Earth 'mentally', as it were, looking for that thought process that you flag up, for example, when you want a drink – which they then home in on. So, what of those spirits?

Well, first of all they have to be broken off those habits they have, and there are teams of spirits who come to try to make them aware of a higher vibration so that they will move on. But, in order to move on, they have to be *desirous* of that higher vibration, and the reason that they are forming thought-connections via the Lower Astral with people on Earth is because they do not *yet* wish to move on.

So, as well as a promoter of Light and harmony in your own life and sending that out into the world, what you also have to see yourself as being is **someone who is cutting off the supply of energy that those spirits need.** Imagine if they could not seek out that shared experience of the drink ...or of the anger ...or of the drugs ...or of the sex ...or of the perversions. Then, in order to continue to have a meaningful existence (as they see it), they would have to actually seek out something else and, therefore, be open to the promptings of the spirits who come to guide them out of their mindset and into the lower cleansing spheres so that they can then start their journey that takes them through to being, once again, free of the clinging effects of the Earth plane.

So, in examining your thoughts, in protecting your thoughts, in giving out the Light and in refusing to give in to temptation (not by resisting it but by realising that, if there is another voice in your head then it is not imagination, it is actually another voice) then you change the world on this level, but you also change the fortunes of the spirits who are still here and wish to experience the lower aspects of the Earth plane time and time and time again.

Today's chapter is, therefore, about liberation ...*liberation* for you in that, through realisation, you now have a way of combatting those aspects of yourself that you wish to refine ... *liberation* for the world in that, in doing that, you become a vessel for the Light, a promoter of harmony and a worker for the evolution of this world according to God's plan and according to the original plan of the angelic host ...*and liberation* in that you are also helping those spirits who have not yet learnt anything better, who have passed on from physical life but have found themselves in an imprisoning state of their own making and who seek to perpetuate that imprisonment because they do not know anything else and have not been open to the spiritual promptings of the souls who wish to elevate them.

There are other influences that we will talk about in coming chapters, but for now I invite questions on this particular topic covered today.

**David:** Joseph, in meditation where you build the golden brick wall, is that something you can do for your entire family or does it always have to be a personal thing?

**Joseph:** That is an extremely good question because in everything we have been talking about today *free will* exists. You *can* place the protection around members of your family, but this also leads to the question of future treatment with regard to people on this level who are completely obsessed with some negative aspect of the physical world and who will not let anyone in. They are, in effect, a physical representation of the spirit attempting to influence them ...or *spirits* because sometimes there are multiple personalities attempting to influence them from a non-corporeal state. You can surround people with protection and with Light, but that does not guarantee that they will be protected. It *does* guarantee, however, that you are giving them a breathing space. And, if you are successful (and you *will be* as you continue to exercise those 'spiritual muscles' in visualising that golden Light around people and around yourself) then, within that golden Light, there is a disconnection from any spirits that may have been around that person influencing them in a negative way.

What then happens with that person and how they deal with that opportunity is entirely up to them, but I will say (as I have said in previous communications) that the more Light you send out to people and surround them with, the greater the breathing space you give them. Then, freed from those connections that may have been with them for a lifetime, they have a greater opportunity to consider a different way of life and to determine that *now* is the time to change their perspective and move away from the negative aspects of life.

It is very difficult, and you realise the nonsense of judging anyone because you cannot see, from a physical level, how many *unseen influences* are connected to someone at any one time. You can imagine how difficult it is to overcome that mindset, if you are constantly being tempted by someone in a non-corporeal state – with more and more additions to the number of spirits that are influencing you. So, you can now look at the landscape of war, the landscape of terror and the landscape of torture and of man's inhumanity to man and realise that the people perpetrating those acts need your Love and need that golden Light …not your condemnation.

In view of what I have said this morning, which of us is blameless and which of us has not been influenced at some time by unseen influences simply because we have cast out our thoughts and attracted someone with inharmonious thoughts, who sees us as 'prey' and a source of energy?

Again thank you, David, for that question because it raises the issue of judgement and the way that we view people. With what

I have said in this chapter about the unseen becoming the seen, you can see that people are *to a degree* responsible for themselves. Yes, of course, they *are* responsible for themselves, but, if there is a weakness, that weakness can be affected by non-corporeal intelligence and intent. And, only in eliminating the non-corporeal connection, can you give the person perpetuating the 'unspeakable acts' (as you might see them) the breathing space to connect to *higher* vibrations – or, at the very least, to a vibration that is not influenced by negativity and disharmony – and, thereby, step back from their attitudes and allow the Light to flood in.

This is why, in previous books, I have always said that the world will not change on a *physical* level. You can apply a 'bandage' to the 'wound' but you will never heal the 'wound' unless you get to the source of the discomfort ...and the source of the discomfort always lies on a spiritual level with each of you because you are spiritual beings. You created this reality as spiritual beings. The only way to change this reality that is based on spiritual principles of creation, is **by applying different principles of creation to it** and by dispelling the disharmony and replacing it with harmony, with Light and with Love that is non-judgemental. It has been said since the beginning of time here: 'Judge not! Love!'

Does that answer your question?

**David:** Yes. Could I follow that up with another comment? If you find yourself in a position where you think you are being influenced from outside – as well as protecting yourself, would you then call on workers in the healing spheres to help that particular source; would you project Light to that source or do you leave it be?

**Joseph:** It depends on your personal evolution as a spirit and understanding of these things. In the early stages, it is enough that you disconnect yourself from the source of irritation and motivation to give *yourself* the breathing space that you need to be able to see, with more harmonic eyes, the true state of your being. Remember that many people who are reading this book will have *never* considered before that there is anything outside of themselves …let alone influences that can colour their lives in certain ways. And, in the early stages of giving yourself breathing space and disconnection, there is only enough energy to maintain 'the wall'.

Remember that once you put the wall up, that wall is also a signal. To use the analogy again, just as your need for a drink (or whatever it is) is a signal, once you change that signal to a more harmonic one – that signal then attracts spirits of a more harmonic, progressive and angelically aware nature, who will add their Light to that wall so that you get longer and longer breathing spaces during which, through your own free will, you can decide how you want to proceed in future. So, the process that I have recommended for souls on Earth to send out Light to other people is, in effect, going on at a higher level around them once they make a conscious disconnection from those thoughts that cause them so much torment. Does that make sense?

**David:** Yes, thank you.

**Jane:** Joseph, if you have guarded your thoughts against negativity and are very positive and enjoy creative things such as beautiful art, can you commune with the *positive* influences in spirit realms so that they can inspire you to do better art? Or, are those evolved spirits less attracted to the Earth because our art isn't as beautiful as the art they can create in the spirit realms? Are those spirits less likely to influence us, whereas people in the Lower Astral can only get their thrills through association with the Earth plane? Are we less likely to attract the positive side of spiritual influence?

**Joseph:** In the normal course of angelic creation, all creation is reviewed and participated in, to a lesser or greater extent, by other members of the angelic host – dependent on whether they find each creative prospect fascinating and of worth to their soul. Do you understand that?

**Jane:** Yes.

**Joseph:** Again, this brings us back to the Fall and the fact that *here* creativity is skewed and that *here* creativity can only be achieved seemingly though struggle, and there is also creativity in a negative way. There is creativity that you would not have in other spheres and other areas of the angelic host because they would not entertain such thoughts. And, such thoughts came about through the perceived need to survive that occurred following the cut-off in consciousness from God after the Fall. (Again, I have to refer readers to the book on the Fall to explain that more fully because, as you are aware here this morning, that is an entire volume.)

Any act of creativity – be it negative or positive – is a signal or marker because that is how you operate as an angelic being. So, your act of creativity that is negative attracts more negativity and your creative act of positivity creates more positivity and attracts fascination and harmony from the higher side of life. So, yes, your positive creative acts attract more of the same ...beauty attracts beauty ...Love attracts Love ...harmony attracts harmony. It cannot be otherwise because it is a principle that is built into you as the angelic being that you really are. Does that make sense?

**Jane:** I probably didn't phrase my question very well ...what I meant was that if I was creating a painting on this level, because of the limited colours and limited subject matter here, I wouldn't attract the interest of many souls from the higher spiritual spheres because they can create much better art *there*. They wouldn't as drawn to our art as much as people in the Lower Astral, for example, would be drawn to alcohol because they can't get the drink sensation from anywhere else. So, I was wondering whether on the Earth plane we are less likely to attract the positive thoughts.

**Joseph:** You are equally likely to attract the positive thoughts. You see how the Field skews your perception of what you are capable of? You are *equally* capable of creating positive thoughts, but you do not believe that because you are held by the Field and because there are negative influences around you in whose interest it is to keep you in that state of belief. Furthermore, it is equally as easy to create positively as it is negatively, but you do not believe that either because of the effects of the Field.

So, your beautiful creative act is just as beautiful here as it is in the cleansing spheres. It is simply that it is masked by the effects of the Field, by the effects of the Fall and by your own disbelief that it can be as beautiful as it is in the cleansing spheres. Do you see that? Every thought that you think is perfect, but you put the spin on it. ...Is it perfectly positive? ...Is it perfectly negative? ... Is it a thought of abundance? ...Is it a thought of lack? It is perfect! Your situations are always perfect, but they are not always perfect with regard to harmony. They are 'perfect' very often with regard to negativity because of the effects of the Fall and because of the drag of the Field.

**Jane:** Thank you very much.

**Tony:** Joseph, I have been thinking about the width and the breadth of the forces upon us from the Lower Astral that can attach, and I am wondering whether children are vulnerable to these forces – things like lack of self-esteem in a child or anger in a tantrum. Could they attract an Astral connection that then can stay with them and form part of their character?

**Joseph:** The Earth under the effects of the Fall and the Field is an *extremely dangerous place*. And, we have to here reference the fact that, in all the books that we have communicated thus far, we have recommended that, upon physical death and awakening in a higher level of consciousness, you heed the advice from the souls around you that urge you not to return to the Earth.

## Do not return to the Earth!

You have to understand that the children coming through grow through a physical process ...child ...teenager ...adult ...middle-aged ...old-aged ...physical death, but all the while they are, in fact, an angelic being. From conception to physical death, they are under the influence of the Field and the effects of the Fall and are to a lesser or greater extent (dependent on their dominant soul vibration and the reason why they have chosen to incarnate here) influenced by negative spirits and by people who have not yet moved on.

So, yes, in many cases children, *are* influenced by spirits who make a connection with them. As a child develops there are dominant traits, and those dominant traits are also influenced by the karmic implications of reincarnating into a physical body. So, if they have had dominant traits that were negative in a past life, then those magnetic forces within them will pull towards them, *inevitably* as they grow, aspects of their past lives that become dominant as things that they need to evolve out of. As a result of this, the child can pull towards itself influences that will attach because they want to experience more of the dominant traits that are drawn towards the child *karmically* because the spirit that the child really is has chosen to reincarnate.

Do you see the *absolute minefield* that this Earth is? And, the thing to do with your children is to bring them up with spiritual values, not to immerse them in the facts, for example, of this chapter until they are ready – but to be aware of the traits that they have and to surround them with Light and pray that spirits from the cleansing spheres come to protect them. As David touched upon in his question, use your ability to transmit Light to ensure that they are given a time of innocence as they grow to enable the spirit that they really are to shine through so that they can *consciously* choose areas of thought that do not lead to connection with spirits from the

Lower Astral or discarnate spirits who have not yet moved on, who would influence them negatively.

Do you see that?

**Tony:** I do. Thank you, Joseph.

Chapter Three
## Children in the Dark

**Joseph:** Chapter three – *Children in the Dark*. In the last chapter, I explained how you are influenced by unseen spirits who have not moved on to where they should be or who have not learned any better with regard to approaching fellow souls who are encased in physical matter. What I wish to discuss today is a further couple of manifestations of energy and consciousness that also influence you.

The first [*laughing*] you will have heard about in your horror films; you will have heard about in literature; you will have heard about in hushed tones in public houses and wherever people gather together, and where, invariably, the conversation moves towards things of the occult and the paranormal ...and these influences are sometimes called 'entities'.

What, exactly, *is* an entity?

Before I explain what an entity is, I have to revisit some terminology that I used in a previous book – *the Fall* – where I explained that the angelic host that is outside of the Earth invested part of its consciousness into the Earth plane as a place that it was going to explore and, in effect, 'gave birth' via spiritual channels to angelic children. In other words, the thoughts of the angelic host projected as part of their consciousness into an arena of experience eventually gives rise to angelic children – to the next generation of offspring from God

46

manifested by the angelic host concentrating and giving form to its thoughts.

**You are an angelic being.** *You*, reading this book, are an angelic being encased in physical matter.

**As an angelic being your thoughts are given form.** Whatever you consider, whatever you project around you and into your worldview is given form. Because you are entrapped within the Fall, your thoughts are mostly negative because of the Field of human consciousness around you. And, so, if you examine your life today as you are reading this book, you will see that there is a tendency to err towards illness …to err towards depression … to err towards a negative view of things, because you are being influenced by a Field of consciousness that wishes to hold you within that negative viewpoint.

Therefore, over a lifetime you begin consolidate those thoughts that you are giving form to. You begin to consolidate, for example, thoughts of illness. You begin to consolidate thoughts of trepidation in certain situations – perhaps you are frightened of a certain area of life and avoid it. You begin to give form to all kinds of negative aspects of life that you don't wish to encounter. As a result of this, because you are an angelic being, you invest part of your consciousness into these thoughts that you reinforce and reinforce and reinforce …day in, day out … year in, year out …throughout your lifetime.

So, as an example, if you are frightened of the dark you project into the ether a fear of the dark that you then give form to as a part of your consciousness. **That fear of the dark then has *a consciousness of its own* linked to you.** You might have a fear of death, a fear of pain, a fear of illness; and, in each of these areas, you are giving birth *angelically* to a child of your own creation and then reinforcing and giving greater sentience to that child as the days pass.

You are also giving a *function* to each of those children ...and that function is to be *exactly* what you have shaped them to be. So, a fear of the dark, for example, creates an 'entity' or connection to your consciousness that has a somewhat separate intelligence that exists to bring back to you a fear of the dark. And, so, each entity out there is fulfilling its purpose. I want you to understand this ...**each entity is fulfilling its purpose by bringing back to you that which you have instructed it to be.**

The entities around you – that are not separate from you *but are distanced from you* in that you have projected them outwards into the Field of humanity – have been instructed by your subconscious fears to bring to you *exactly* the fears that you have given them life through. So, you have around you at any time further projections out into the ether that are your 'angelic children', and those angelic children exist to serve you by bringing to you those aspects of yourself that you have projected into them, which are usually ...fear ...negativity ...dread ...upset ...trepidation ...and also *temptation*. **One of the biggest entities that you can create is the entity of temptation –** whereby you push away from you the thoughts that you most fear will come to haunt you ...*because you fear you may give in to them.* And, in projecting those outwards into an entity over years of living here, you then become tempted because you have created the means of tempting yourself. With other entities, you have created the means of making yourself afraid ...the means of bringing pain to yourself ...the means of bringing illness to yourself. And, all these entities you sustain by pushing life-energy into them via filaments that connect you to each individual entity.

Now, the traditional response to having something that is outside of yourself tempting you or making you afraid *is to resist it* and to put up a barrier between yourself and it. But, in doing that, you fuel the entities with more of the original fears and more of the original upsets that you created them with in the first place ...*so they become stronger*. This, I hope, presents to you a scenario that is far more terrifying than any of your horror films, but I present it to you to:

Make you aware of it.

Make you aware of how to combat the entities that are around you that you have created.

**...And you combat them by *not combatting* them.**

You combat them by *loving* them, by reprogramming them and by understanding that these are aspects of yourself that, through fear, you have projected outwards into the ether and given 'birth to' as manifestations of your angelic power – and that you can, at this point, surround and infuse them with Love to give them a different directive. Understand that they are a part of you and embrace them to you, not as something that will take you off the track of goodness or spiritual evolution – but as something that is not to be feared and as something that can be *held*. Once you hold the entities to yourself in Love, you then dissipate those original instructions from those manifestations around you and infuse them with Love that *then comes back to you as Love from the entities*.

They are not in truth 'entities' but 'children' – potential angelic children that cannot be given full form because of the effects of the Fall and because you do not remember the Fall you, therefore, do not understand that, in the angelic realm, you give birth to further generations of angelic beings *simply* by placing part of your consciousness into different spheres and allowing that consciousness to explore those spheres for itself and take on sentience and individuality.

This is why I call this book *the Spaces Between* because I want you to understand that all these processes are going on *despite* you thinking in a constricted, societal way. These processes continue because at your core you are what you have always been ...an angelic being that exists to explore the constructs and creations that you put around yourself in order to glorify God. You also exist to become *more* ...to become more as an individual and to become more in the form of the offspring *spiritually* that you create. And, you create those offspring quite naturally by investing power and energy into aspects of your life that you think are important. Unfortunately, in the case of entities, you think those negative aspects are so important that you give them *particular* power and sentience.

So, do not be afraid of what are sometimes described in spiritual circles as 'dark forces' – those dark forces are only dark because you have programmed them to be dark. Programme them to be Light and they will dissipate and disappear from your lives, and your fears will melt. You will evolve spiritually and will gain the confidence to say: 'This is no longer a part of me! Love is a part of me. My angelic children surrounding me are nothing but Love.' And, if you give out that Love and Light ... *Love and Light* are what will come back to you via those 'children' or sentient probes that you have created and sent out around you, which are joined to you.

If you were to see yourself as an angelic being encased in matter on Earth, the nearest analogy I can put to you is that of a pincushion – where you are the pincushion itself and the stem of pin is the filament that leads to the head of the pin, which is one of those angelic children that you have partially created ... *partially created* (and more on that later in this chapter).

So, you are not alone, as we said in the last chapter, because of the unseen spirits that try to connect with you because they wish to relive certain experiences. And, you are *never* alone – regardless of whether you are married, single, have physical children or no children whatsoever – because you are always creating your next expression of angelic intent around you.

I now wish to move on to the second area that, again, is investigated in horror stories and films and is condemned by religion as something 'out there' that you need to fear ...**I want to talk about demons.**

First of all, the question is: **'Joseph, do demons exist?'**

And, the answer is ...**very definitely, yes** – although their origins will *startle* you.

Their origins will startle you because *YOU* – as humanity since the time of the Fall – have created them, not specifically as part of this civilisation but as part of *past civilisations* that should have known better. And, you have created them thus: certain adepts or angelic beings in past civilisations, who retained some of their conscious memory of how the angelic universe manifests and operates, and with a specific purpose in mind (i.e. the control of other souls through power-seeking) sought to manipulate and control the process by which angelic children were produced and also sought to manipulate and control deva energy. So, by joining together as groups, those souls would seek to create sentient angelic children by drawing on their own angelic material and on deva material, which was trapped through certain rituals, to produce distortions of angelic children that would operate and work for them according to their own desires ...**and thus demons were created.**

There is now a further question. In the case of entities and demons, *you have created children* ...either partially in the case of entities, or completely in the case of demons. You have created sentient beings – just as you create sentient beings by being an angel and projecting into a theatre of experience. You create children. These beings exist.

**What do you do with them?**

Assuming (as we have explained in past books) that we are all attempting to escape the effects of the Fall – what of the demons? What of the entities around you? They exist and, *in Love*, cannot be left in God's universe in a Fall situation.

First of all, you have to understand that the entities that you create around you *are a part of you* and are not fully formed angelic children. They are partially formed angelic children because you are seeking to create the next generation of angelic children within a skewed and limiting landscape and, so, they are not fully formed. It is vitally important that you send Love to the so-called entities around you which are extensions of you because, in sending Love to them, you not only neutralise the negative aspects of what they put out, but you *reabsorb* them into your own being so that, when you move on, you take with you those aspects of your angelic personality as a part of you, and you extricate yourself *fully* from the effects of the Fall.

In previous books you have asked me: 'Why are people pulled back to the Earth plane when you explain to them in *such detail* that they should not come back here? Why are they pulled back?' ...Can you see *another* reason now? They are pulled back because of the lures of the Earth plane, but they are *also* pulled back because they have partially created angelic children from their own angelic being that pull them back as a child's cry in the dark that says: 'I am still here. Where have you gone, Father? Where have you gone, Mother? Come back to me!'

So, I wanted to reveal a further expansion of why people are pulled back to the Earth plane. They are drawn back because of the voices in the dark that pull at them as their own angelic children. So, it is important that you love those negative aspects of yourself and love away those fears ...or, at least, embrace them and understand that *they are a part of you* so that you then evacuate this planet, at the end of your earthly tenure, as *a complete angel* at core that can then move on through the rescue spheres and out into Infinity.

With the demons it is a different matter ...these beings have been created to serve man within a skewed theatre of the Fall, and they exist as fully formed deva energy given purpose by groups of souls on Earth. Once these beings have been 'left behind', as it were, when the effects of the Fall move on, there will be a special team entrusted with ushering them safely out of the physical matrix of the Earth so that they, too, can make *the choice* once they get to the rescue spheres to either dissipate back into deva energy, whilst retaining a portion of their individuality, or to move onwards as angelic children to the point where they become bright and shining angels (just as you are) and can move on into Infinity.

Again, I titled this chapter 'Children in the Dark' because **these beings are *your children*.** In the case of the demons, it is also upsetting because their intent has been determined for them in the past by the groups that controlled them – occult groups who have used them to further their own ambitions. So, are they 'evil'? Are they dark? …Only because that is a projection that has been put onto and through them. They are expressions of God filtered through souls who have been mistaken because of the effects of the Fall and, therefore, the demons have to be given the opportunity to come out of that darkness.

So, what will happen is that, at the point that the human race has extricated itself from the effects of the Fall, the team will surround the demons and eradicate their original intent. The groups that controlled them will no longer be there – and would no longer wish to control them because they are moving on through the rescue spheres and into Infinity as evolving angelic beings. The team will remove from around the demons that negativity, and then they will be ushered into a parallel set of rescue spheres and given the opportunity to evolve. The devas that they are a part of will be asked whether they wish to take into themselves those demonic forms or, alternatively, allow those demonic forms to move onwards as an expression of the devas' energy (now removed from the wishes of mankind) …or, if you like, *as the devas' children*. Within those demonic forms, are the most beautiful, wonderful spirits because they come from deva energy …from the selfless energy of the devas who create the landscape through which you move.

A *huge* subject that I wished to cover this morning and a *huge* realisation for you that, unlike the rest of the physical and spiritual universes, **the so-called evils, perversions and darknesses that exist outside of yourself have been created by *you*** …either individually as thought given form according to your fears …or, going back in time, as the result of groups wishing to have beings *at their behest* that would further their seeking of power following the Fall and the human spirit being trapped in matter as a result.

Have I covered everything that I wish to cover on these subjects? No, because there is bound to be so much that will need answering. I will attempt, at this point, to answer your questions and, perhaps, they will prompt me into looking at areas that I have not explained fully this morning.

**Tony:** Joseph, the demons act out the will of the occult groups that you mentioned so, once they have power, how do those demons affect human beings?

**Joseph:** You will see from this morning's chapter that there are underlying currents that society knows nothing about but which occult students will know something of, and that for millennia there have been groups, who have sought to overpower other groups and empower themselves. Demons are an embodiment of magical intent and the wishes of groups to have controlling forces that can do their bidding and which are stronger than the individual.

And, so, the groups would gather together to give group-power to their *perverted* angelic children (i.e. 'perverted' from the point of view of the instruction that goes out to create that child). Those demons would then be used to control areas of power and areas of intent and would be drawn upon when groups sat in circles to control areas of the Earth. Originally, wars and battles (which, of course, in themselves are as a result of the Fall) would be fought on *two* levels. They would be fought on the conscious level of man against man with weapons ...but would also be fought with the help of demonic forces to attack at a psychic and spiritual level to pull down into darkness the morale and viewpoint of other factions. So, war and battle would have been fought on two levels – on the level that you can see visually and on an intention level via the use of demonic forces.

You have to understand that **these demonic angelic children still exist** ...*still exist!* There are still pockets of intent and, behind the scenes, there are still occult groups that work connected to the Field and connected to their demonic forces in order to influence this world in a negative and power-seeking way. These aspects of life still exist. For most of mankind, there is no consideration that they exist *except* in literature, but for certain factions it is their intent always to work as part of the Field (and, in a way, in worship of the Field) to make sure that the chaos on this level as a result of the Fall continues.

Does that make sense?

**Tony:** Is there anything we can do to protect ourselves?

**Joseph:** Protection is something that should be an aspect of each chapter of this book, of course. With regard to demonic forces, it all comes down to the message that has been brought through since we began these books ...and the message is that *Love changes all things*. The ultimate protection is Love. The ultimate protection is Light. But, in the case of the individual who is a spiritual student and who is seeking to transmit Light, I would suggest that the transmission of Light out to the world on all levels is *ALL* that should be attempted and that **UNDER NO CIRCUMSTANCES should anyone attempt to directly combat the groups or the demonic forces.**

It is not a matter of combat. It is a matter of sending Light out into every expression of life across the world. Otherwise, the person who directly seeks to combat or to change demonic thought or occult-group thought then becomes a target, and that is not what this book is about. This book is to make you aware that the world that you consider to be so solid, so rigid and so reliable in the way that it unfolds day-to-day *is anything but!* And also, for those who have read *the Fall*, to further expand on the consequences of the Fall, and to explain that there is so much more going on within this sphere as a result of the Fall than I first told you.

I wished this information to come out in this further book; wished to say: 'Look how much of a task there is in front of you, and look how important it is for you *each day* to send out your Light ...to send out your Light into every dark corner of the world, to channel God-Light and to change this world.' And, you can see why this world is such a contaminated place but also a *quarantined* place from the rest of the physical universes, and you can see the great consequences of the Fall over millennia ... and millennia ...and millennia where you have become more and more entrenched in a negative way of life.

I am telling you these things, not to frighten you but to impress upon you the need for soldiers for the Light ...the need for souls to escape this place ...and the need for you to understand the angelic children that you give birth to. You should also understand **that the only true negative, evil and bad aspects of this world lie within the *physical minds* of men and women,** that the demons are blameless and that the entities you put out are as a subconscious desire for you to fulfil your mission as an angelic being to give birth to the 'next generation', as it were, of angelic beings. All this has become distorted because of the effects of the Fall. Do you see that?

**Tony:** Thank you, Joseph.

**Jane:** Joseph, could I ask a question about our little angelic children that are attached to us like 'pins in a pincushion'? Just occasionally, I have had thought-forms stuck to me, which Michael has then thankfully removed, querying whether I have recently spoken to someone who is depressed or negative. So, how do those thought forms become attached to us if they are still also attached to the person they have emanated from?

**Joseph:** I have to smile at this point because I may have said it in my mind or may have said it in words, but this section is one of three chapters, and [*laughing*] the third chapter deals with exactly your question.

**Jane:** OK, thank you.

**Joseph:** There is a further chapter, and the three chapters together will cover what is out there and influences you that appears to be unseen.

**Jane:** Could I ask another one, then? You said that the demons were produced in a previous civilisation – so where did the demons go during the stasis following the last cataclysm when the world was being re-formed to sustain life again?

**Joseph:** The matrix was always present, and I have spoken before about devas and deva energy producing the landscape against which you can register yourselves as physical beings. The dormant demon energy was held by the deva – or devas – because sometimes it was more than one deva. The ancients knew how to contact specific devas to create specific entities for specific reasons. And so, they would put into the demons they sought to create a mix from devas that they had in a way 'enslaved' in order to create *exactly* the beings that they wanted with the right degree of energies in them for specific purposes. So, at the time of stasis – just as the thoughts of mankind are held within that stasis and when you are born back into the Earth plane *you attract more of the same* because the matrix is still there – part of that matrix was the demonic form and the deva form that held that demonic form whilst it was not being instructed by the groups that had formed it. Do you understand?

**Jane:** Yes, thank you.

**Joseph:** A final question, please.

**David:** Joseph, when people do choose to reincarnate back to Earth – and you have referred to karma and the picking up of our old vibrations – those 'partial children' now explain how part of that happens because, as soon as we reincarnate, we make a closer bond with them, don't we? And, then they start carrying out what they were originally programmed to do.

**Joseph:** Yes, not only that but, because you have created them and because you are their angelic parent, they 'lie in wait' for you in anticipation of your return so that they can gravitate towards you as their angelic parent because they are not fully formed.

Because of the effects of the Fall, *individually* you are not fully forming angelic children (I am not talking about demons here). In the normal course of things you would, as an angelic parent, project part of yourself down into a sphere that you and a number of the angelic host had created. At a certain point, you would then break that 'umbilical cord' between yourself and the angelic child because that angelic child would gain sentience to such an extent that it had earned the right to be individualised and would *wish* to be individualised. So, it would always be linked to you, but there wouldn't be an energy-link pushing from the angelic parent to the angelic child. That energy would be self-sustaining in the fully formed angelic child, if that makes sense.

**David:** Yes, it would have the God-within…

**Joseph:** It would have the God-within, and it would have been pushed forward to go forth and experience …just as God said to the original angelic host: 'Go forth and experience! You are part of Me, but I give you individuality. Go forth! You are now *the captain of your own ship.*'

What happens here on Earth?

First of all, this knowledge that we have covered today is not understood so the process goes on, but it is not a *conscious* process. It is not as though the people you meet in the street realise that they are giving form to their own thoughts. So, you do not have that volition that you would have from an angelic parent, who is not encased in matter within the effects of the Fall, to explore and then to let loose part of itself as an angelic child.

Secondly, because of the skewing of energy on this level, you are only partially forming those angelic children, and they are still linked to you by 'umbilical cords'. Again, with the pincushion analogy, you are still connected to each of those 'pins'. You cannot release them and they cannot release themselves. And, so, they are extensions of yourself that are not quite angelic children and not quite independent.

So, when you move from this level to the next level of consciousness upon physical death, if you have not absorbed *through Love* those aspects of yourself that you have not been able to free as angelic children, they remain in thought and partial consciousness within the matrix of the Earth. When you are *pulled back* because of that need to be with those children, they re-attach to you and are ignited once more. They become your fears and, yes, I *am* saying that the fears you have this time round in your incarnation, you could have had last time round …and the time before that. And, the desires that you have, you could have had last time …and the time before that …and the time before that because you have constructed these things. Once you move back into the arena of the Earth plane as a spirit encased in matter, you then reactivate those parts of yourself that are partially conscious within the matrix of the Fall.

This is why it is so important that you acknowledge your spiritual heritage and love those aspects of yourself that you fear and those aspects of yourself that give you problems. You then are able to take with you *a wholeness* when you exit this world – rather than an expression of yourself, which has that pull with it because you have invested so much in aspects of the Earth and in your fears and negativity and have left those fears and negativity here with links to you that will 'call to you in night', as it were, that will disturb you and will give you that impetus to reincarnate once more so that *strangely* you can be with your fears because you know on a subconscious level that those fears are expressions of yourself.

Is all that making sense?

**David:** Yes, it sounds like 'better the devil' you know, and so you reincarnate because that is what you are happy with.

**Joseph:** It is information that I can only give you at this stage, having given you all the other information on the Fall and how you operate within the Fall. This book was always intended to be a further illumination into the frightening aspects and consequences of what the Fall has produced as an area of being. It is often said in your world that you are in 'Hell' now ...and, indeed, you are. But, in understanding that 'Hell' you can transform it into 'Heaven' and you can *very quickly* (except you will not believe that because you are so enmeshed in negativity) turn the Earth and yourselves back to what you originally were and to what you are supposed to be now ...and still are at core.

I am sorry but the energies are waning, and I have to relieve Michael of his duties once again until we next meet.

## Chapter Four
## Guess Who's Coming to Dinner!

**Joseph:** Chapter four. I am going to deal with another *serious subject* this morning, but in doing so I want to begin with a humorous title for this chapter. This is something that I gave Michael a few weeks ago as the theme for this chapter, and he thought I was kidding ...and I *was* because I wanted to say something funny – and so the title of this chapter is: *Guess Who's Coming to Dinner!*

**Guess who's coming to dinner** – which, of course, is a reference to a popular film from some years ago that was often quoted in cartoons and television programmes as a joke. *Guess who's coming to dinner* because, having spent two chapters talking about entities, demons and discarnate spirits who can influence you, I have to say to you that from a certain point of view you, as an angel enclosed in physical matter, represent a delicacy ... represent food ...represent a dinner ...represent a wonderful meal!

**Now, who on Earth would want to *eat* you?**

**Who on Earth would want to take away all your energies?**

The Earth is a strange place when you begin to view it from a psychic and spiritual point of view because, from a spiritual point of view, you are constantly putting into the atmosphere *that which you believe to be true and that which you fear*. And, because you are angelic children, you 'give birth', as it were, to further angelic children. But, within the confines and results of the experiment that was the Fall, you only *partially* give birth to further children (as we discussed to some extent in the last chapter). So, your children are not the wonderful, glowing angelic children that they should be as a part of you that you have projected further out into the ether to become *independent* and to reflect God's glory. You give birth, through the natural mechanism that you exhibit as an angelic being ...to your fears ...to your depressions ...to your anxieties ...to your views of the world – not fully but *partially*.

And, so, you are constantly sending out as a background aspect of yourself ...an image of fear ...an image of trepidation ...an image of depression ...an image of illness. And, because you constantly feed these partial fears, worries and negative views, *you partially give birth to them*. Those embryonic angelic children (in the way of thought that will eventually give way to form) mingle and mix across the Earth psychically ...**and have to have a form.** They are given a partial sentience by your fear today, by the fear of the person next to you and by the fear of people across the world constantly projecting and personifying those fears, upsets, depressions and illnesses. So, within this 'soup of thought' that you have projected out as part of your natural ability as angelic children, *there is partial sentience* ...partial personification of fear ...partial personification of depression ... partial personification of need ...and partial personification of greed.

In many, many, many instances that partial personification coalesces here and there into what I have to describe 'feeders' or semi-sentient beings that exist to consolidate your fear ... consolidate your depression ...consolidate your illness ... consolidate your view of these things, and to serve you as your partially-formed angelic children.

But, having been given sentience, these 'semi-beings' need energy in order to survive and in order to focus on what they see as their *need* ...and their need is to amplify your fear ...to amplify your depression ...to amplify your illness ...to amplify your negativity ...to amplify your anger. Now, in order to do those things and to exist as what they are, they have to have a source of energy.

**...And the source of energy, dear Reader, is *you* and people like you.**

For example, if you are depressed for any length of time – be it through illness or circumstance – then you emit a vibration at a lower level of energy than you usually do as the angelic being that you are in full health. That vibration connects to and attracts feeders of equal vibration. They are attracted to your Light – not as a fully conscious thing but as a magnetic attraction with a limited degree of sentience. They then attach themselves to you. If you were to look at these beings, you would see that some of them have tentacles and some of them appear to be like a slug that is grey or black in colour with a changing form. But, they are able to latch on to a similar vibration (as all things do) so that they can take energy from that similar vibration.

So, as an example, in your depression you will attract one or more of these feeders – these partially-formed, semi-sentient, embryonic angelic children – and they will subsequently attach themselves to the point on your etheric body from which they can draw the most energy. That is usually one of the major chakra points, and you will find that they attach themselves to your forehead, to your throat, to your heart-centre or to your solar plexus. They will magnetically connect to you and, from that point onwards in order to draw the low level of energy that they need to maintain themselves and to survive, it is in their interest to keep you (in this example) depressed and to keep you at that lower level of energy, because a higher level of energy is of no use to them. A higher level of energy does not feed them; it is 'above them', so to speak, and they cannot connect to it. So, they keep you focussed on that lower level of energy *so that you can maintain them and they can maintain you in that state of mind*, and on and on goes the cycle.

What to do about these beings? What to do about feeders? How do you, first of all, detect that they are there, and how do you detach yourself from them and they from you?

Well, first of all, we have to go back to the state of meditation. **It is so important that you meditate daily** and take yourself out of the 'fast lane' of this life and spend some time reviewing the state that you are in – not just physically but *spiritually*. In meditation, you come to a point where you can determine whether the thoughts that you are having and your predominant feelings and moods are solely yours, are partially yours or belong to something else. And, at that point, in daily meditation you will also be able to see with your third eye the feeders attached to you and where they are. You will sometimes feel a tightness across the throat that signifies that one of their tentacles has connected itself there; or you will feel a heaviness across the forehead, as though you are wearing a hat, which denotes that there is a connection to a feeder at that point; and there are various other points across the body.

Having determined that you are 'not alone', as it were, and are providing a 'tasty snack' for some of these beings, you then have to deal with them. The most efficient way to deal with them is to use the action of your *physical* hands and arms and to see yourself pulling away the feeder from the point at which it has attached itself to you. If you reach out with your *psychic* senses, you will feel the width, breadth and form of the feeder, and you can put your hands around it and then gently draw it away from the chakra. As you do so, you will normally notice that the main body of the feeder is not the only aspect of it but that there are tentacles attached to the chakra in question. Keep pulling outwards from your body until you feel that you have moved the feeder far enough away from your body so that the connection to your chakra detaches.

**...And at that point you find yourself with hands full of feeder!**
You have got the being away from you in that it is not drawing
energy any more, but you have not dealt with it *and it is still
there.*

So, now hold it and use your ability, as an angelic child
connected to God, to put Light into it – not the low level of
vibration that it has been attached to you by and feeding from,
but a *higher* level ...White Light ...God-Light. See, in your mind's
eye, the God-Light infusing that feeder and see the feeder
becoming lighter and lighter and lighter. Then, there will come a
point at which you will feel the weight in your hands dissipate
and you will feel the feeder disappear. You will feel it disintegrate,
as it were, into the White Light and it will, most certainly, be
disconnected from you so that it can no longer connect to you
and you are of no use to it.

This exercise should be done at least once a week and should
*certainly* be done whenever you feel that your mood has suddenly
changed and there is no apparent reason for it – if you wake up
depressed or fearful, for example, for no apparent reason and
you didn't go to sleep with that weight upon you.

As with all physical life here the feeder has a need to exist, and
remember that *you* have partially created it. So, there is a
*responsibility* (even to these feeders that you could call 'psychic
ticks' that connect to people) to restore this Earth to a balance
of vibration that excludes that type of sentience being formed.

As I have said, the feeders are a coalescing of your fears and
worries and your aches and pains, but they are also a pocket of
expression from the Field, which is set to negative (as we have
discussed in previous books). It is as though the Field is using
that analogy of the pincushion that I gave you in an earlier
chapter and putting out aspects of itself that are partially sentient
and partially aware. And, so, you can regard feeders as little
pinpoints of coalesced Field-energy that are having a high old
time by connecting to you ...but the irony is that **they were**

created by *you* in the first place – as was the Field of consciousness. So, we are back to *the project* that I have given you from the beginning of these books which is the need to project Light into the Field; and also not to be disturbed if you find yourself connected to a feeder or 'psychic tick' but to love it away and to love the Field away through the projection of Light.

In your dealings with people, be aware that when they react badly to you oftentimes it is because *they too* have unseen 'guests' feeding at the 'table' of their spiritual and psychic energy. And, so, in dealing with people in a potentially explosive situation where there could be an argument or worse, before your meeting with these people or at the time when they are acting unreasonably, project enough Light to surround them and infuse their bodies with Light so that their ticks dissipate. The feeders can only connect to a *low* level of energy. When you are depressed ...when you are fearful ...when you are worried ... when you are ill, the amount of Light you exhibit is shrouded, is shadowed and becomes darker and greyer – and it is that Light that allows the feeders and ticks to maintain themselves. They cannot cope with a higher level of spiritual energy.

And, so, you send Light to people that you suspect have these 'infestations' (for that is what they are) and you send Light out into the Field. What happens to the feeders is that they are not dissipated, as such, but are *transformed*. The dark can only resist the Light to a certain extent and then it becomes infused with the Light and changes its intent and vibration totally. So, when you are sending Light to an individual to get rid of their ticks – you are not destroying the ticks but are transposing and changing them into something better. You are returning them to a more balanced and harmonious creative atmosphere.

The preceding two chapters and this one (if you take notice of what they are saying to you) must make it seem like you have suddenly been placed in a *very* precarious and dangerous atmosphere ...and, yes, you have; but I am not telling you these things to depress you [*laughing*] because, if I depress you, then you will attract feeders! I am telling you these things in order to make you *aware* of how things are here and how to detect signs that will indicate to you that, perhaps, you have an obsession that is born, not of yourself – but of yourself *plus* somebody else in whose interest it is to draw you towards that obsession.

Also, things are not what they seem on a global level where you have conflicts because, behind those conflicts there can be unseen entity and *demonic* representation furthering the conflict in the interests of the Field by *influencing* the people at the head of the conflict and the people behind those heads of conflict to act in a manner that rationally, as spiritual children, they would not act in.

I also want to say to you that ...your fear when it becomes amplified ...your depression when it becomes amplified ...your illness sometimes when it becomes amplified, is not always as a result of your thoughts or your body deciding to give in. It is rather that you have things, which have attached to you that maintain you at a low level of energy for as long as they can in order to survive and maintain themselves.

So, please take heart! I cannot change the way that things are other than by instructing you to send out the Light, but I can change the way that things are by making you *aware* of how things really are *spiritually*. You will see thus far in this book that your day-to-day existence is not what you think it is. It is not the nine-to-five existence. It is not the work ...and the relationship ...and the leisure ...and the saving of money for the future. That is surface. Beneath the surface there is so much going on, and there are things going on that are *detrimental* to your spiritual health and have been detrimental to the health of this planet, to the health of nations and to the health of the individual for millennia.

**It is time to *expose* this information.**

**It is time to *equip* you.**

If you are setting out on a long journey, you take with you the things you will need to sustain yourself and you are wary of the dangers that might lie on the path ahead. And, this is what I want you to be – aware of the dangers but able to transmute those dangers ...*able to transmute the darkness into Light.*

And, so, [*smiling*] I do not want to conclude this chapter by making you think that perhaps you are a delicious meal for something as you read this, but you *can be* and *you often are.* Many of your emotions are amplified negatively by so many outside influences. This is not to excuse the negative things that you do so that: 'It's all right – I can do X, Y and Z because I am being influenced externally.' But, it is to make you aware that it is important to try to hold your core emotions in a harmonious state because, when those emotions start to slide towards the *negative*, you present all kinds of opportunities for the unseen world to attach to you and to give you more of the same – to make you more depressed and to make you more ill.

Often in illness, you would cure yourself if you could *effectively* get rid of those ticks and feeders that are attracted by that low level of vibration your body is giving out because of the illness; and you would raise your vibration. Often all that is wrong is that the body cannot cope because there is so much external influence draining it and it begins to shut down. If those external influences were not there, then the body would be quite able to repair itself.

So, there is a great importance in being able to discern what is happening with yourself and with other people – and don't forget we have mentioned in the chapter that you can do this on behalf of *other people* too. In illness situations, if you are sufficiently psychically aware and you do this through repeated meditation, you will be able to see if there is something influencing or depleting another person. Then, if you ask them to sit quietly with you for a moment, you will be able to remove the ticks and mites on their behalf and help to restore that person to health ... or help to restore that person to a better frame of mind ...or, in some cases, help to prevent that person from taking their own life. With people who commit suicide, in many instances, their view of life has been tainted to such an extent by those unseen influences around them that they feel the only way out is to terminate their existence – which, of course, they cannot do.

So, not only are these last three chapters there to warn you – they are there *to arm* you so that you can work on behalf of others, as well as yourself. And, if you are a true spiritual seeker *that* has got to be your aim, not just to enlighten your own existence – but to bring Light into the existence of the people around you ...then to move on from that to bring Light into the existence of nations ...and to bring Light into the flashpoints that sometimes occur where there is so much weight of the unseen negativity around nations that they wish to strike out at another nation. *All* that can be prevented if enough of you give out the Light and if enough of you *without judgement* realise what is happening and work to dissipate the aspects of the unseen that are controlled by and drawn into the Field of negativity of mankind. You can work to dissipate those and to change this world.

Are there questions, please?

**David:** Joseph, from personal experience I have noticed (and I think Michael, Jane and Tony will probably agree) if we go into somewhere that is heavily populated – such as a city centre – we often come away a few hours later feeling drained. Is that because of these feeders, or is it because of the depression that is caused by feeders on the people that are around us?

**Joseph:** There are several reasons for feeling depleted in any crowd of people. First of all, as you become psychically and spiritually aware, you become aware of *the clatter of the human mind*. When you find yourself in a crowd situation, it is as though you have walked into a room that is full of the old-fashioned type of computer that chattered away – whirring and clicking and checking a thousand things a minute – so you have the *sheer cacophony* of the human mind, which is why we always advocate meditation. As individuals you do not know how to become quiet, and it is essential that you become quiet in order to harmonise with your true spiritual self. So, in any crowd situation you find yourself with many, many people who are giving out this atmosphere and projection of chatter, busyness, noise and confusion. So, that is one reason why you feel depleted in a crowd.

Another reason is that in any crowd there are people whose background desire is to find a way out of fear, a way out of ill health or a way out of depression. Subconsciously they are seeking energy that will restore them and subconsciously they are sending out requests: 'I need energy! I need this type of energy to be well. I need this type of energy to restore myself. I need this type of energy to get rid of fear and depression.' So, latching on to you on a subconscious level, you have connections with people who require energy, and you are depleted in crowd situations for that reason.

And, [*laughing*] then you have people in a crowd who have souls with them from the spirit side whose interest it is to keep them set to negative. You also have people in a crowd who have mites and ticks attached to them that are looking for various low vibrations of energy. There are *all kinds of agendas*, and you have in microcosm in a crowd what is happening across the world – which is what I have been trying to describe to you over the past three chapters.

So, you have a combination of things and you have to be aware, when going into a crowd situation, and visualise yourself surrounded by the highest vibration of Light that you can possibly imagine and draw out of yourself, and then seal yourself into that Light as though you were in a force field. Then, when you have come out of a crowd situation, it is best to sit for a few minutes to examine your physical and etheric bodies to see if anything is attached to you.

Again, we are down to the importance of meditation and the ability to see what is happening with you. You owe it to yourselves, but there is such a resistance to meditation. For most people it is the crowd situation that they crave – not the silence, not the introspection, not the connection with God. But, it is vital *...vital at this time particularly...* to divest yourself of anything that has connected to you and to be aware that you can get connections to these entities, feeders and discarnate spirits in crowd situations. Many people seek crowds because they do not wish to be alone, and the *irony* is that when they come back *they are not alone* ...but not in the way that they would want 'company'.

Does that answer the question?

**David:** It does. Thank you very much.

**Tony:** Joseph, in the western world we take enormous amounts of medication for various things – often to 'prevent' illnesses, and we also have another culture that takes recreational drugs and alcohol. This is a very big issue in the western world but, by doing this, does it increase our vulnerability to feeders?

**Joseph:** Absolutely it does! There is more that we will come on to as the book progresses, but first of all let us look at prescription drugs. You have a prescription drug that might have been given to someone in good faith by a doctor who firmly believes that the drug will help that person, but *the drug has an intent*. If you look back at the history of the drug, it might have been invented with the best of intentions, but then it goes to a company whose objective is to produce the drug so that people become dependent on it ...because *dependence on the drug equals 'pounds, shillings and pence'* for someone somewhere along the line of manufacture.

So, the intent behind the drug is not pure, and every drug that is manufactured is controlled by that impure *core intent* because there is that background influence and residual vibration (almost like 'homeopathy') inherent in it. So, before the drug is even taken, you have – as you are holding that drug in its beautiful little packet – that background intent. Were the intent to heal someone, there would be a completely different feel to that drug, but the intent is not solely to heal someone ...a large percentage of the intent is to make money.

So, you are putting something into your body that already has that impure signature-intent with it. Then, because of the unnatural man-made substances in it, that drug alters the vibration of the body because, in most instances, the body is having to fight the effects of the drug to some extent. The drug may do something that helps dissipate the illness, but it will have side effects that have to be combatted. And, because the body's strength is going into fighting the effects of the drug, it lowers the body's vibrational rate ...then, at that point, you have feeders and ticks attracted to that lowered vibrational rate which attach themselves to you ...*and down you go again.*

**...And what is the solution in the western world?**

**The solution is to give you more drugs!**

The solution is not to look at you holistically to see if there is something attached to you and to remove it. The solution is to give you *more* drugs with more of that signature-intent that pulls you in a downward spiral. That is why so many people depart this planet years before they would have done had they not been given that sort of blinkered treatment.

Similarly with recreational drugs, there is a connection with souls that have taken these drugs, who say: 'I want to be out of my head. I want to be in another state of mind.' So, the signature with the drug is that it is going to put you out of your mind. Also, if they are recreational drugs that are *illegal*, there is the signature of the system that brings them to you; and that system is, once again, focused on *money* at any cost and *dependence* at any cost. So, those vibrations are inherent in the recreational drugs that you take.

You can apply this to alcohol or to anything that gives you an obsessional need of that object. You have to view things holistically and see that each aspect of life that you consume has an intention behind it. And, so, it is important that you make life choices about what you consume and ingest based on how *ethical* the source is: 'How much do these people *truly* care about me? Do they care about producing an excellent product? Or, do they only care about making themselves rich and about making souls dependent upon that which they manufacture?'

Do you see that?

**Tony:** I do. So, with that intent in the pharmaceutical drug, if the readers blessed their pills – would that raise the vibration of the medication they are taking?

**Joseph:** It would. It would certainly dissipate the core intent inherent in each of the pills *to an extent*, but you also have to consider what the drug is doing to the body. In a spiritual society you wouldn't need drugs. In a spiritual society you would ingest Light and others would bathe you in Light to remove from you that which is causing you the disharmony. You are not at that stage and so, of course, at certain times there has to be something that will ease the pain and the symptoms, but the purer and more natural the substances you take, the less detrimental the effect on your body. So, where you can and if you are able (and you have to *feel able* and, through meditation and prayer, *feel it is the right thing for you*), if you can find a natural alternative that hasn't been corrupted and polluted through process – then these are the things that you should go for if you need to take something to restore your body to health. Do you understand that?

**Tony:** Thank you, Joseph.

**Jane:** Could you just clarify something, please? In your pincushion analogy in the last chapter, you described how a person's dominant thoughts become partially formed angelic children that are still attached, whereas I get the impression that the feeders and ticks have become independent somehow. How do they break away from someone's original thoughts of depression or whatever?

**Joseph:** They are the result of *background* thoughts. You may get up in the morning and think, 'I am perfectly fine,' and that is your conscious thought, but you have background thoughts that you have reinforced over the course of your life to varying degrees. You might have a fear that you have not dissipated from twenty or fifty years ago. You might have a depression that is only sparked off by your memory of a certain event that occurred some time ago. They are not dominant thoughts, but they are a 'leakage' out into the Field of the things that identify you as 'you'.

You cannot exist in isolation, you see, because you send out into your aura – and then from your aura into the greater physical world and etheric worlds – all that you believe to be true and all that you are. This is why we know all about you because it is 'written' in your aura. So, as we talked about in the previous chapter, there are those dominant aspects of yourself that you are feeding all the time – either consciously or semi-consciously – which then feed back to you. But, there are lower levels of fear and depression that come from this life and also residual vibrations from past lives that leak out into the greater Field ... and the Field has use of them because they are negative.

So, there are your thoughts of negativity leaking out and other people's thoughts of negativity leaking out. There are millions of people around this globe, and they are pouring into the Field *exactly* what the Field wants ...*negativity*, but negativity that is given a further consolidation – not so much as to be an aspect of you that is fed back to you (as we have said in the previous chapter) but to become semi-aware. It is not the awareness of a human being, but is a response-awareness in the case of a feeder or a tick. At its basest level it is: 'I must survive! I need a similar level of energy to feed on in order to survive.' And, so, you let go of these things daily and conjure more of them up, and they consolidate and cluster. Your residual fear links with someone else's residual fear of a similar vibration, and when there is enough of that vibration within the Field – which is itself sentient – you get a kind of semi-sentience and form.

You may wonder why a feeder looks like a slug or an octopus and why it has tentacles and tubules. It has these things because, once it has gained this base semi-sentience, it then adjusts itself to the most efficient form it can have in order to draw energy from a human being. It has to have a form so that it can clamp on to you, connect to your principal chakras and not fall away from you. Drawing on the vibrations emanating from people all the time, it has enough sentience to form itself into the most appropriate shape and form to achieve what it wants to do … which is to draw energy from you and survive.

Do you see that?

**Jane:** Yes, thank you.

**Joseph:** Because the energy is rapidly dissipating (and I am afraid that Michael will have an 'interesting' time of it, and I do apologise), I wish to conclude by saying that we are going to move on to other aspects of the world that will open the eyes of readers and will make them aware and armed, as I have said, in a complete way as to *what is really happening across this planet* that they appear to live on in a certain three-dimensional way. But, I also have to stress that this book is one of joy and one of Light – as all my other books are. So, we are dealing with some dark subjects, but we are dealing with them in order to turn them into Light.

## Chapter Five
# The Illness Agenda

**Joseph:** Chapter five – *The Illness Agenda*. I want to open a new section of the book now, because I want to make you aware of your place in relation to the world. You probably think that you work in isolation, that your existence is your own, that you do not affect other objects and that other objects do not affect you. What I want to show you over the next three chapters is that *quite the opposite is true*, and I want to open by discussing illness and disease.

In my first communications [*reference to **Revelation**]* I quite rightly said that you cannot be ill; that, as an angelic being at core, *you cannot be ill because you are perfection personified* – literally! So, illness is a misconception and something that you believe to be true, but further to that statement I want to look at 'dis-ease'. I want to look at illness and some of the viruses and the afflictions that you contract.

In the beginning, when the devas created the landscape of this world and the life forms that would eventually house the spiritual angelic form, there were only *benevolent* life forms. I want you to understand that ...**only benevolent life forms**. It is because of the effects of the Fall that animals prey on other animals. It is because of the effects of the Fall that there is a power-seeking and a perceived need to absorb energy.

In the beginning, when the devas were *delighting* in creating different life forms and different expressions of 'what could be', the life forms existed in harmony with each other ...and that included the microorganisms that you hold responsible for disease. At the time of the Fall, there then ensued a perceived need for power by those angelic children that had decided to pursue a different path of creation and, as a result of which, had cut themselves off in consciousness from their God and from the knowledge that they were, in fact, angelic beings. They began to perceive lack and would look at others and say: 'I need the energy that you have. I need the power that you have. I need to control you so that I feel secure and so that I have enough energy to take me through life safely, and I have gathered around me that which I need to survive.'

At that point with each angelic child lusting, to a lesser or greater extent, for power, the Field of human consciousness – that had already been turned to negative because of the effects of the Fall – became *stronger*. The perception of mankind was that *it needed* ...it needed power ...it needed energy and, as a result of this and the chaos that ensued following the decision that led to the Fall, *beings began to prey on beings*.

**There was no meat eater before the Fall**. There was no need to digest heavy matter. There was no need to take from another in order to exist as an individual. But, as a result of the Fall, all that changed – and poured into the Field was a global desire for power and a global perception that energy was needed. As that perception was absorbed by the Field, it was fed back to the current and successive generations, who then made it a subconscious 'fact' – as they saw it: 'I *do* need power. I *do* need to absorb power. I *do* need to take what others have to fortify my position as I travel through, what I perceive as, a small life with no spiritual aspect to it and with no expansion of that life once my physical frame has been left behind.'

**That perception then applied to the less individual life forms.** Living within the Field were the creations of the devas that had not taken human form – the various animal forms and the flora and fauna. They, too, absorbed this supposed need to survive and supposed need to prey on others and take what others have in order to survive. ...If you believe that you need to survive but do not consider that there is a spiritual option to do so by drawing energy from the God-*within*, then you look *without* to others on your plane of existence. As a result of that, the animal and plant forms all began to vie for power and to prey on each other to claim their 'corner' of this globe so that they could survive.

At that point, the microorganisms that you see as being responsible for disease also began, as a matter of survival and at a group-conscious level, to prey on other life forms – the other life forms being hosts that they then made the centre of their universe so that they could absorb energy. In addition to this, once the fallen angelic children began to become ill, they believed that the microorganisms responsible for the illness had power over them and were negative things that sought to overcome them.

So, into the subconsciousness of mankind and into the Field of human consciousness, was introduced the added belief that illness was something that, not only sought to pull someone down – but was also 'evil' and a negative force. That thought was reinforced and sent into the Field and fed back to the human beings living around the globe at that time ...and also to the microorganisms, *giving them an agenda to become exactly what they were perceived to be by humankind at that time and in successive generations.*

And, so, coded into what were formerly harmless microorganisms was an agenda to take people and animals down, not just to survive – but to destroy and obliterate. This was not the original agenda of the microorganisms but an agenda that was imprinted onto them by the effects of the Fall and also by subsequent observation of what illness did, which has been reinforced ...and reinforced ...and reinforced ...and reinforced to this present day.

So, you have illnesses that attack you and, first of all, you look at them negatively which, of course, you would if something is attacking you. You then also believe *subconsciously* that the illness has an agenda to defeat you and cause you to depart this physical world. And, because you believe that, you *accelerate* the effect of the illness on you and you further consolidate the view that the illness is an evil thing. Societies existed in the past that regarded illnesses as the work of the devil or of evil spirits, and *all* these views of illness as being a negative thing – past and present – reinforce illness as being a negative thing *and give illness force.*

I would like you to consider that the viruses and organisms you see as causing illness are *still benevolent at core* and at core have no interest in hurting, destroying or despatching you. I would like you to consider that, just as those microorganisms have been programmed by the progress of time and consolidation of thought, you can overlay and infuse them with a *different coding.* You can recognise them as what they once were and can instil Light into them which will recode them so that, not only can they not harm you – but they *have no wish to harm you.*

Every time you look at an illness with your own eyes or through the eyes of the medical profession, you are seeing something that is a threat with the potential to destroy you. That is the only way that you view it, and that is, unfortunately for the most part, the only way that the medical profession views it *the instant* it is diagnosed – as something that is negative, destructive and something to fight. What you have to do with illness (and what the medical profession will *eventually* have to do if it wants to conquer illness) is to recognise the God ...the good ...the *benevolence* in the illness and not view the illness as something that sweeps through the body and destroys it.

Am I suggesting to you that if you are brought low by an illness or have a potentially life-threatening illness (as you see it) that you ignore it? No, but I *am* suggesting that you ignore the evidence of centuries that says that this thing is going to destroy you. I *am* suggesting that you start from scratch and say: 'This microorganism, this virus, this invasion of my body does exist, but it is neither malevolent nor benevolent. It is something that I can encode in my daily meditations to give it the correct spin and the correct force.'

In any illness *you choose* what the outcome is by your perception and your strengthening of a certain set of values that you donate to the illness, because *the illness is sentient* in that the universe is sentient. And, this is what this section of the book will expand upon – the fact that objects around you are sentient. You may not think of a virus as being affected by your thoughts or as having any kind of intelligence. It has an intelligence influenced by the global waves of thought that persuade it to act in a certain way, and have persuaded it to act in a certain way for generations ...upon generations ...upon generations.

There is not you and the illness, with one affecting the other from the point of view of the illness having the upper hand. There *is* you and the illness *but you are linked*. There *is* you and the illness with you able to communicate with the illness and able to reason with it and say: 'I accept that you are there, but I also accept that you are able to respond to my wishes and to the charge that I put into you, and that you are able to respond to my observations of you as either a malevolent or benevolent force. *And, I choose you to be a benevolent force.* I do not put up a resistance to you, but instead, through my imagination, I infuse you with Love and Light. By doing so, I sweep away the effects of millions of years that have instructed you to act in a certain way and you, being intelligent as part of global intelligence, have obeyed those instructions. I personally give you different instructions. I see you as part of deva creation and as something that is benevolent, something that is beautiful and something that was brought forth, initially, not to destroy but as something to examine different forms of expression of deva energy in an evolutionary expansion to seek out forms that could house angelic spirits.'

Devas, of course, are also angelic spirits, but with deva creation there is a 'hive-mentality' that connects the expressions of creation that devas bring forth ...the animals, trees and flowers, etc. We talked in *the Fall* about devas being trapped as the creators of the backdrop against which you express yourselves. So, the original life-energies that were brought forth as different expressions of animal forms and various other forms of life were *benevolent*. There is never a thought in a deva's mind of: 'I shall create something that is malevolent.' And, there is never a *new form* that is introduced into the matrix. What I am saying is that **all forms of life have been here since the beginning of the creation of this world** ...all forms of life *including* the microorganisms that you see as causing disease. So, when you say that a new disease that has been found to cause harm to mankind – no! What has been discovered is a *new encoding* of those microorganisms to group together in a way to attack you that hasn't been tried before. (Oh dear!)

...Because, mixed in with the negative thoughts in the Field are aggressive and violent thoughts, and those thoughts affect those most basic of life forms and encode them differently. So, there is no such thing as a 'new disease'. There is, rather, a new expression of malevolence, via the thoughts of mankind through the Fall, that encodes itself onto microorganisms giving a different result when they attack the human body, but they are the same microorganisms and the same expressions of deva activity. They were originally created to explore the expression of form around this globe and are not malevolent beings.

Of course, in your enlightened view of illness you also have to shut out the views of those around you, because your illness – whatever it is – will not be viewed in isolation. It is not just you viewing it. It is you ...plus the medical profession ...plus your friends and family viewing it, and they are reinforcing the negative view of the illness. It is very important, if you find yourself becoming ill, that you spend time in quiet meditation (which is a key feature of this book) and you connect to the God-within and infuse your illness with Light. Surround yourself with

Light and send Light to the people who are treating you, to the people who are part of your family and to the people who are part of your friendship circle. Surrounding them with Light, say: 'Thank you for your view of my illness, but it is only *your* view of my illness. It is not *my* view of my illness. On a subconscious level no longer view me as being ill. Thank you.'

Now, this will seem like an extraordinary turnaround in the way that you view things but, nevertheless, if there is ever to be progress against disease you have to understand that disease is controlled by the Field, is controlled by the thoughts of mankind and that **you have power over what happens in your body**. Tremendous power! More power than the consolidated views of mankind and more power than the illness you perceive as attacking you ...*because you can draw on the God-within*. You are an angelic being and you, as an angelic being, were created perfect. You are perfection personified. This will help you in your view of any illness that may come to you during your lifetime.

You also have to understand that there is a view that 'even if you survive' an illness you will be disabled ...will be weak ...will have aged. All these things are further views of the effects of the illness that need not be there and should not be taken for granted. You, in the measure that you believe and send Light to what you perceive as being wrong with you, *can cure anything* because, ultimately, there is nothing to cure.

**All that needs to be cured is a viewpoint**. All that needs to be cured is the quality of vibration that links you to the illness that has attacked you, as you would see it ...or... 'made a connection with you' is a better phrase. That is what needs to be cured. It is as though there is an argument where you and the disease have differing viewpoints. What you need to do is to make the disease see things from your point of view, not through anger or through upset – but by simply sending Light to the illness and infusing that illness throughout your body with Light to bring it back to its original coding, which was to be a benevolent being that existed, not to destroy *but simply to experience*.

There are, of course, other aspects of illness; and I am not talking about breaks or damage to the body here – although those things can also be repaired by viewing the body as being perfect again and by communicating with the cells in the body. Because of the effects of the Fall, the cells in the body are also encoded with a disbelief in repair because generations and generations of mankind have said: 'You will only heal at a certain rate and to a certain percentage. You cannot repair yourself. We have evidence.'

What evidence? When, what you would consider to be 'miracles' occurred in the past, those miracles happened because there was a greater belief in the person being healed – *as being perfect* – than that person and the people around them had in the effects of the illness. There was a greater belief in the Light that was within.

I also have to tell you that at times during mankind's evolution... (I don't want to say 'evolution' – that is the wrong word because you have not evolved since the time of the Fall! Oh, you have bright, shiny things to play with, but you have not evolved. You are still the same as you were at the point of the Fall.) ...In the dim and distant past, there were times when illness was also used as a weapon by those who wanted to attack and who desired great power. This is not something that has happened for millennia, but it did exist in the past. There were times when creations of the deva (as we talked about with demonic existence in a previous chapter) were used *very specifically* to target people to bring them to their knees. There are echoes of that in the illnesses that you perceive and suffer from at this time. There are still echoes because anything that you have encoded into the Field that is negative has had millennia to become embedded within the Field and within perception. You are so used to looking at things in a negative way that, in almost every decision you make, you weight up the positive and the negative ...and you almost always err on the negative side. That is how long you have had the effects of the Fall around you.

My purpose in communicating this book is to make you aware of these things and then to give you the ammunition to change things for the better. Which of you does not want to be healthy? Which of you wants to be ill? Which of you does not want the ability to negate the effects of illness ...to talk to an illness, dispense with it and restore yourself to health? These are the gifts that are available to you when you tune in to your true angelic self.

So, I would ask you to look at illness in a different way from the moment you read this chapter and to understand that nothing out there – from a microbe to a lion – is your enemy. It is only your enemy because you have decided it is your enemy, and because you have decided that animal 'A' eats animal 'B' eats animal 'C'. You have decided that certain expressions of life are dangerous. Initially, all expressions of life on this globe were benevolent ...*and they still are*. It is only your instruction to them that needs to change. Your instruction to them should be one of Love.

Again, we are down to you needing to spend time on a daily basis (sometimes almost on an hourly basis, if you can afford a couple of minutes each hour) to redress the balance. Look at that phrase ...**redress the balance**. This is what you are looking for – *balance*! In an illness ...in an aggressive situation ...in violence there is a lack of balance. Once you bring balance into the situation, through transmitting Light into the negativity, you restore harmony – and in harmony there can be no violence.

We will look at other aspects of your world in the next two chapters with regard to you not being at the mercy of them but having an influence on them.

The thing I want you to, please, take from this chapter is the knowledge that illness is not what it appears to be. It is not a given thing that an illness can attack and destroy you. It is not a given thing that because an illness in the past has resulted in a certain outcome for people that that outcome will happen to you.

It is not a given thing that there is a certain amount of time for which an illness lasts. An illness only has a priority to make you ill for as long as you acknowledge that priority, and the priority goes back to the time of the Fall when illness was viewed as something 'evil' and that volition has been imprinted into the makeup of the illness.

Questions, please!

**Tony:** Joseph, in this arena of microorganisms our thinking is a big problem because sometimes there is a positive advantage to being ill. People can feel loved and are given attention through having an illness. Our thinking is our worst enemy and we have a lot of work to do, haven't we?

**Joseph:** Your *physical* mind (as we have said in many of the books) is your worst enemy. You have a heart-mind that connects you to God, and it is that transference of volition and thought from the head-mind to the heart-mind that is *the key* to all this, because all that I am saying to you is *known* via your heart-centre. The head-mind will say: 'What Joseph has just said about illness is rubbish.' But, it is in the interests of the head-mind to say that because it is keyed into the effects of the Fall. The physical mind is keyed into and influenced *almost totally* by the physical society that you see around you. So, it is in the interests of that mind to keep you believing what you believe at present.

What people have to do is to be brave enough to explore and discover for themselves that there is another seat of intelligence – *angelic intelligence* – and the seat of this intelligence is at the heart-centre. And, I would say to readers of this book: 'You have nothing to lose and everything to gain by exploring that possibility.'

There *is* a lot of work that needs to be done, but the work needs to be done from *within*. The greatest challenge that we have as communicators is persuading people to spend some point in their day going within to discover that the universe is actually within them and not outside of them. People will think of a million excuses for not doing this, but it is *the only way* to discover who you really are ...to reconnect to the knowledge within you ...to reconnect to the God within you ...to reconnect to the angelic intent and identity within you. But you have to do it. There is no other way. I cannot reach inside you and say: 'Here is your heart-centre!' **You have to discover it yourself.** It is your right, through God's free will that pervades the universe, to do it for yourself, but *you* have to do it; and the benefits are wonderful – not just to free yourself from your perceptions of disease and illness but also to free others.

You are quite right, Tony, in saying that there are advantages to illness in that people draw attention to themselves and say: 'Focus on me. I need help. I don't need to do this and I don't need to do that because I am ill.' But, by going within, you discover that you have all the Love you need. The greatest aspect of Love is to give it out – not to seek it. You are seeking something that is yours all the time. And, when you discover that Love through the heart-centre, you discover that there is so much Love for yourself ...but there is also so much Love that you can give out that it bubbles over and extends into the universe and is transmitted to everyone that you meet. The greatest gift you have is to say: 'I don't need this crutch anymore. I don't need this illness. I don't need to look at myself as being unloved.'

The reason you look at yourself as being unloved is because you are operating, for the most part, through the physical mind and the physical mind says that you lack ...and you need ...and you want ...and that no one understands you ...and no one gives you what you want. You are looking outside of yourself for the things that you want, and [*laughing*] the things that you want *you don't need* because they are with you in here [*pointing to the heart-centre*]. What you need is to take the time and to have the discipline to commune daily with what you really are.

You are an angel that is blindfolded. You walk through life blindfolded. You are an angelic being and, from birth to death, so many of you are not aware of that. You are not aware of this glorious, immortal inheritance that you have. Doesn't it make sense to actually investigate that possibility – investigate what you are and discover for yourself?

Does that answer your question?

**Tony:** Thank you, Joseph. In actual fact as 'spiritual doctors' that is exactly what we should be getting over to people rather than intervention.

**Joseph:** Spiritually minded doctors should be looking for the God and the good in each situation. Their perception of illness should be something that can be persuaded to change *through Light* to benefit the patient. Spiritual doctors should not add negativity to their diagnosis. Their diagnosis should simply be factual: that a person is inflicted with this particular ailment at that time. But, they don't do that and, again, it is the fault of the Fall and millennia of thinking in a certain way. What they do is to make a diagnosis and then superimpose onto it their view of how the illness will react and what will happen to the patient within a certain timescale. They do not know that! They only 'know' that through their negativity, which is as an effect of the Fall. They *should* say: 'This is what I perceive you to have. I can now treat this and can get *you* – because you are the greatest doctor in this situation – to treat it through a change in perception, attitude and approach to this illness.'

Do you see that?

**Tony:** I do. Thank you, Joseph.

**Jane:** Joseph, this is just a comment that people could practise and prove it for themselves. They could start now by building up a track record in dealing with the smaller ailments (such as a headache or eczema) and they would get used to the fact that they *can* heal their body. Then, if something more major comes along later, they would have that reinforced belief, whereas if they just left it until they got cancer, for example, it would be too overwhelming.

**Joseph:** It is never at a point where it is too overwhelming. It is the body and the physical mind that are overwhelmed. The angel that you are is never overwhelmed. The angel that you are knows that you are not ill. It is not a matter of faith – it is matter of *knowing* in the extent that you open up to your angelic capabilities.

So, yes, it is quite right that you can practise by visualising away …and yet 'away' is the wrong term. I should be telling you to *embrace* the illness, not to acknowledge its effects – but to embrace it as a 'friend' and to put your angelic arms around it to love it into a different frame of mind. And, that is what you should do. In your visualisation you should view the illness as no longer invading the body, but *you should also love it.*

If you do not love it, you are putting up resistance against it and are instructing it to be what it is. You see, an illness is being what it has been encoded to be. The illness is not 'evil' but is looked upon as being 'evil' and is given power by the patient and is given power by the doctors, which then harmonises with a belief in the illness that goes back for millennia.

What you have to do is say: 'This cannot harm me. This is just another expression of life. This is my friend and I love it. I harmonise with it. I do not resist it. I acknowledge it. I infuse it with Light and with Love.' It is so much easier to infuse something with Light and with Love if you see it, not as your enemy but as your friend.

And, yes, there is the complexity of *why* has a person attracted an illness at a certain point in their life? It is a complex interaction, but we are looking at *one aspect* of it and the basic aspect of illness we are examining today is the fact that illness is *programmable*. Not only is illness programmable, but it has been programmed towards the negative side for millennia.

You have the physical and mental understanding *but not the spiritual understanding* of doctors, nurses and research scientists; and then you have the interests of companies and those who invest in illness. With the best will in the world, those who research, market and produce the drugs that purport to combat the illness *have an investment in that illness*. And, so, part of their subconscious approach when they are at the office day after day developing, promoting and sending out the drugs is: 'This is a good thing! It is good to have this illness because the drugs that I sell to combat it give me the power that I need to get through my life comfortably.'

And, so, we have come full circle ...we began the chapter with a discussion of how there was a perceived need for power and that you had to prey on others in order to feed that power, and here we are in what you perceive as 'modern times' with the same need going on but this time dressed up in suits and driving nice cars to an office. It is the same negativity and the same mistaken need that goes back to the time of the Fall. Do you see that?

**Jane:** Yes.

**Joseph:** But, yes, people should start small if they so wish and say: 'Today, I am making a friend of this particular headache or this ache and this pain. Today, instead of using the drug, I am going to infuse it with Light. Today, I am going to make a friend of it; and I am going to love it and love my body better. I am going to love that illness so that I am negating its effects and it will have no further effect on me. And, if it leaves my body, it will have no further negative effect on the global consciousness.'

So, you are consolidating your little corner and making strong a view that illness is not what it is perceived to be, and you are eliminating that negativity from your own body, own aura and own life. But, you are also sending out a view into the Field that illness is not what it is said to be. And, if enough of you do this (and this has been a theme in many of the books), you consolidate and change the way that things are perceived.

**David:** Joseph, as science puts forward its theory of evolution that flora and fauna change form in order to adapt to circumstance, climate and environment – that just seems to back up what you have been saying. The devas behind the flora and fauna are trapped within the Fall so the forms they put out reflect the sense of lack by searching for energy outside of themselves rather than from within. So, in a sense the theory of evolution backs up what you are saying.

**Joseph:** 'Evolution' is not the term I would use. I would say *mental evolution* because evolution presupposes that things are adapting and getting better. The mental evolution I am talking about is the construction via thought into form that has occurred since the time of the Fall. As you say, there are life forms that adapt in order to consume energy or to become the top predator, but you have, at the core of those life forms, *benevolent expressions* of deva activity.

I wish I could share with you the *joy* that is felt by the devas in creating, in examining and in putting forth part of themselves as a myriad of different life forms and experiencing how those life forms fit together. In other spheres and on other planets, there is not this violent backdrop. There is not the need on the spiritually advanced worlds to consume and to dominate. There are simply different expressions of life that are examined in joy.

And, if those expressions of life are no longer needed, then they are withdrawn by the deva. Nothing is lost. The physical expression may become 'extinct' as you would understand it, but the energy has not been harmed. The energy has been brought back in by the deva to be put out as further examination and expressions of life – some of which will eventually be chosen to house angelic beings who are travelling through those worlds that they have created, in conjunction with the devas, in order to experience certain aspects of creation and certain opportunities. They can then move through those spheres and grow and can, of course, leave angelic children in their wake – with angels giving birth to angels as we explained in *the Fall*.

Much of evolution is as a result of the negative views of mankind being put onto various life forms and the dictate that you must survive ...must consume ...must have territory. All these things are beliefs that came about because of the Fall, and they are imprinted on the less individualised life forms, which are brought through constantly and maintained and enjoyed by the devas, but are then (as we have discussed with the microorganisms) imprinted by the dominant wishes of mankind. So, there is this 'sticky coating' of *you have to survive and adapt* imprinted on the life forms. But, that adaptation is not for the sake of exploring beautiful new aspects of that which was before which has become something more – adaptation is solely to survive, and that is not why deva expression is given form.

Deva expression is given form to examine different opportunities and different ideas ...always with Love and always with God at heart to provide different backdrops for angelic beings to move through, to revel in the *beauty* of form brought forth and to say: 'God, look what I have created! Look at this wonderful animal. Look at the beauty, the Love and the perfection in it. I love it. You love it. It loves all other forms of life.' That is *at core* what deva activity is for and there is, unfortunately, a convergence of intent that is superimposed onto life here because of the effects of the Fall.

Does that answer your question?

**David:** It does, thank you.

Chapter Six
## Your Dance with Reality

**Joseph:** Chapter six – *Your Dance with Reality.* First of all, I must express my delight at being able to come through and speak to you once again, although you know that from my point of view it is not an interrupted journey – it is a *continuous* journey.

I want to begin this chapter by asking the reader to imagine it is a *typical* day – and the word 'typical' is important. It is a typical day for them. They get up in the morning and, perhaps, stub their toe on the corner of the bed. Then they eat their breakfast quickly, which might result in indigestion as they sit in traffic going to work in a car or bus, where it seems as though the vehicle doesn't go fast enough and things don't go according to plan. They then find themselves, maybe, in an office where they work for most of the day, and during that day there are various mishaps ...the computer doesn't work as it should ...they bang themselves against a desk ...perhaps there is a minor altercation with fellow workers ...they rush down a lunch that, again, doesn't agree with them. They then sit in the car or bus to come home, but once they are home there are other trials to deal with ...the washing machine isn't working properly ...the television doesn't show what they want to view ...there are various things that need to be repaired and sorted out.

It is, as I have said, *a typical day*, and during that typical day that person's view of what happens to them is that ...this is the way the day is ...this is the way that objects react ...this is the way that people react …this is the way that society reacts …this is the way that the world reacts. They see themselves as going through a set of circumstances and that those circumstances are just 'the way things are' and in no way attached to them and in no way a part of them.

**I wish to tell you this morning that you *influence* everything and every object that you come into contact with during every waking moment and every sleeping moment.**

With every object that you encounter, as soon as you attach relevance and consciousness to it, *you begin a dance of energy with it* – something that I could describe as the 'energy exchange'. And, were you to look with psychic eyes, you would see people sensing and reacting with a myriad of objects during every day, and with each object there is an exchange of energy.

In the example of a cup, the moment that you look at it energy goes out from you and does a spiritual 'handshake' with that cup, which alerts the cup to the fact that you are observing it and alerts the cup to the fact that you need a reaction from it. Now, that reaction *should* be: 'I am a cup and I am here to serve you until such time as you don't want me to be a cup.' But, unfortunately, with your psychic handshake there is also transmitted an expectation of what the cup will give back to you.

So, you observe the cup, but you do not solely want a cup. You want a cup that will react to you according to your worldview of how cups and every other object that you encounter during your daily lives should react to you. If you expect the cup to be cumbersome …if you expect it to be too big or too short …if you expect it to spill its contents …if you expect it to react with you negatively *that is exactly what the cup gives back to you* via this spiritual 'handshake' that took place the moment you observed the cup. In other words, you tell the cup what it is to be, not only an object that you recognise through society as something that holds a liquid – but also with regard to how that cup treats you and what you can expect from it.

Now, each object that you encounter *should be dormant* until the time that you encounter it and project consciousness, awareness and observation onto it and through it. Unfortunately, you have the expectations of millions of souls who are also observing cups throughout the world and dictating subconsciously what a cup should be. So, your brand-new piece of crockery is already pre-programmed to react to you in a certain way *before* you even buy it and add it to your home.

**You do a 'dance' with each object that is around you – *every single object*!**

You activate every single object and then, when you take your vision away from it, that object should become neutral and passive but, because of the effects of the Fall …(the 'original sin', if you like, whereby matter was altered by the angelic children in a certain way so that they forgot who they were and forgot their connection to God-consciousness and God-creativity)… each object is pre-programmed and *is not neutral*. Each object contains within it the wishes of all the souls that observe it as a certain type of object in order to react with them correctly when observed…

I hope that is making sense. I am aware of background interference [*reference to noise disturbance from next door*] so I am trying to push through that. Let me reiterate…

In an ideal creative society, every object should be neutral until activated by the observer. However, as a result of the Fall, flowing through each object is a background predisposition to act in a negative rather than a positive way. So, when you connect to that cup by observing it, if you are connecting to it with an expectation that it will react to you in a negative way …*you are enhancing and reinforcing the negative vibrations that are already in it*, so what you get back is a negative response rather than a positive or neutral one.

And, so, there is this delicate dance with every object and every situation that you come across during your day-to-day lives. With what I have just said, first of all there is a realisation that, if you are the observer and instructor as to what each object does for you, **you are *in command* of the objects that you direct your observation towards.** You then can turn around your expectation of those objects and can create a *different dance*. In this dance of creativity that comprises each of your days here, you can take command. You can decide that instead of it being a typical day (and I referred to 'typical' as being an important word because your idea of the typical day is probably one of it being a negative day) ...instead of it being a 'typical day' you will say to yourself: 'Today is going to be *an atypical day* until I have sufficiently reprogrammed my own personal field. Today, I am going to be aware that *I lead* in each dance – I lead in each connection to each object so that each object is going to respond to me in the way that I want it to respond. In other words...

'I am not going to stub my toe on the bed.

'I am not going to have a breakfast that causes indigestion, because I will observe the ingredients and see the God-content in them and say that those contents cannot possibly lead to indigestion for me.

'I will sit in the car or on the bus and will decide how I will react with the other drivers or people on the bus ...and I will react with them by seeing the God-consciousness and the positivity in them and by allowing that to be fed back to me via my observations of the people around me.

'I will see my job as being a creative, positive thing. I will infuse every aspect of it with God-creativity. I will see my fellow workers as people who react to me in a positive way – people I don't argue with and people I observe as having God within them. Therefore, they will react to me on an angelic level and there will be harmony within my workplace.

'I will see my home as a spiritual fortress and the objects and people within it will react to me on a God-level and on a level of positive creativity; and they will bring back to me that God-energy, that Love and that harmony so that I rise above my expectations of what happens within my own home.'

I am saying to you that you are in charge of, not only your own life and your own body – but you are in charge of the reaction you get back from *every single object* that you encounter day and night throughout your life.

What you also have to bear in mind is that observing the God-within eliminates the negative charge that is inherent in objects because of other people's observations of them. So, you have to use that God-charge, that God-observation, that positivity, that Love and that harmony to observe objects, people and situations in that way in order to overcome the inherent negative charge within them because of the change in vibration that came about because of the Fall.

[*At this point there was a short pause in the communication.*]

I am taking Michael deeper into the trance state because I want to combat the noise that he is picking up on a physical level [*reference to the slight disturbance coming from the people next door*]. There is more that I wish to say on this subject this morning, and I apologise for the interference.

I want to talk about the nature of your reality. Having spoken about the fact that you can encode your reality with a certain set of values, I now want to talk about what *is* and what *is not* there.

You see everything as solid and as permanent but, as I have said, in an angelic state of creation (as opposed to your state of creation that has been polluted by the effects of the Fall), the landscapes and the objects that you see around you are not actually active in your life until you observe them. They lie there as a background of information to allow you to experience *and nothing more*.

Do you see how you have invested too much in your material objects as a result of *this* spiritual reality? You look at your objects and you, not only expect a reaction from them in terms of how you interact with them, but you solidify them and put onto them an importance that is not there. They are only your 'tools' to allow you to experience as you pass through various landscapes spiritually to evolve as a soul. They are not meant to be the be-all and end-all, and they are not meant to be *as solid* as you observe them to be.

In other spiritual spheres where the angelic children have not been polluted by the effects of the Fall, it is possible to determine the *degree of solidity* or 'reality' that is attached to each object, depending on what you want from that object. So, as an example on the Earth plane, you might look at your car and to you a car is a very solid, metallic thing that you can push your hand up against but no further because it is tougher than your hand – and that is because you observe it as something that is always so.

If you were reacting on another material sphere of spirituality, you could determine that that 'car' would be a car that could take you somewhere on one occasion and then be a background object on another occasion. You would rank it in terms of its solidity and its permanence at any time, dependent on what you wanted from it. So, you might want to use the car for a journey and it would be very solid, but then at the end of your journey, you would get out of your car to meet with someone. That car would still be within your observation but would be phased out of the *importance* of your observation, which would then be centred on the person that you are with and not on the car. And, as a result of this withdrawing of a hundred per cent level of observation of the car, the car would be less permanent and would fade into the background until such time as you wished to draw it out and go back home.

Now, if you have read my other books, you will realise that that is the way you operate in the spirit realms to a finer degree. And, I am not talking about cars, but I am talking about objects that you can bring out of the 'ether', as it were, observe them for the time that you want to use them and then put them back into the ether. What I want to explain (and I have touched upon this in the other books) is that there are other *material worlds* of existence where more spiritual values hold sway than they do with your rigid belief in materialism on Earth. In other words, there are other beings on other planets that view materialistic objects as graded objects ...as things that can be extremely solid or as things that can be semi-solid, dependent on the amount of observation that they put into them.

And, you might think: 'Well, that is an amazing thing – whereas I am sitting on a chair watching television and can feel my feet on the floor. I have a car outside. I have a house around me and I live in a town.' Yes, but there is *no difference* between those beings living in other worlds with that ability to vary the amount of solidity that they attribute to objects and with you here, except with your belief ...*except with your belief*! I am trying to get at your core belief and say that that belief is changeable, and I am not doing that to destroy your view of reality ...I am doing that to allow you to *change* your view of reality.

Again, referring to my other books, I have said that if you put Light into the world and if you see the world that you want to see and infuse that new vision with Light then you change the world. In this chapter, I am attempting to explain why and I am attempting to *shake away* your view of the world as being solid, as being immutable and as being something that you are at the mercy of. All these objects around you, *you have created* and you have created originally *spiritually*. Every object has to first exist as an idea and it is then given form, but you decide how much solidity that form has.

So, as an exercise I would like you to go through a typical day and decide that the typical day is not typical and to look at your reactions to the objects around you. What do you expect from them? You expect them to work in a certain way because they are designed as certain types of objects, but what do you expect from them *spiritually*? And you will look at me wide-eyed and say: 'Nothing, Joseph! What are you talking about – *what do I expect from them spiritually?*'

And, I could say: 'Would you ever expect Love from your cup? Would you ever expect healing and Love from your meals? Would you ever expect harmony from your car? Would you ever expect peace, tranquillity, silence and a connection to the spiritual realms via your home?'

...No, you have never thought in this way, but I am encouraging you to think in this way so that you can change your view; you can change the way that objects and people around you react to you and, ultimately, you can change your world.

You are not at the mercy of a negative world *unless* you decide that it is a negative world. You are not at the mercy of the thoughts of society *unless* you decide that the thoughts of society are also your thoughts and you are buying into them. You can change yourself.

**You exert energy.** If I could show you the equivalent of a 'spiritual X-ray' in the example of the cup – the cup exists in a neutral state when you are not looking at it. You then decide that you need the cup, so you approach it and the moment you are aware of the cup, energy from your core or solar plexus reaches out towards the cup, envelops it, infuses the cup and activates the cup as a 'cup'. Not only that but at that point – based on your core values, beliefs and expectations – the cup decides what it has to give back to you. So, this dance of energy between the two of you goes on until such time as you put the cup down.

**Your energy is stronger than the cup's energy.** Your energy is the creative energy that, *en masse* as spirits, created the cup in the first place. So, if you want to change the day that you are having; the life that you are having; the experiences around you and the way in which things react to you – you have to *consciously* use that dominant energy in a different way. And, you use that dominant energy in a different way *by changing your expectation* ...by expecting the cup to react to you in a positive way ...by expecting the cup to react to you in a spiritual way ...by expecting the cup to react to you in a harmonious way ...and also by expecting the cup to have no more value than being a cup. It is not a dominant and decisive object in your life unless you make it so – neither is the car, neither is the house and neither is the wallet.

These things only have the weight that *you* put into them, and they return to you that expectation of them being important or that expectation of them being elusive or that expectation of them being supportive to you in your life. You are supportive of yourself. You are dancing with the whole of your personal world. Remember that you *lead* in that dance and that you can dance a *different* dance. Remember that everything that you observe exchanges energy with you. You energise it. You bring it to life when you observe it and put it back into neutrality when you turn your back on it. And [*laughing*] then there is the old quandary from the point of view of earthly mentality...

**Do things still exist when you don't observe them?**

**When the cup is behind you or in the cupboard – is it still there?**

It *is* there as an expectation and it *is* there because it is also infused with the expectations of billions of souls that there should be a cup in your cupboard. But, if you expected there only to be a cup when you observed a cup, your cupboard would, in fact, be empty. There would be no cup until such time as you observed it – expecting it to be there only when you needed it.

**This also explains why you are running out of energy.** I have explained that you are running out of energy because you are trapped in a Field of negativity. But, within that Field of negativity, you have billions of souls expecting all those objects to be there ...hundreds ...millions ...trillions of objects and maintaining them in energy needlessly when they are not part of their conscious observation.

As spirits, ultimately, what you should observe objects as being are background tools or aids to your journey through a physical level and nothing more. In that way you conserve energy. You conserve energy personally; you conserve energy globally; and you do not run out of energy, which gives you more time to change the dominant energies and beliefs of the Field.

So, an awful lot to consider and, hopefully, I am shaking your view of what reality is. Your reality is not permanent. Your reality is contained within you. Your reality is not neutral because you project onto your reality expectations of that reality. You encode reality with what you expect to get back from reality.

**And, your reality is *changeable* – that is the important point.** Your reality is changeable according to your view and expectations of reality. You can expect something different – something positive and wonderful from reality after reading this chapter, and into the dance that you have with every aspect of reality, you will start to build something positive and harmonious into your life.

And, when you have changed your own life and put into perspective the materialism around you, then you can start to change the lives of others by beaming out Light from your solar plexus. This then illuminates and puts into perspective *their reality* so that they can shake themselves free of this dependence on a materialistic viewpoint of life and dependence on a negative viewpoint of life that they expect and, therefore, create to be there day ...after day ...after day ...after day.

Can I invite questions on this topic so that we can further illuminate it for the readers, please?

**Tony:** Joseph, I am looking forward to listening to the recording again afterwards, and I understand a lot of what you are saying. I am interested in this core belief about the materialism that we all have. Does it mean if we could change our belief at a core level that we could literally walk through walls?

**Joseph:** You are a creator. Each of us is a creator of worlds, and what I am saying is that we create the level of spiritual reality needed to take from each particular journey that evolves our soul the best aspects of it in order to have the greatest opportunities for growth. Over the millennia, you have solidified matter through your core beliefs as inhabitants of this planet globally, and *you continue to solidify it.*

**The matter around you is becoming *more* solid.** What I mean by that is, it is becoming more important and more weighty in your minds, so you continue to regard matter as having more importance and you make it more solid. You cannot walk through the wall at the moment, but if you *truly* approached the wall from a spiritual point of view (observing that wall via this dance of energy between the wall and yourself) then you could pass your hand through it and could move your body through it. You could disperse it and you could bring it back. It is only there as an aid to your spiritual progression. And, there will be many who read this and, at this point, say that that is impossible. Yes, it is impossible because you have just said that it is impossible. So, by saying it is impossible, you are reinforcing your belief in the wall as being solid, being immutable and being something that reacts to you in a certain way.

What you have to do is to observe the wall from a spiritual point of view. The way to detach yourself from the materialism around you (and by 'materialism' I am talking about your reaction to whether something is solid, changeable or is really there) you have to, again, go into the stillness of meditation. Once you have become still, you have to look with your *psychic eyes* at the room where you are meditating and see the energy that pulsates through every object. And, independently of the physical mind, observe that wall until a point where you can see it as nothing more than a lattice of energy that has been put together by the spirits that shaped this world – *yourselves* – in order for you to travel through this world and to experience. The wall is not solid. Your bodies are not solid. The Earth is not solid. But the wall, your bodies and the Earth are solidified by your beliefs since the Fall, and have become more solid.

It is also important that I talk about *emotion* because you attach emotion to material objects too: 'I can't walk through the wall because the wall will hurt me and I will be upset and in pain.' So, you attach an emotional charge to something that is there only to place you in time and space (neither of which exist in the way that you observe them either [*laughing*] but that is an address for another time). You place yourself emotionally within and against objects, and you believe in them from an emotional point of view and you solidify them. You make them heavier, you make them your gods, you make them your masters, you make them something that cannot be altered and cannot be rearranged into what you want them to be.

So, all that energy ...in the wall ...in the objects in your cupboards ...in the car ...in its engine ...in all the myriad pieces of technology you have *is locked in* and you are not drawing on God-energy to create new objects. You are drawing on a finite well of energy, but you have already locked in an increasing percentage of that energy into the objects that you already have **...so you are running out of energy.**

Not only that, but you have the belief in the material as being solid from the past. You have this Field of energy in which there are layered memories from the past that also contribute to the solidity and unchanging-ness of every object that you have because that is ingrained into you. It is ingrained into you by society so that you grow with this expectation that everything is solid. That expectation is then *reinforced* by the vibrations that permeate every wall, every cup, every car – that say that every wall, every cup, every car has always been as solid as it is today. Does that make sense?

**Tony:** It does, indeed. Thank you, Joseph.

**David:** Joseph, as it happens, yesterday I was putting a cup away in a cupboard when I caught it on the cooker hood and knocked a chip out of it. The first thing I did was to curse the cooker hood for being there and then moan at the cup – so what you are saying I can understand. The point I am trying to make is, rather than seeing what is really going on, it is becoming increasingly difficult because we are expending energy on saying that the cup is in the wrong place and the cooker hood is in the wrong place, and so on.

**Joseph:** Yes, that is an isolated incident in one life, but when you multiply that by the number of cups that have been smashed on cooker hoods and cursed at the same time, you have this build-up of observation that says that every cup that you take out of every cupboard will smash against the cooker hood. You are creative spiritual beings and over time you are building into those objects an indication of how they should perform for you. And, yes, you are right in that you are running out of energy because you are increasingly expending energy in solidifying your view of the world as being negative, as being set against you, as being wrong and as being disharmonious.

I hope that you can see and I hope the readers will see (if they have read the other books) that I am further illustrating in this chapter how the end can come quickly if you are not very careful and *if you don't change*. I have said for some years now through the books that you are living on a finite amount of energy. Not only are you living on finite energy, but you are expending it more and more quickly because you are inventing more objects to attribute weight and solidity to. So, you are growing in terms of objects and solidity around you, but you are shrinking in terms of the energy that is left with which to change those objects and to change the nature of your world.

*Unless* you imbue those objects, people and situations with positivity and with God-Light from *outside* of the Field, it is inevitable that, if you continue along this path, there will come a point where there is no energy left with which to create new scenarios and the old scenarios will come to a halt.

## *It is inevitable!*

It is a very important point. Do you see that point? It is *extremely* important that I get this across to people. My reason for this book is to say: 'Look, the world operates in a different way than you think it does,' but also to expand on what I have said before, to give a further hint of how to change the world and to give a further hint that, if you do not change the world in this way, *inevitably* it will come to a standstill ...*as will you on a physical level*. Because you are drawing from a finite Field of physical energy, you cannot continue to expend ...and expend ...and expend energy and solidify ...and solidify ...and solidify the wrong aspect of creation without there coming a point where there is *nothing* left on this level and *nowhere* for you to go except into stasis.

It is extremely important that each person reading or listening to this does their level best to work for change. It having been explained to them as to how the world works, there is the opportunity to work for change. It is no use saying: 'I will leave it to someone else.' It is no use saying: 'I will leave it until tomorrow.' Simple changes, through meditation and the way that you observe the world and observe everyone, leads to a big change in the way that energy reacts with you and leads to a big change in the perception of the world – both for yourself and for everyone else in this world. It is *vitally important* that each person reading this puts the time in.

## The time for change is *now!*

And, initially, if you can't do it for everyone else – do it for yourself! In doing it for yourself and changing your perception spiritually, you will eventually do it for everyone else because you will crave that harmony for everyone else, and you will lift yourself above the materialism that locks you into this culture of self. The culture of self has to end. The culture of materialism has to end. This Earth has to get back to the way it was when you first created it as the angelic children you were before the time of the Fall.

**Jane:** Joseph, this is a slightly trivial question and is concerned with poltergeist-like activity. Sometimes in my house, objects have inexplicably moved – such as finding a shoe positioned up against the back of a closed door, or something from a cupboard being in the middle of the floor, or losing an earring in the car only for it to be found two weeks later in a completely unrelated place in the house. On those occasions, I assumed it was spirit activity where someone was trying to give me some sort of message. So, how does that work? Is it because *they* believe that they can move whatever physical object?

**Joseph:** You have to understand that with a spiritual viewpoint of life and the afterlife, you and others like you *lessen* the hold of the Earth on you. You lessen your viewpoint of the Earth as being all there is. You are not as interested in materiality as many people are. As a result of that and as a result of working spiritually on a regular basis, your vibrations are used to elevating themselves to a higher level of consciousness.

Now, on that higher level of consciousness – just as we are today, there are various sounds and sensations of the spiritual world going on. They are not dead worlds activated only when you look at them. Once you get into the spiritual spheres **there is creation going on** *writ large* (which we will talk about at a later stage). So, at any time interpenetrating your world and interpenetrating you at times, there is 'spiritual activity' as you would describe it. There are the thoughts and intentions of the spirits that are around you who are trying to contact you, trying to uplift you and trying to instil more spiritual knowledge into you so that you can spread that spiritual knowledge globally.

So, at times when the 'veil', as it were, is thinned because you have shifted your vibration from this material level to a higher spiritual vibration that is also contained within you, people are able to impress their presence upon you – but not totally as they would do if you were talking to them spirit-to-spirit. And, so, that information is translated into the knock on wood or the rap on a table, because it is a translation filtered through the energies of the Field that can get through to you, but not in its purest form. In its purest form, there would be someone that you would see quite plainly and quite solidly, who would then explain to you why they were contacting you and what they wanted to say to you.

Does that make sense?

**Jane:** Yes.

**Joseph:** Are you sure that makes sense?

**Jane:** Er... I can understand the knock on wood, which is a slightly frustrating thing because you know someone is around but you don't know what they want. I just wondered how spirits actually managed *to move* physical objects.

**Joseph** [*laughing*]: This goes back to exactly what we have been talking about. They can move objects because the objects are not solid. They put out a pulse of energy. There is an energy exchange on all levels of consciousness, so the energy exchange that we have been talking about this morning – this dance of energy between you and an object – also takes place in the spiritual realms between spirits and the objects that they create and then put away when they no longer need them. It is a burst of volition. When you take the cup out of the cupboard, you are translating that volition into flesh and blood ...a motive that makes you stand up, go to the cupboard and physically take the cup out. But, in your spiritual nature as the God that you really are, you simply take the cup out of the cupboard *by wanting to take the* *cup out of the cupboard.* You don't have to move flesh and bone – these are things of the Fall.

Also, any spirit that is making contact has to *punch through* the dense Field that is just as solid as the car because you on Earth have made it so over the millennia. You have said: 'This is the way things are. There is no afterlife. These are the solid things that are around us. This is our reality and then we die!'

So, again, because of the effects of the Fall and because you cannot put away your 'toys' once you have finished playing with them, you have created this heavy, dense atmosphere. It reflects itself in the density of the objects you have around you, but it is also in the atmosphere. And, those who rebuke spiritual communication and say: 'Why is it so difficult, and why don't they say *this* and why don't they say *that?*' ...don't realise that *they are contributors to making that communication difficult* because of their expectations from the Field ...their expectations of life ...their expectations that everything should be so dense ... and their expectations that it is difficult.

The spirits that come through have to fight against the solidity and gravity of the objects within the material Field. This is why I can only communicate with you for a certain amount of time. This is why it requires power from your side as well to allow the communication to take place. This is why Michael is fatigued to the extent that he is after each trance session because his body and his psyche have to fight, not only the materialism of the world to punch through and connect with me – but have to fight *his own expectations* as a spirit immersed in the effects of the Fall. He has to raise himself up to the point where he breaks through his expectations on a physical and mental level of how society should be and how 'reality' works so that he can connect with me.

Does that make sense?

**Jane:** Yes, thank you.

## Chapter Seven
## Inner Reflections and the Hall of Mirrors

**Joseph:** Chapter seven – *Inner Reflections and the Hall of Mirrors*. How tall are you? How much do you weigh? How important do you think you are with regard to your size and your weight as part of the global family of mankind? How important do you think you are with regard to the solar system ...or the universe ...or spirituality? And, how do you view your life – would you say that most of your life takes place outside of yourself or inside of yourself?

And, at this point, many readers or listeners will say: 'Joseph, what do you mean by *inside of myself*? If I go to work, the work is around me. If I go to an office, I have to travel across town and my work colleagues are outside of me; and that is an exterior experience. The same can be said of my relationship with my partner, my children and my friends. They are *all* outside of me, and I connect to them outside of myself. What is within me is simply a monitor of how I am ...whether I am well or ill ... whether I am happy or sad ...whether I am progressing or holding myself back. That is the only extent to which I regard myself as having an inner world.'

**I wish today to change that perception *totally*.**

**I wish you to understand that the world exists, not outside of yourself at all but *within* yourself.**

I wish to tell you that the solar system exists, not outside of yourself but *within* yourself.

I wish you to understand that the physical universe exists, not outside of yourself but *within* yourself.

I wish you to understand that the spiritual universe and your connection to God exist, not outside of yourself at all but *within* yourself.

I had better explain. You are a concept of God. God encapsulates everything that God is. How could it be otherwise? God contains God. God is the extremes of God, the interior of God and everything in between. God *IS*. God is ALL. You are an expression of God. Therefore, what you perceive as being outside of yourself is a *projection*, yes, of the things happening in your life ...but is, in reality, taking place *inside* because you are the consciousness of God. Therefore, anything that happens to you in your life is expressed inside your soul and spiritual core.

Let me explain this a little more...

The aspects of your life that I have mentioned ...your relationships ...your work situation ...your perception of where you are with regard to how your life is progressing – all these things are internalised. You connect to other spirits, not by the exterior world at all but by the interior world at the point at which you and those other spirits (particularly those closest to you) are one. And, you will say: 'Well, I can see a person outside of myself. I can see a world outside of myself. I can look through a telescope and see the stars at night. I can look on my computer and see galaxies and other solar systems.'

*All these things* – from the person that is seemingly stood in front of you ...to the world backdrop that you have of landscapes and workplaces and cars and food ...to other people ...to the planet that you stand on ...to the planets in the solar system – *are a reflection of what is going on within you.*

Now, there is a lot of scorn poured on astrology and the concept that the stars can predict what is going to happen to you in life. I would tell you that *astrology in its purest form is absolutely correct*, because the positioning of those outer bodies are a reflection of what is happening inside of you. That is why they can seemingly predict what is going to happen to you. From your point of view of looking at stars astrologically, they seem to forecast what happens in the future, but what they are *actually* doing is reflecting back, like a mirror, what is happening in your life according to the decisions that you have made and the path that you are currently on.

The people around you in life are there as a reflection of your triumphs and ...(I don't want to use the word 'failures') ...the areas in your life that you need to improve, hone and polish. So, the people around you are not there by coincidence. They are around you through family and friendships links, yes, but that is a physical link. On a *spiritual* link, these people are there to tell you something about your life and for you to tell them something about theirs. They are further 'mirrors' that show you what is happening within your core.

The situations that you find yourself in in life and the situations that most think are random and are the act of a cruel God or a cruel society, are there as 'mirrors' of what is happening inside of yourself and are situations that you need to concentrate on and to evolve through.

**You are *everything* ...and so is everyone else.**

And, the reason that I mentioned height and weight at the beginning of this chapter is because most people regard themselves as a tiny speck in the universe. Most people regard themselves as someone who, for example, can't walk through disability ...or can't talk properly ...or can't go out because they feel too overweight ...or can't achieve anything because they have a restricted personality ...or can't communicate well with people. What I want to say to you today is that you are *all-powerful*.

**You are *all-powerful* because you are *all things*.**

When you go for a walk in the morning, the trees that you come across, the birds that are singing, the sky above you and the Earth beneath your feet, the animals that you encounter and the people that you say 'Good Morning' to ...*are all you.*

How can they be me, Joseph? How *can* they be me?

**...Because there is only one organism.**

There is one God expressed as billions and billions of angelic souls; and in the case of the Earth expressed, unfortunately at this time, as billions of angelic souls who decided long ago to take a turn in the path that took them away in consciousness, not only from the fact that there *is* a God but *more importantly* from the fact that they are a part of that God and that God is a part of them. What I want to do today is to expand your consciousness, and I would like you in your quiet times ...(and, yes, Joseph always speaks about 'quiet times' because in the stillness you have a *unique* opportunity to connect to spiritual concepts and to connect to yourself within) ...I would like you to consider your oneness with everything.

In a meditation, for example, you could see yourself in your heart-mind going on a walk that you normally take physically. During that walk, I want you to look in your mind's eye at everything that you encounter ...from a telegraph pole ...to a wall ...to a person ...to a dog ...to a leaf ...to a tree ...to the sky, and to concentrate on each object from the point of view of the God-within and the heart-mind. Relax as you look at those objects, and you will receive a signal from them that tells you that those objects are no different from you and *are actually a part of you*. I want you to experience oneness, and I also want you to experience and understand the power that you have as a result of being everything.

You see, you have 'little points of everything' across your globe, and those 'little points of everything' are externalising and sending out into what is really a 'hall of mirrors' – what they perceive the world to be. So, you have billions of souls perceiving the world as a violent place …you have billions of souls perceiving the world as a place of opportunity to take advantage of others …you have billions of souls perceiving this world as somewhere that illness exists that needs to be abolished through external means. You polish certain of those 'mirrors' by your belief and you externalise a contribution to how the *illusion* of this planet, its landscape and your external society function.

So, I want you to consider that *if* you are everything – *which you are* – and *if* everything is contained within you – *which it is* – you have the ability to colour that 'everything' as you see fit. What a marvellous gift, Joseph! What a marvellous gift to be able to send out into this external world your personal view of what you want it to be. So, the peaceful world that many people say they want, you can help to create. The non-violent world that many people say they want, you can help to create. The spiritually aware, caring and unified world that many people say they want, you can help to create. And, you don't create it by going out into the physical world but by going into the mystical, God-potential world that exists within you, and by realising that your dreams and solidification of ideas within externalise themselves and push out into the world *that which you believe to be true and that which you want to create.*

So, if you are a stranger to *the Joseph Communications* you should find this a revelation (and, there is a deliberate pun here with my first book [*reference to* **Revelation**] because I like puns). You are not today – sitting listening to or reading this book – the small, confined, powerless individual that you may or may not believe yourself to be. You are everything. If you are listening to this book …you are part of the computer system that allows you to listen to it. If you are reading this as a paperback ...you are part of the book, part of the paper and part of the words because you have contributed to creating these things, as you have from the time when you became individualised as an angelic being, as a facet or 'mirror' of God.

So, imagine instead of this dull world ...where you see people taking opportunities to use others and draw from their power ... where you see people limping along because they don't have the perception of health that they should ...where you see people worrying about economics and money ...where you see people investing in politics that do not ultimately change anything – **you have the power to change these things.** You have the power to visualise and to create *your* world on a daily basis. Now, aren't you a powerful being!

In addition to this, I want you to look at your exterior world in a different way. I want you to look at the principal things that are happening, both in your personal world and in the world at large, and to understand that these things are reflections of yourself. These things are there, not to trouble and challenge you in a negative way, but to say: 'This is happening to you because you perceive in a certain way. If you change your perception, then the things happening around you will change accordingly.'

So, I am saying there is a 'well' of God-power within you; I am saying that everything is within you; and I am saying that, by dipping into that 'well' and bringing out different concepts to the ones you are used to believing, you alter the challenges around you. The financial difficulty will go away – not by addressing it physically but by addressing it spiritually. The relationship difficulty will go away – not by addressing it physically but by addressing it spiritually. *First and foremost spiritually* ...and then what those challenges present to you on a daily basis you deal with, but you continue with your view of how you want things to be.

Of course, there is a danger there because you *may* want the whole world to serve you and bring you what you personally want. So, in changing that landscape by going within, you have to first connect with the knowledge and truth of the heart-mind and not with the desires of the head-mind. Approach the God-within through the heart-mind. Let go of self! If you are God and if you are everything – why would you confine yourself in your meditative times to the little self? Why would you want to be the little personality when you can take so much joy and bliss in being a weave of everything …in being part of the dream of God and the dreamer *as* God?

So, in changing your landscape you have to, yes, address the challenges that come to you because they prevent you from operating spiritually to the full, but then you have to also connect with the God-within and say: 'What do You want, Father? What do I as You want, Father?' See the two steps…

Step one: 'What do *You* want, Father?'

Step two: 'What do *I as You* want, Father?'

…And, what you want is harmony. What you want is peace. What you want is growth of spiritual knowledge. What you want is healing for the world. What you want is reconstruction of the matrix of the world so that it can be the shining sphere of experience it is supposed to be.

Those are the things that you will discover you want when you put the ego and the little personality aside. Those, then, are the things that you need to bring out into your dream and externalise. You fill your body with Light and with the desires that you have on behalf of the God that you are …and then you send them out into the illusion and the aspects of the planet that you see around you.

And, you will say: 'Joseph, I am doing this but there are so many others who aren't.' Well, yes, they *are at core* because each person – being part of the universe, being part of God and being God – creates in the way that I have explained earlier in this chapter. Each personality is creative; and here is something for you to think about ...each personality *at core* (because they are part of God) creates as God creates and has a desire to create bliss and to experience harmony and potential. That core experience is always there on a subconscious level, but what happens is that most people *unconsciously* bring out (because they cannot help but be creators) that core experience but filter it, blacken it and darken it by what they expect to receive via the ego and their small vision of what should come to them today and in the future.

So, the core volition is always God-volition and cannot be anything else, because your consciousness and your ability to create comes from that God-point ...and that God-point knows nothing about violence ...that God-point knows nothing about petty or global disharmony ...that God-point knows nothing about illness ...that God-point is a pure, creative point of bliss existing to explore and to grow through harmony. But, then that God-point becomes polluted (exclusively here, as far as I am aware) by the effects of the Fall where you chose to create in a different way.

You may put this book down or switch off the recording and think: 'Well, my life has not changed.' **If it has not changed – change it!** *Be joyous* because you have the power to change it. *Be joyous* because, no matter how black the world seems and no matter how dark society seems – you, as everything, have the potential to change it on an hourly ...daily ...weekly ...monthly ...yearly basis. *Be joyous* because you have that opportunity, but you have to invest time in it.

In understanding that you are all things and that you are an encapsulation of the universe and an encapsulation of God, you have to invest time in exploring the *true* area of your being. And, the true area of your being is not outside of yourself at all but *within*. So, you have to get to know your inner self and you have to invest time in stillness, in meditation, in contemplation and in experiencing the connection. You will know when you have connected to the God-within because you will feel that rush of energy ...you will feel that peace that you will not experience in any other situation ...you will feel that definite connection ...and you will feel your senses expand.

Isn't that a better scenario than continuing with your life as it is at the moment? To swap your life of fear, violence, lack, illness, anger and pain – for a life of bliss that you will then pour forth into your houses, into the people around you, into your work situations, into all other challenges in your life and, ultimately, out into the world to change it into a shining, harmonious sphere – isn't that a wonderful thing? Isn't that worth investing time into?

Now, I can take you so far and get you to contemplate the concepts, but I cannot get you to do the work. And, *it is work* – not nine-to-five work, but it is a matter of spending some time daily with ...I was going to say 'your God' but it is spending some time *with you* because you *are* your God (and always have been and always will be) and you can change what for you and for many people is, almost certainly at times, a bad dream and, almost certainly at times, a nightmare.

Before I end the chapter, let me talk for a little while about *the hall of mirrors* and by 'hall of mirrors' I mean that when you look at any situation in your life – be it somebody that you connect with, or a challenge at work, or an illness, or your attitude towards global concepts and trends – you are looking at a reflection of yourself. And, so, in certain mirrors you will see a distortion of yourself ...taller ...or smaller ...or fatter ...or in a comical stance. **Everything outside of yourself reflects yourself.** And, so, you look at the world and you see the planet at the moment that is polluted and is dying in certain areas. You see certain animal species becoming extinct. You see diseases in plants and trees. You see the seas clogged up and poisoned. All those things are a reflection of what is wrong within the God that is you and within the God that is everyone else. Let me explain that more fully...

You are God. You are a God-filter, and so what you see is a *distortion* of the way that you filter God out into the planet and out, ultimately, into the universe. So, the planet dying shows that your creativity is dying. The elimination of certain species means that spiritual aspects of yourself are becoming unavailable to you physically and mentally at this moment. Everything is a reflection of what is happening within you. So, you have to bring revitalising energies outwards – energies that will re-foliate the world, that will cleanse the oceans and that will purify the skies. You do this by bringing through those visions from within and making them reality.

Back to astrology – the pulls and the pushes of the planets around you are according to your wishes of how you perceive yourself within. 'Are you saying, Joseph, that *I* steer the planets, that *I* decide their orbits and that *I* put comets in certain positions in the sky?' ...Yes, that is *exactly* what I am saying!

I am saying that you have created this area of space. You originally created it as an area in which to examine God-potential and bring greater adventures to the God within you. You have skewed it. You created the planets, but you affect their orbits. You affect the patterns that they weave throughout space. You create those trajectories. If there is a wobble with a star or an ellipse with a comet, you have created it ...and it is *significant*. As an angelic being [*laughing*] you can read these things. As an angelic being, you would instantly be able to read what is happening in your world rather than ignore it. All these things are 'mirrors' reflecting what is going on inside yourself.

**There is nothing, ultimately, except God and except *you* as God.**

...What about all the other souls, Joseph? It is the same equation because you are a part of all the other souls. You can condense down and condense down and condense down and, finally, there is only one organism …only one expression of life and it is *you* …and you …and you …and you. All the 'you's that you meet during the day, *they are all You.* All the 'you's that you talk to on the telephone, *they are all You.* All the people that you will ever meet, *they are all You.* All the things that you come across, *they are all You.*

**There is nothing but You.**

**There is nothing but God.**

And, if you realise nothing else from this chapter and fail to go within, *if you realise that everything is you – you will change your dream instantly* because you will not be able to harm anything, you will not be able to argue with anyone and you will not be able to be violent towards anything. How can you harm yourself? How can you harm the 'you' that exists around this planet as all the seemingly different personalities but which are, in reality, all 'mirrors' of you?

Are there questions, please?

**Tony:** Joseph, a lot of religious orders sit back and believe that there is going to be 'the chosen one' who will rebirth and save us all – a Maitreya or a Jesus that will return – but I think this chapter makes it very clear that actually it is up to us to make the change and to do the work.

**Joseph:** The power is always in your hands. It is an interesting term – 'the chosen one'. *You are each of you the chosen one.* There is *only* the chosen one. You are chosen because God has chosen to give you the illusion of individuality.

To put things right here requires a shift in consciousness, and so many people resist that shift in consciousness because they are slowed down, enthralled and distracted by the physical and mental Field that they are apparently living in. So, to incarnate

119

here you are instantly surrounded by the drag of the physical and the effects of the Fall that change this world into what you perceive around you.

Each soul, as we have said throughout the books, *has to find its own way out*. We can give advice and point out the truth of the situation, but at some point *each soul* has to make the realisation that they are God, that they are an expression of God – an angelic being – and that the power to change things lies with them, both individually and globally contributing to all the other 'you's that exist around the world. You have the power to pull yourself out of this situation and to change the situation around you. No one else can do it for you because you are God and are, in effect, saying: 'This is how I want to be until I want to be something else.'

**Until the point at which you want to be something else, you will remain as you are.**

If heavenly prophets appeared now in shining robes in front of you, they could not change you into the angelic being that you truly are at core *unless* you wanted it and *unless* you understood totally, absorbed totally and projected totally what they were saying to you. That is a big step because most people are viewing religious salvation from the point of view of the Field and, therefore, feel that someone will come along, and they will not have to do anything but will be scooped up by wonderful, caring, loving hands and placed on a higher sphere of elevation. That is not the way things work. **Ladies and Gentlemen, that is not the way that things work!** You have to revert to what you were and what you still are *personally*. You have to take that step.

A wonderful question, Tony, a wonderful question! You are externalising into the 'hall of mirrors' so you look into one of those mirrors and you see a saviour ...not realising that the saviour is you. Do you see that? **The saviour is you!** It is a further projection and a further externalisation with regard to the effects of the Fall. You expect the saviour to be outside of yourself, but the saviour is within yourself because you are all things. And, this is what the truly spiritual messengers over the aeons have said to you: 'You are your own salvation and everyone else's.' Does that make sense?

**Tony:** Thank you so much, Joseph.

**David:** Joseph, you use the term 'hall of mirrors' – are you actually referring to the Field in that?

**Joseph:** I am referring to everything. I am referring to the challenges that come to you in life as reflections of what is really going on within you and the point you are at with regard to spiritual evolution at any one time, but I am also referring to the greater aspects of Creation. As you get further out into the universe, the effects of the Fall are diminished, but there is still the 'machine' in place reflecting aspects of what is truly happening at your God-core. That 'hall of mirrors' rings true for every aspect of Creation outside of the Fall too, and that is why the angelic beings create spheres of experience so that they can travel through them and have reflected back to them certain scenarios in order that they can grow.

The whole of God's physical and spiritual universes are set up as this giant 'playground' or giant 'hall of mirrors' that reflects back to its inhabitants a measure of progress and also opportunities to progress further that are expressions of the desire of each individual angelic being to progress in a certain way. So, the gigantic 'hall of mirrors' of Creation reflects back, not only progress but the *desires* of the angelic beings because, having progressed to a certain extent, they wish to express and progress *more*; and each group of angelic beings or group soul wishes to progress in a certain way that is delightfully and exquisitely *different* and, yet, enhances the desires and wishes of the other individual angelic beings and group souls. Do you see that?

**David:** Yes.

**Joseph:** So, not only are the spiritual and physical universes set up to allow angelic beings to view their progress and to create opportunities for further progress, but *the outer reflects what the inner wants to do next,* showing a scenario that the inner wishes to examine and to progress through next. This, of course, is because there is nothing 'in reality' outside of the angelic beings because they are part of God. There is nothing except expression outside of the angelic being and then, ultimately, as we have said in other books, there are no angelic beings [*laughing*] ...there is only expression given form ...only volition given form ...only God given form.

That might seem terribly frightening to the readers of this book: 'What do you mean there is nothing there?' Of course, there is *no-thing* there because, at the heart of everything, there is God. God brings forth the 'mirrors'. God brings forth the individualisations. But God is always God. God is examining Himself. God is progressing Himself. Just as the world around you is, ultimately, an illusion and a temporary sphere that was originally created so that you could examine the reflections in that particular 'hall of mirrors' and move on – the whole of the universe and the whole of Creation is such. That is a wonderful thing because it means that, at certain times, the experience can be collapsed and that those individual points of God – the angelic beings – can then create something entirely new to continue to progress themselves and to continue to progress and evolve God. That is a huge concept but do you understand that?

**David:** Yes, and it is just in this little corner of the universe where we have become enmeshed in the reflection rather than realising that we are all projecting.

**Joseph:** You cannot find the door out of the 'hall of mirrors'. The books are about giving you *the door... the corridor and the door at the other end* to escape it and to get back into the greater 'hall of mirrors' where you came from.

**Jane:** Joseph, this is just a quick question on astrology – presumably we only influence the planets that are close to the Earth, otherwise we would be interfering negatively with the spheres of experience of other angelic groups. So, is it just the planets on our skewed vibration that we influence?

**Joseph:** ...What is the analogy I can give? If you have a bath of water and put a drop of ink into it – that ink spreads out and becomes clearer, doesn't it? There is a darker centre and then it becomes clearer and clearer until the rest of the bath is only influenced to an infinitesimally small degree by the addition of that drop of ink. Would you agree?

**Jane:** Yes.

**Joseph:** Now, this is what is happening with the Field, where you are putting that drop of 'ink' into the 'ocean' of Creation. You are quite right in that the planets in your solar system are the closest to you and are, therefore, influenced the most. And, they influence you the most by the way in which they travel and deliver a view of the unseen. But, the rest of Creation is also influenced to an infinitesimal degree by what happens here ...as *here* is influenced to an infinitesimal degree by the rest of Creation. So, in the same way that gravity works, the rest of the planets and stars in this particular universe and in the other universes are influenced to a tiny, tiny, tiny degree by what happens here.

So, looking out into space, if you knew how to read the signs spiritually, you would see that the other solar systems and galaxies are also teaching you something. In the normal course of events, you would be teaching them something as well, but all you are teaching them is: KEEP OFF! ...STAY AWAY! ...DON'T DO IT THIS WAY! But, that in itself is a lesson because if, as a result of the Fall once it is cleared up, the rest of Creation takes on board the reflection that says *DON'T GO THIS WAY* then there has been a triumph, hasn't there? Do you understand?

**Jane:** Yes. Presumably, it is mankind as a whole that influences our little bit of space because an individual wouldn't be able to cause the wobbling of a planet or a comet.

**Joseph:** There is no individual. Your collective thoughts and skewed vision are enough to influence the spheres around you, because remember that the Earth as a sphere was created by you and is positioned with other spheres of experience that, in the normal course of events, you would move on into and through in order to enhance your experience and the experience of the Whole in certain ways. So, the...

[*At this point there was a short pause in the communication.*]

...I am sorry I am reaching the end of my energy level.

So, the individual is not an individual. The individual contributes, yes, individually but also as part of a group soul. We have talked for many years about group souls and how decisions are made as a whole but also with the agreement of individuals. Because you see and accept society as it is, you buy into the group vision that, therefore, has the power to influence those planets. Do you see?

**Jane:** Yes.

**Joseph:** So, in that respect you as an individual are all-powerful because, as a contributor to group consciousness, you are maintaining the planets in that way. But, I have to end this by saying that each of you is all-powerful so when you change your viewpoint and put out into the ether a reflection of yourself that is holier, more blissful and more harmonious, you are beginning the movement that changes the path of those spheres to reflect back to you a change for the good. Does that make sense?

**Jane:** Yes, it does. Thank you.

**Joseph:** It is difficult to get across ...you are that point of 'ink' but, instead of it being ink, it is a point of Light. That point of Light then spreads out and influences the reflections that come back to you – only infinitesimally if you do it individually – but when that point of Light links up with other points of Light, then the course of the heavens is changed by you thinking, acting, creating and reflecting back in a different way.

## Chapter Eight
## The Banishment of God
## and Sawing the Lady in Half

**Joseph:** Chapter eight – *The Banishment of God and Sawing the Lady in Half*. What on Earth are you talking about Joseph? Why title this 'Sawing the Lady in Half'?

Well, I have to bring to mind a conjuring trick that has been popular over the past few decades of your present existence on Earth, and that is the trick of sawing the lady in half. This, as you know, involves a lady being placed in a box on two trestles and the magician taking a saw or sheet of metal and dividing the box right down the middle, and then pulling the two halves apart so that the lady is apparently in two separate sections – and yet she can wiggle her toes in one section and can move her head, arms and hands in the other section. Then she is joined back together, the sheet of metal is removed, the lady is taken out of the box and is, of course, whole again.

What on Earth has that got to do with *the spaces between*?

Patience, Reader, and I will bring you back to this image later in the chapter.

I want you to consider, now, the false gods of ancient Rome and ancient Greece. I want to take you back for a moment to a time when on every street corner, in every household, in every town square and looking down from every temple there would

126

be images of gods, and these gods would represent *super aspects* of the human condition. There would be a god of speed ...a god of great strength ...a god with great creative abilities; and other powers would be manifest through these idols that were placed around society at that time.

Have you ever considered why the images of the gods were created and why it was so important to have statues depicting deities outside every meeting place and on every street? It goes back to the time of the Fall and the separation *seemingly* in consciousness from God that occurred at that time. As a result of the Fall (as discussed in previous books) *souls lost their conscious contact with the God-within.* They lost sight of the fact that they were angelic beings and that they were a part of Divinity and, yet, on a subconscious level that knowledge was still there eating away at them. That knowledge that they were incomplete was manifest in their actions as a result of subconscious desires.

So, it became necessary, after the time of the Fall, to create and believe in a god that could not be a god *within* an angelic being but *outside* of an angelic being. All those aspects of the angelic being that had seemingly been lost ...the ability to create ...the ability to cover great distance in a fraction of a second ...the ability to have great strength ...the ability to have great destructive and creative powers – *all* those things were projected onto supposed deities. And, those deities were given substance as statuary that the worshippers could look to, believe in, pray to and have faith in rather than approaching the God-within.

That subconscious desire to express, appreciate and *worship* Divinity ('worship' in the sense of laying, in front of Divinity, the fruits of your experience) has continued to this day. However, there is a paradox in that mankind senses there to be a lost Divinity somewhere in its consciousness, and yet as it currently heads towards destruction and the end of society unless it changes, *it seeks to banish God.* As society has seemingly advanced technologically and scientifically, it sees no reason for the Divinity that is *within* to exist or to acknowledge that Divinity. So, gradually, it has put aside its false gods of ancient times and has decided that it no longer needs the God *that subconsciously it knows it does need* – thereby setting up a further schism within itself with regard to harmony and its connection at a subconscious level to all things.

Having said that there is no room for a God in life and in approach to others and in seeing only a physical universe ... nevertheless, each angelic soul has within it that core understanding that, at its heart, *it is God*. What a paradox! What an irony! It is banishing God, saying that there is no God and (like some of your writers) goes to great lengths to convince those who are in two minds about whether there is a Divinity that they are ...A) *Stupid* ...and that B) *God cannot possibly exist.* There is a schism because, at core, the angel knows that it is part of God ...that it *is* God.

**Having banished God, mankind still needs its false gods.**

So, instead of the statue of a winged god or the statue of a mother god that takes care of the Earth – as expressions of the Divinity *within* that were expressed *without* in ancient times, you today have a focus on and a preoccupation with aspects of materiality ...*and you make them God.*

Let us look at the shining gods of modern times. Let us look at *the spaces between* and discover what you consider to be God. ...You consider the shining piece of metal that is parked on your driveway or in your garage to be God. ...You consider the pieces of paper in your wallet and the coins in your pocket to be God. ...You consider the souls who have indulged in the entertainment industry to be God with lifestyles that should be followed. ...You look at the phones in your pockets and the computers on your desktops, and you consider these things to be God.

And, so, the false gods of old are the false gods of today in new guises. You consume, and you pursue, and you worship, and you devour these false gods because of a *need* that is within you to acknowledge that you are part of God and, more importantly, from your point of view at this current time, *that God actually exists.*

And, you may say at this point: 'Joseph, I don't believe in God.' **...Belief has nothing to do with there being a God.**

And, you may say: 'Joseph, I have read literature that says there is no God and I am convinced.' **...And conviction has nothing to do with there being a God.**

And, you may say: 'Joseph, I have a god in my religion that acts in a certain way and excludes parts of mankind.' **...And the way that your god behaves according to your religion is nothing to do with God.**

Let me bring you back to the image of the lady in the box who is seemingly sawn in half by the magician. To all intents and purposes, from the viewpoint of the audience, that person has been cut in two, and yet she can still move her arms, legs and feet despite being severed in half ...because, in reality, she cannot be cut in two. She has always been a whole person. It is a complete illusion. And so it is with you and with God. You cannot help being part of God, and God cannot help existing in you and cannot but exist. Your belief has *nothing* to do with the equation. Your biases have *nothing* to do with the equation.

As an absolute spiritual fact: **THERE IS A GOD.** Not only is there a God, but **YOU ARE THAT GOD.** Not only are you that God, but **YOU HAVE NEVER BEEN SEPARATED FROM THAT GOD** – that God still exists at your core.

In banishing God and trying to rid yourselves of God from the equation, you banish part of yourselves, and so the disharmony that you feel with the world increases. I tell you that you will never find harmony in others ...you will never find harmony by seeking out materiality ...you will never find harmony in viewing this world as being only a physical place and there being only a physical level …you will never find harmony until you rediscover, accept, examine and communicate with the God-within.

Open your mind to the possibility! You cut yourself off aeons ago, but you only cut yourself off on a surface level, and that is how you are approaching all things at this time – *on a surface level only*. You expect that surface level to bring you satisfaction, to bring you happiness, to bring you peace, to explain the mysteries of the universe. That surface level cannot do any of those things, because it is an encapsulation of mind and of intent from the time of the Fall. Outside of this bubble that you think is 'reality' exists the greater reality, the true reality, the angelic reality …a universe of wonders …a planet of wonders … individuals of wonders …a mechanism of wonders that you have closed your mind and your access to.

One of the greatest things I could ask you to do in this book is for you to examine *the possibility* of there being a God …not the God of religion …not the God of the statue in the town square …not the God of acquiring wealth and possessions … but the God that flows through you and gives you the peace of knowing that you have always existed, that you will always exist, that you are connected to all things and that you are on a wondrous journey.

And, you will say: 'How, Joseph, do I discover this God because I don't believe in Him?'

Stop believing in the disbelief! Stop shoring up your insistence that there is no God! The God-within is found through a seeking in meditation, a seeking in the silence, an asking to understand and an asking for reconnection. The God-within does not require belief. Whether you believe in the God-within or not … **the God-within exists and cares not whether you believe in Him or not** but cares that one day you will come back to your connection with Him and continue your journey as the angelic being that you really are by rediscovering and acknowledging that connection.

That connection has to be made in silence. That connection has to be made in inner contemplation. Ask to *sense* the God-within in your quiet times and meditations. Don't expect a voice. Don't expect an externalisation within yourself of God, because that is another mistake that spiritual seekers make. They expect the God-within to feel like an externalisation within their inner world. In other words, they expect to go into meditation, to receive visions and to be talked to by *another personality* within that bubble of meditation that they have created, as though there is them and also someone else. No! There is no one else.

When you discover the God-within, the God-within flows through you. Yes, your mind will be used to influence what the God-within is saying to you. Yes, it will seem at times as though you are being spoken to, but you are being spoken to by yourself – *your greater self*. You are contacting your greater self and there is no separation. If you think of God as separate from you, even within your meditations, then we are back to the illusion of the lady sawn in half. We are back to that whole being feeling it necessary to investigate itself through the illusion of it being two parts of the same thing, rather than one part of the same thing.

You have to seek the God-within as a knowing ...a sensation ...a harmony ...a warmth ...a peace, and you have to acknowledge that those urgings and feelings are not separate from you but *are* you. You are God.

So, to return to the lady who has been cut in half – that is how you are operating at the moment. **You are not Yourself**, and I say that with a capital 'Y' because the 'Yourself' has been separated from you by your own beliefs over countless millennia ...your belief that God is, first of all, *outside* of yourself and needs to be worshipped ...and, secondly and currently, that there is *no* God and that you had better satisfy yourself through materiality because there is nothing else that will bring you harmony.

**The thing that will bring you harmony is reconnection with God.**

So, we began with a conjuring trick and we are ending with *a reality* because there is magic for you... There is magic for you to discover in those times when you feel that this world is pressing in on you and you feel that you don't have the armament to allow you to go through the challenges that present themselves to you. *There is magic waiting within.*

And, you will say: 'What are the benefits of connecting to this God that you say I am part of?' In connecting to the God that you are part of, you see a way through all challenges ...not the way through challenges that you have attained to this point in your life ...not the way through challenges which means making a blind decision and hoping that that decision is the right decision ...but a way through challenges that means you can go within and *know totally how to act in any situation* and move accordingly through that challenge with no harm to yourself and no harm to the others who are linked to you in that challenge.

The God-within will also give you comfort with regard to those whom you feel you have lost, because that two-halves-of-yourself viewpoint tells you that people are lost when they die to this place. The God-within will bring you knowledge that those people are, not only continuing to exist but, at times, you can contact them and have an unspoken dialogue with them which will help you with your life and reconnects you to them so that grief disappears.

**The God-within in *all* situations is the source that you should go to.**

In the present upheavals in your violent areas of the world, if those leaders would consult the God-within rather than the false gods of what they hope to attain by being aggressive and by taking land and lives – then those violent times would disappear, and the world and its countries would be restored to harmony.

As a result of that, the planet *itself* would be restored to harmony and the planet would react in harmony with your knowledge of operating from the God-within. In other words, you would not have the violent eruptions of physicality around the planet that occur now because the Earth would be in harmony with you, you would know how to interact with the planet and the world would start to re-form itself into the paradise that it once was, the paradise that I have talked about in other books and the paradise that we are trying to bring back to you.

**You have not gone *too far* down the road but you have gone *far enough*.**

Look on a certain day at your dependence on materiality. Look at your investment in materiality. Look at how you react with regard to status on this planet according to what you can draw to yourself. Look at the effort that you put into drawing those things to yourself – effort that could be used in silence to help the world and to reunite its angelic children. Look on a certain day and begin to notice how tied into materiality you are ...and try to withdraw.

Try to withdraw for a few moments. Consider the connection that you have lost and consider that *all the world's ills* are because you have, not only externalised your God (the God that you are and the God that is a part of you) but, in recent decades, you have pushed out that externalisation too. You still operate it because you are still placing onto external sources that need to connect to God. You are still investing in the car, in the house, in the money, in the power. Consider that you need to invest *within*. Consider that, if you invest within and recognise your wholeness with all things, then all those false gods and that banishment of God will disappear.

I cannot give you another message. I cannot say that it will be all right if you believe in each other and continue to banish God. **It won't!** It won't because you are like the lady in two halves –

still connected, but you are not acknowledging that the other half of you is God. It will not be all right until you acknowledge God, because God is what you are. And, I know that you have been put off by religions with regard to how God is …God is vengeful …God is judgemental …God will send you to Hell …God doesn't want you to act in this way …God doesn't want you to act in that way.

**That is religion and, as I have said in other books, *religion is nothing at all to do with God*.**

**If you want to know what God wants – go within.**

What God wants is what *you* want at God-level, but you will never know what that is until you go within, until you consider that there *is* a God and until you reunite Yourself. And, in reuniting yourself with God, you then see everyone else you meet as part of God too, and …you let go of your judgements …you let go of your need to defend your own corner …you let go of your power plays …you let go of your disharmony …you recognise the God in all things and in all people. In doing that, you break the banishment and you bring God into the equation a little more than He was before you recognised your reconnection to Him. In doing that, you can then wield the God-Light we have talked about in other books …*and you change things*.

Questions, please!

**Tony:** Joseph, the route to that God-within is through silence, as you have said quite clearly. A lot of your readers will say: 'Well, I sit in meditation but I can't stop the thoughts coming in – such as making tea for the family or having to do this or do that.' How can people achieve the silence that is required to access their God-self?

**Joseph:** They have to regard that searching and meditative time as *sacred*. Again, you can see a reflection of what that time represents, for example, in people's need to go on holiday and to get away from the job, from their situation or, in some cases, from the family and to go as far away as possible to be in a different situation where the sun will shine, the food will be wonderful and there will be no worries. And, for a time when people go on holiday, that is so because for a few days there are no worries. They are *in a different state of mind* and they are able to let go [*laughing*] ...**and that is an externalisation of what they need to do in their meditative times.**

In their meditative times they have to be brave enough to let go, for a short time, of the challenges and thoughts that are around them. They have to understand that they are using that meditative time *to alter the very situations that are causing them so much trouble.* They should regard that meditation as a holiday from the world and as an opportunity to be peaceful in the 'Divine sunshine' ...on the 'Divine Li-lo' ...in the 'Divine hotel' ...eating the 'Divine exotic food'.

If they can use that as a starting point, which should be easy because they are used to thinking in that way, and they regard their quiet times as *needing to get away* and as a 'holiday time' when they can quite naturally push away those thoughts, then they will benefit greatly. Otherwise, to take their thoughts into meditation is blanketing their ability to commune with the God-within. The God-within operates *by permeating the spirit* requesting help, advice and direction. If that spirit is already saturated by a negative viewpoint, then what room is there for a further viewpoint? You have to empty the vessel in order to pour into it 'better wine' and more glorious vibrations to drink in. Do you see what I am saying?

**Tony:** I do. Thank you, Joseph.

**Joseph:** This is what they should aim for ...a daily holiday ...a daily respite ...a daily bathing in the eternal sunshine of the God-within that restores. You cannot seek change if you are always taking with you the 'un-change'. You have to put aside what is seemingly not changing in order to allow change and possibilities to take place.

**Tony:** Thank you, Joseph.

**Joseph:** Further question!

**David:** Joseph, when people do go into the silence and communicate with the greater self or the Divine, isn't there sometimes a temptation to demand answers and to expect something there and then, instead of letting things come out in the fullness of time?

**Joseph:** Yes, there is, and there is a very important point here regarding the demand for answers because, metaphysically speaking, an answer is also a concept that you hold in mind and expect to be able to access as a fully formed, instant response within, isn't it? You take the situation in, and the answer is something that you are expecting to form within you. People have to understand that God and, therefore, you (i.e. the people reading this book) do not operate in that way on an angelic level.

You *know* what the outcome to situations is at God-level and at an angelic level. You *know* what the outcome to situations is by connecting to the God-within. You do not expect an answer. You expect to reconnect to the harmony of the God-within and, by doing that, the seemingly exterior situations will conform to their best possible configuration in order for you to evolve as the spirit being that you really are. It is a matter of dipping into this 'well of energy' so that the energy can permeate the situations around you, and those situations can reconfigure to give you the optimum opportunity to evolve and to become more than you were before you sat for the 'answer'.

An answer is also something that you expect, more often than not, to be in a certain way. Many people go to speak to God and expect an answer that conforms to their *conscious view* of what should happen. In other words, 'God, You must serve me in a certain way because this is what I need to happen and this is the answer that I want. I want someone to get better in a certain way. I want money for a certain situation. I need guidance as to whether I should tread path A or path B.' So, you already have in your mind a certain outcome that you want, but the 'you' that wants that is only the surface you. What does the angelic you want and what does the angelic you need?

The angelic you needs and wants the God-view. The God-view provides a path, provides the next step and provides what is right for you. And, by *what is right for you* I mean what will bring you back in the quickest time to a knowledge of you being an angelic being, to a knowledge that once you leave this Earth you should not come back and to a knowledge that you were part of the Fall experiment that went wrong, and it is now time to drop that experiment and to return to the bosom of your angelic family.

So, expect the unexpected! That is a phrase used on Earth – *expect the unexpected*. Do not expect the God-within to work with you in the way that you consciously *wish* the God-within to work with you. Expect the God-within to work in a way that you, as an angelic being, *need* the God-within to work with you. The two are not necessarily the same thing.

Expect no answers – expect *guidance*. Expect no conclusions according to your viewpoint, but expect a moving on according to what is right for you as an angelic being and what is right through you as an angelic being experiencing the right conclusions that affect *every other angelic being around the Earth*.

You have to understand that you are approaching God from your corner, but there are millions and billions of other corners. You are a part of all those other corners, so what affects you in this life seemingly personally affects every other soul. You have to approach the God-within knowing that …what works within you …what works within your town …what works within your county ...what works within your nation ...what works within all the nations *is for the good of everyone at a God-level.*

As with the illusion of the lady being sawn in half, just as you cannot be separated from your God-within, you cannot be separated from the God-within that is within all the other angelic beings – both around this world and throughout the universes. This puts into perspective the scale of the challenges that you are going to the God-within for answers to, doesn't it? There has to be a greater view and an acknowledgement that God's view is the *only one* that matters. There has to be an understanding that there *is* an instant answer, but that instant answer is the harmony that you receive from communing with the God-within and allowing that harmony to work itself through the physical and mental situations around you for the good of all. Is that a sufficient answer?

**David:** It is wonderful. Thank you.

**Jane:** Joseph, you are probably advocating that readers do two different types of meditation. One is where we sit for ourselves for our own spiritual evolution through being in touch with the God-within, and the other is where you advocate that we sit to send out Light to the world. So, presumably they should be done in two different sessions?

**Joseph:** What we are talking about and what this book is providing is an insight, both for those who already send out the Light and for those who have not yet considered doing so. The point of *this* chapter is not to preach to the converted but to say to those who are picking up this book for whatever reason has drawn them to it: 'The God that you think doesn't exist and have pushed away does, in fact, exist *and is you.*'

Now, that is a sea change in thinking and attitude, and you have to become acclimatised to that. You have to become acclimatised to the concept of there being a God. You have to be brave enough to drop the concept that you have, perhaps, believed in for decades – that there is no God. You have to become acclimatised to looking beyond what the human mind has produced as evidence of there being no God. You have to look beyond what the human mind has produced as a religion and a specific approach to God. You have to discover the harmony that is within, discover the feelings that are within and discover that *surety from within* that there is indeed a God ... and that takes time.

Once that has been established, or if you are already an acolyte in spiritual matters, then you have no need to constantly commune with God to see if God is there. You commune with God as your daily source of direction, and you commune with God as your daily source of Light that you send out to other souls in order to give them enough illumination to see past the physical mind and the physical attitudes to rediscover that they are part of God too. Do you see that?

**Jane:** Yes.

## Chapter Nine
## Meeting Your Co-Stars in the Story of Your Life

**Joseph:** Chapter nine – *Meeting Your Co-Stars in the Story of Your Life*.

All the world's a stage! What a wonderful statement – 'all the world's a stage' because all the world *is* your stage and you are the star of your own production. You are the star of your life, but every production – every television show and every film – has to have a star and has to have co-stars. There are co-stars in your life that you will never have considered before because, if this is a production ...who sets the stage ...who builds those sets ...who allows you to work against the backdrop of this world?

The answer to that is that you are not alone as a species *spiritually* on this planet but are a cohabiter of this planet with deva life forms and deva energy.

So, initially, you have the matrix of Creation that emanates out from the Godhead. Then, within that matrix of Creation or temporary arrangement of seeming reality, you have the bubbles of reality that are created by the angelic host in order that the angelic host might experience and, as a result of that experience of passing through the 'playgrounds' that the angelic host has created, bring more experience to the Godhead. The Godhead then pulses out further refined realities based on the input of the angelic hosts that are, in reality, the Godhead issued forth into His own Creation to experience.

In the normal course of things (which does not apply to this planet because of the Fall) a portion of the angelic host determines that it will create a sphere within which experience can be dipped into by other members of the angelic host. That sphere takes shape over a period of 'time' because of the will of that segment of the angelic host to put forward a *certain projection of reality made form* that that section of the angelic host feels will result in new experience for those members of the angelic host visiting that reality.

So, in complete agreement and harmony, a sphere is produced via the creative wishes of that segment of the angelic host wanting to create that sphere. Having created the sphere, it is at that point a ball of energy containing within it *the potential* that that particular sphere has to offer. Then, certain members of that section of the angelic host that we can describe as 'devas' (and devas are angelic children – just as you are) go in as the 'architects' and 'sculptors' of that sphere. So, you have a sphere with a set of experiences built into it and you coalesce that sphere into a slightly heavier area of semi-physical matter. Then, in conjunction with the rest of the angelic host creating that sphere, the devas work to furnish it with an environment within which the rest of the angelic host can experience. The devas define the mountains …decide what the plant life should be like …decide what the marine life should be like …decide what the surrounding atmosphere should be like …and refine all aspects of the unseen into the seen to provide a series of 'stage sets' against which the angelic host visiting that sphere can experience.

There is no difference between yourself as a member of the angelic host as an angelic child and the deva as a member of the angelic host as an angelic child *except in preference of creation*. In other words, there are certain segments of the angelic host that prefer to bring experience to the Godhead via visiting spheres of creation across the universes; and there are certain segments of the angelic host who prefer to bring experience to the Godhead by creating different expressions of the Godhead against which the Godhead can react in Its form as the angelic children. The

Earth was created by the angelic host and, as we have discussed in previous books, that is no insult to the held belief that God created the sphere. Of course, God created the sphere …He simply created the sphere as extensions of Himself that are the angelic host.

So, the angelic host creates a sphere and says: 'Here is a sphere that we wish to create in this manner in order that a certain set of circumstances can play out upon the angelic children visiting that sphere so that they might learn and grow and bring back to the Godhead the results of having passed through that sphere.'

That sphere is then given greater solidified form (although not as solidified as the Earth plane) by those members of the angelic host that we describe as devas and that you would understand as nature spirits or elemental spirits. They are not 'elemental' in that they are different from you – they are elemental in that their expression against the sphere is of a more rarefied solidity than yours. In other words, *they exist within the fabric of the sphere.* They withdraw from the rest of Creation and confine themselves to the fabric of the sphere for a measure of time (just as you withdraw from the rest of Creation for the duration of your incarnation on the Earth plane). During that time, the devas interact with the sphere to give it form and a particular reality working with the dominant elements of that sphere.

For example, on another planet you will have a different set of elements to the fore and, rather than water and earth, there will be different compositions to work with. The devas work with the compositions that are inherent within the wishes of that sphere to be a certain specific area of experience. Then, based on the elements of that sphere, they bring forth life, expression and *a total backdrop* – which, in the case of the Earth, is from the water that you drink …to the soil that you walk on …to the clouds in the sky …to the winds that blow …to the rain that falls.

Not only are those background elements created by the devas, but the framework within which a more solidified expression of reality can be understood is also brought forth, and by that I mean the structure of the life forms that you see across the planet that are other than yourself (I will return to that later). So, from an insect form ...to a mammalian form ...to a bird form ...to grasses ...to trees ...to flowers – *all* those expressions are brought forth as projections from the deva. Each form – from an insect to what you would consider a more advanced form such as a gorilla or large cat – contains the energy, will and expression of devas.

When you are looking at an animal, you are looking at an individualisation of God – just as you are an individualisation of God – but you are also looking at an individualisation of God that belongs to a greater individualisation of God. You are looking at a putting forth of a myriad of forms from many individualisations of God with each one expressing an individualised intelligence, but each one also expressing the intelligence, creativity and essence of the deva.

Each animal form is linked and is maintained because of a wish to put forth *correct form* into a sphere. Each form is examined and then allowed to continue to express itself as an expression of the deva until such time as energy is withdrawn from the sphere, the sphere is collapsed and the angelic host then take that experience of the history of the sphere and its life forms back to the Godhead.

What I am explaining is why certain forms exist because you may, perhaps, question what is the use of an insect ...what is the use of a mouse ...what is the use of various other forms? Those forms, initially, have been brought forth in joy (because all deva creation is joy) as potential expressions within a certain sphere that can eventually house the angelic spirits who will travel through the sphere in order to gain experience. As we have said in previous books, there has to be a host body for the angelic child to inhabit whilst moving through a sphere in order to experience in slightly more condensed creations of Light. So, based on the structure of the sphere, the devas examine the best forms that can eventually house the angelic children who will visit the sphere.

Now, in many, many cases a type of human form *with two arms, two legs, a head and a torso* has been found to be the ideal form to house the travelling angelic spirit visiting a sphere in this particular physical universe. This is why when other inhabitants of the universe are seen by anyone *psychically* (although I have explained in other books why this is not usually the norm), they resemble what you would call the 'human spirit' in form – although it is not the human spirit but a universal spirit. Nevertheless, despite that being the template used to a great extent throughout the spheres, the devas – when creating the backdrop or 'stage sets' of a new sphere – examine *through joy* all the variants that are possible in order to find the ideal frame to house the angelic spirits visiting that particular sphere. Having examined all those possibilities for the sheer joy of creating for themselves and for the Godhead, those other forms that are not the ultimate vehicle for the visiting angelic children are maintained. The flora and fauna and every expression of life is maintained and brought forth by the deva until such time as the sphere is non-operational, is collapsed and new spheres are created.

There are certain points across a planet, which are the energy points of the deva. It is as though the devas cluster together in creation at certain points across the sphere and then send out and interlock their creative wishes to cover the whole sphere. That is how they enable the 'reality' to take place and the backdrop to appear between those points, thereby allowing the angelic children visiting the sphere to move freely through that sphere without (and I don't wish to be humorous) 'bumping into a deva', as it were. There are points, nodes or concentrations of deva activity. In other words, there are places within the sphere where the deva lives, has its being and transmits from.

In the normal course of things on planets that are not affected by the Fall, those areas of deva concentration are easily seen by the angels visiting that sphere and are respected and *avoided* – just as you would avoid walking through a power station or a boardroom. If a skyscraper was placed in your path and you knew there were people working within, you would not constantly attempt to walk through that area.

On Earth things are different because you have lost sight of the fact that the backdrop is created for you by the devas. So, because your angelic memories have been cut off from you, you do not recognise those areas of heavy deva concentration, and you bring through them the pollution you have around you as a result of the Fall that took place so long ago. You are taking your pollution into highly spiritual and creative areas, and your pollution disturbs and pollutes, to a certain extent, the rays of deva vibration that are sent out between deva clusters and makes the ability of the deva to put out form in its purest form less effective for a time. Now, I hope that this makes you realise *two* things.

I hope, first of all, it makes you realise that you are not alone on this planet and that there are other creative forces that *allow you* – out of their Love for you, their Love for God, their Love for creation and their Love for the planet ...to live ...to breathe ...to exist here ...to have the backdrop of nature ...to have the backdrop of other forms that bring you delight. They allow you to have that! In the case of the devas that are clustered around the Earth, those devas were not a part of the conscious decision of the angelic children to create the effects of the Fall. And, yet, because they have begun to maintain this sphere in Love of God and you and each other, **they *choose* to maintain this sphere for as long as it takes *despite* the harmful effects of the Fall that impinge on them.**

So, they have entrapped themselves through *free will* in order to see through this sphere of creation ...either to its reinstatement as what it was supposed to be so that they can see their glorious creations shine out again ...or to see through creation here to the end of the cycle and then start again so that the angelic children can be brought back out of stasis to, once again, play against this backdrop that is given to them freely and in Love *and this time* try to get things right and negate the effects of the Fall so that the planet can be restored.

In saying this, I want you to understand the dedication, the Love and the commitment of the devas on your behalf. So, *respect* is the first thing I want you to bear in mind when considering the devas ...when considering a tree ...when considering a mouse ...when considering a bird ...when considering the rain or the snow or the wind. Respect! Not to see this planet as your 'plaything'. It is your plaything in that originally you came here to play and to experience, but it is not your plaything in that you can trample through every aspect of it without a consideration for all that has gone into this planet in order that you can experience. That is the first thing I want you to consider.

The second thing I want you to consider is that when you approach nature, you do not know where the centres of deva activity are. If you are psychically aware you will know, but the average man or woman under the effects of the Fall will not consider or sense where the clusters of deva activity are taking place. If you take into nature pollution – either psychic or physical – you interfere with the patterns of creation that emanate from the deva clusters and, as a result of doing that, the creative lines of the Earth become polluted. The devas know what they are doing! They know when it should rain ...they know when it should be sunny ...they know when it should snow ...they know where the continents should be ...they know what the balance should be ...*but the balance becomes skewed because of the pollution of mankind.*

I hope you see that. I hope you understand that in thought, word and deed you pollute the background **...you pollute the co-stars in the story of your life.** You set out to have this wonderful story that you star in, and yet you destroy the backdrop that is around you and alter the course of your story *negatively* by bringing pollution to the co-stars who are allowing you to have the story in the first place.

Do the aspects of deva creation have a soul? Does the mouse have a soul? Does the tree have a soul? Is there a spiritual content beyond what you see when you look out on nature? …And the answer is YES because every life form is given life by the deva that creates and imbues it with life on behalf of the Godhead. So, from the tiniest insect to the biggest whale in your oceans, those aspects of creation have soul and have spirit because they are projections of angelic deva-intent – just as you have a soul because you are a projection of God-intent given form as angelic children.

**So, if you harm an insect …or a whale …or the ocean …or the trees …or the clouds –** *you are harming devas.* **You are harming your brothers and sisters.** They might have a different 'job title' but they are your brothers and sisters. Do you, in the normal course of your life, wish to harm another human? Do you wish to harm a child, or another man or woman? Do you wish to harm *anyone*? Then, there should be *no difference* in your intent not to harm when applied to a deva. You should not wish to harm any expression of deva activity.

I will ask you something else – do you wish to take a knife and fork and eat your fellow man? This, because of the effects of the Fall, has actually happened in the past, hasn't it? But, would *you* wish to take a knife and fork and eat your fellow man, or would you feel that this was an abomination? Would you feel that this was a horror story? *And, yet, you do it with aspects of deva creation.*

**With aspects of deva creation you blindly, numbly and** *cruelly* **attack that which allows you to have life.**

And, you will say: 'Well, the mouse doesn't allow me to have life.' Yes, it does because the mouse is one of the creations of the matrix of deva activity that gives *the complete form* to this planet. You cannot attack or harm *any* aspect of deva activity without affecting, damaging, polluting and corrupting the backdrop against which you ideally live in balance.

You may say: 'Well, I only eat salads and vegetables.' And, at this point, there has to be an understanding that you have entombed yourselves in heavier matter for the moment because of the effects of the Fall. As a result of that, unfortunately, there has to be an intake of Light via a physical form. In actuality, were you to open yourselves up to your angelic heritage, you would exist on Light only, but that is not possible for the vast, vast, vast majority of mankind. So, unfortunately, you have to intake some of the deva matrix that is around you. But, in doing that, if you eat the simplest foods and less complex expressions of deva creativity and, *crucially, if you thank God and thank the deva for allowing you to have these aspects of creation that will keep you alive on this planet, then you are doing the least damage.*

In other spheres, the need to eat to consume energy as you do is not there. That need to consume energy is only here because of the effects of the Fall. You have to be aware in your eating and in your approach to nature that *all this is provided for you.* There should be thankfulness in your day for the backdrop that is provided for you. And, if you come across areas where you feel you should not go, then do not go there. If you appreciate nature then leave no footprints and leave no pollution. Understand that *your thoughts* also attack the backdrop of creation. Your thoughts should be of the purest form and should be thankful and respectful with regard to the surroundings that allow you to continue your life on this level.

Open up your view of life as a result of this chapter, please. If you have never considered that there is anything of equal value to yourself, now is the time to do so. If you have only considered that the human form must be preserved at all costs, now is the time to realise that *all forms* need to be preserved at all costs – not just yourself but the devas that provide the backdrop and the planet itself.

You are one unit. You have brothers and sisters that are creating different aspects in order that you can travel through them and experience, *but you are one unit*. You cannot look at the clouds ...and the trees ...and the fields ...and the oceans ... and the streams ...and the rivers and say: 'These things are less than me.' They are part of you because they are part of your brothers and your sisters; and you and your brothers and sisters – the devas – are an equal part of God brought forth with a creative task to bring more experience back to God *equally*. Therefore, if you follow that to a logical conclusion, the forms that the devas produce as part of the matrix of the creation of this sphere *are as important as you are*. They are extensions of your 'arms' and 'legs' and so each life form should be approached with the respect that comes from knowing that that life form is part of a deva.

I must conclude this chapter by saying that when life forms are terminated here, either through natural causes or through cruelty, *that essence* that was the life form returns to the deva. It is drawn back into the deva to be pushed out as further life forms. But, the *experience* of that life form is taken in by the deva and can be projected outwards again to interact with the angelic host or to interact with those who are psychic enough to be able to tune in to, for example, pets that are given as having returned through mediums. What happens is that aspect that is still individual and yet part of the deva, is able to project itself again to say: 'This is the life I had. This is who I am. I still love you and I still react with you.'

You see in the deva form an illustration of what happens to you in angelic form because in angelic form you, as an expression of God walking this Earth, eventually go back through the cleansing spheres and out into Infinity to become part of the angelic host again ...yet all those individualisations of you are still available despite you being a greater being in total. Also you group together within group souls, and yet are still individual – you contribute to the group soul but are still an individual.

So, every expression of deva reality and every life form maintains its experience, to a lesser or greater extent, with regard to reacting with the rest of the angelic host and can be called forth. It is part of the deva experience but is still an individual when called upon to be an individual.

**Respect the devas!**

**Understand that you could not 'act out your play' here were it not for the devas.**

**You owe them *everything*.**

As I dictate this chapter, there are terrible earthquakes and storms with terrible destruction around the Earth. That destruction has been caused, not directly by the devas and not by the Earth being angry or callous with the life forms that inhabit it ...but simply because the matrix of deva vibration has been disturbed. It has been disturbed *physically* by mankind, has been disturbed *mentally* by the thoughts of mankind and has been disturbed *spiritually* by the intent of mankind. It is terrible that people blame the violence that happens naturally on some unfeeling God, or on fate, or on an Earth that doesn't care – when none of these things are true. Mankind has caused, does cause and will cause (until it learns better) the disturbances in the matrix of the sphere.

At deva level on other spheres, these things do not exist because there is a balance. There is balance because the devas and angelic children cohabiting in a sphere understand that they are there to experience. They cohabit peacefully and harmoniously in order that that experience might be presented to those angelic children to the best extent.

**If you want to stop the violence through nature – stop the violence through mankind.**

**If you want nature to respect you – you have to respect nature.**

Questions, please!

**Jane:** Joseph, could I ask a question about the origin of the deva? In *the Fall* book you described how the angelic host gives birth to the angelic children through thought. So, is the deva also given birth to by the angelic host through thought?

**Joseph:** In order to create a sphere you have certain workers. You have the majority that wish the sphere to be in a certain way – so, running through the angelic host wishing to create that sphere, is the *higher intent* of the sphere. Then you have the members of the angelic host who actually create the sphere as a matrix of potential and energy. And, then the devas solidify that energy into coherent form that can be seen by those travellers who will eventually move through it.

The devas are part of the angelic host; they are just different workers. If you like, the devas have *'a brown jacket on with some pens in their pocket and they set about painting the stage, putting together the sets and making sure that every area is covered from every camera angle'* …thereby creating a wonderful temporary construct of reality through which you can travel. But, they are issued forth from the Godhead – just as you were issued forth from the Godhead. They have chosen to contribute in a certain way. There is an argument for us, at some stage, to create a chapter (not in this book but, perhaps, in another) on angelic intent and the various mechanisms of angelic intent. You have certain specialists, and the devas are specialists in a chosen and particular way. Does that answer?

**Jane:** Yes. So, in the normal course of things, they would go from planet to planet, but on ours they got trapped because of the Fall.

**Joseph:** They are trapped by Love and by volition. They understand that, in order for the angelic children to come out of the dream of the Fall, there has to be an evolution of thought against the backdrop of the planet as it exists. Were they to withdraw that backdrop, there would only be stasis because there would be nothing against which the lost angelic children could play to realise that they are lost and come out of that wilderness. So, the devas are trapped in that they had created a certain backdrop at the time of the Fall, which they now maintain through free will and will not come out until we have all come out. Do you see that?

**Jane:** Yes, thank you.

**Tony:** Joseph, as you were relating this chapter, my metaphor was of the human body where we have an energy system with meridians taking neural signals all around, and we have chakras which are major energy points within that neural network – is that how deva energy travels? For example, we have beautiful red beech trees around the Sanctuary… is it right, then, that they would be individual as a tree but also part of a network that allows the deva to connect through that particular aspect of nature?

**Joseph:** Yes, it is an excellent analogy and I thank you, Tony, for reminding me of it. It is an excellent analogy because you can liken the planet to a body with, as you say, chakras and energy centres, and those chakras and energy centres equate to the clusters of deva activity on the sphere from which energies criss-cross the planet.

Were you to see the sphere from an angelic viewpoint as it actually is with regard to deva activity, you would see a sphere of Light. But, within that sphere of Light, you would see threads of energy of different colour and intensity emanating from a cluster that would resemble an interplay of different energies coming from a pinpoint. Again, we get back to the *dot within the circle*, which applies to the planet and which applies to deva activity. I am trying to describe something that I can see and understand that doesn't easily translate into words …but you would see a blossoming of energy from the deva clusters that then lances out as threads that interconnect and entwine together from the other points of deva activity to create a criss-crossing of reality that is woven. It is a weaving of reality in a certain way that is maintained from the points of deva activity.

So, the trees in your Sanctuary will be maintained by a specific point of deva activity, and yet will be connected to all the other trees around the globe. The mouse that I have mentioned today is maintained via a specific number of devas but is also connected to every other form of life around the globe …to other mice and to every other form of life as a result of these criss-crossing threads of deva activity that maintain the reality around the world.

These threads of activity also maintain, criss-cross and permeate the human body. **The human body is created and maintained through deva activity.** There is no exception because every framework inhabited by angelic intent is created by deva activity. So, when you respect the deva activity around the world, you are respecting the health of your own body. You have the phrase: *be in tune with nature*, and being in tune with nature is a very important thing to do because if you balance outside – you balance inside. In respecting and doing no harm to nature – you balance, respect and do no harm to your physical frame.

Readers, I hope you understand that your physical frame is maintained by the very deva activity that for the most part you ignore; for the most part you don't believe in; and for the most part you damage by the way that you live your existence here.

So, if you wish to be healthier, yes, you go within and transmit the Light out into your body and out into the planet, but you also maintain, respect and love the devas that are around you that allow your frame to maintain itself. **If you pollute them – you pollute yourself.** You transmit a sickness out into the world and, as a result of switching off some of those connections between the devas because of your pollution and colouring some of those threads darkly, you stop the maximum amount of energy maintaining your physical frame …*and so you damage yourself.*

There is only one organism, as we have talked about today. There is only that one organism – whether it is expressed as an angelic child or whether it is expressed as a deva creating and maintaining the sphere. **There is one organism.** You have to respect the whole and have to understand that it is only one organism. You have to treat it as one organism. See the whole universe as being your body, see the whole universe as being you and see the whole universe as being treated by you as you treat yourself in physical frame ...then you are on the road to rediscovering who you really are ...then you are on the road to brightening some of those threads that have died and been disconnected ...then you are on the road to elevating the sphere back to what it was and elevating yourselves back to what you were.

**Tony:** Thank you, Joseph.

Chapter Ten
# Vapour Trails and the Universe Within

**Joseph:** Chapter ten – *Vapour Trails and the Universe Within*. If you look up at the sky on any day you can see planes flying across the clouds, and you can see vapour trails behind them as though they have left something of their essence behind as evidence of where they have been. If you were to examine those vapour trails, you would find that they stretch back far further than you imagine – past the visible into the *invisible* – with particles issued from the back of the jet engines that still exist as a 'marker' displaying where those planes originated from.

In your physical life you obviously interact with people on a daily basis and those interactions, you might say, are markers to delineate your passage through your physical life. You have connected with people and, as a result of that, their markers have been altered because they have dovetailed with yours. But, on an energetic level, far more is taking place than you can actually see at any moment in your life because there is *an energy trail* that you plough through your physical life – the equivalent of a vapour trail that says where you have been. If you were to look at this trail *spiritually* you would see a line of Light that stretches back seemingly 'behind' you into seemingly the 'past' that zigzags and connects with other lines of Light, which are the vapour trails of the people you interact with, and, as a result of connecting with those trails, it bends itself into new, delicate and always beautiful configurations.

Not only that, but all those vapour trails that stretch back from you, from your family, from your friends, from your workmates and from all the other people you connect with – those trails then split off and connect to other people and actually *link to the paths of the whole of mankind.* So, from a spiritual point of view, you can look at those vapour trails and see billions and billions of intersecting and connecting lines of Light that delineate *exactly* what has happened to a person during their lifetime.

Now, we have to extrapolate back from that because that line of Light representing your interactions during your present incarnation actually stretches back *beyond this particular life* into a pattern that has been formed by the other lives you have lived before this one. So, with spiritual eyes, you can see the line that stretches back along the length of your life …which then connects with the lines that stretch back from the people around you … which are then surrounded by the lines from people that are running concurrently with you or are ahead of you or are behind you in terms of their lifespan on Earth …but the line also stretches back into the life that you lived before this one when you were surrounded by other circumstances and other people's lives …that then stretches back again into the life before that one …and so on …and so on …back to the point of entry into this level when you were an angelic child that began to express itself in physicality.

I hope this helps you to understand why it is possible for you to have a life review when you return to the spirit realms because that energy has been recorded, not by anyone sitting in judgement of you or by 'CCTV cameras' looking at you from every angle – but has been recorded *by you* as a matter of spiritual construct and as a way that things operate on a spiritual level.

I hope this also allows you to understand (and I feel this is something that hasn't been explained fully in spiritual literature to this point) *why* the **Akashic Records exist** and how you can have access to them, because those lines that stretch as energy trails behind you *are accessible*. They are accessible by you, first and foremost, and most importantly **they are private to you** unless you seek to make them 'public', as it were. This is why it takes quite some 'time' for people who are not ready to access that life review to view it because they resist. And, if they resist, there is 'no power on Earth' (if you will forgive the pun) that allows us to gently coax them into looking across that most recent line of energy to see the impact of that line upon themselves and upon everyone else. So, it is held private.

And, *each* energy line is private unless a spirit reaches a point where it says: 'I have achieved much in my life. I have achieved positive things. I have achieved negative things. My life is unique but others can learn from that uniqueness, and so I allow other souls access to my 'vapour trail' – my passage through a physical universe.' And, at that point, there *is* access to the Akashic Record of the individual but *with permission*.

So, in the spiritual realms there is an area (and, again, this is relative) people can go to if they wish to access a certain situation unique to a soul that is held within that soul's Akashic Record. If that soul has given permission for that record to be accessed, then there is an area that souls can go to to access that information. Now, because you have been on Earth for some time, it often presents itself as a hall where you can access a book in a booth, and that book represents the life track of a particular soul or souls ...but that is not actually what is going on. What you are doing is *with permission* tapping into the energy line that still exists stretching back into the 'past' (as you would view it) that connects that soul to the actions it has undertaken in various lifetimes in order to become what it is today.

So, you will see on certain days (although 'day' is a relative term) souls accessing record books in a vast hall and taking in and then *reliving certain situations* – not 'reliving' as in they have already lived them, but reliving the experiences of a particular soul whose Akashic Record they are seeking to access. So, the book opens; the spirit invests his or herself into the book and is able to track back down those lines to certain situations that they feel will be of benefit in understanding more about themselves and the physical universe, and also *in this case* extricating themselves from the physicality of the Fall and moving onwards into Infinity.

**Where does that record actually exist?**

That record of energy (because you *are* energy) exists within you. It is not that you are looking back at a past that is separate from you, as though you could walk down a lane and access the various houses you have lived in in the past. **That record is held *within you* and is part of your energy wave as a spiritual being.** But, when you choose to either look at the path of your life in a life review or to share it with others, you *externalise* that part of your being. So, you are helping to create the 'physicality' in terms of the spiritual realms that are seemingly around you by what you have within you, because your records and experiences blend (as they do on Earth) with the records and experiences of everyone else to create reality [*laughing*].

As an angelic being outside of the effects of the Fall, your energy signature of who you are and what you have experienced (i.e. the experiences you have had up to this point in the NOW that you are experiencing *now*) is woven into the area of physical and spiritual universes that you exist in to a certain extent. **You create the fabric of the universe by who you are and who you have been.**

So, there are 'angelic Akashic Records', if you will; and, at a level where angelic beings create planets and galaxies and universes, the thread from you as an angelic being that goes into the creation of planets and galaxies and universes can be seen and *recognised* – almost as though you were Picasso or Gauguin or another artist. In other words, other angelic beings can see your artistic touch running through the universe. They can look at a planet and say: 'Yes, I recognise the handiwork of a particular angel in the creation of this sphere,' because that is *how unique* your personal energy-pattern vapour trail is.

But, there is a greater implication here because, whilst you are weaving those vapour trails through planets and galaxies and universes, **you are becoming more unique in the way that you create.** You are able to access your own Akashic Record and say: 'I like that aspect of creation. I would like to expand on that aspect of creation.' And, more and more, you come to a point where – rather than there being millions and trillions of filaments in a project that you have undertaken (those millions and trillions of other filaments representing the creative vapour trails of other angelic beings) – there are less and less and less vapour trails *until you create your own masterpiece.*

That is where the vapour trails are leading to ...the point where you have become such a creative artist in physicality and in spirituality that **you are capable of creating your own spheres and galaxies and universes *yourself.***

And, that Akashic Record held within you becomes a realisation that the universe you eventually create *has been there within you all the time,* and what you, as an angelic being, have been expressing is your Oneness from within and without. You are becoming a greater creator. You are joining with other more-experienced angelic creators to create new universes, new planets, new areas of creation and to share that record that is within yourself with other angelic creators ...and with your God.

Such a vast subject! I wish I could share with you the insight that we have into how this looks and actually take you into the Hall of Records and show you that, initially, no angelic being creates on its own. The society around you on Earth, if you were to see it spiritually, is represented by lines of colour and Light ... and sometimes by lines of darker shades that are absent of Light. There is an intermeshing of all these vapour trails that creates what you would call 'history' and is set as history by the way in which your vapour trail and the vapour trails of every other angelic being on Earth have meshed together to produce form.

This brings us back from what seems like a complex, *complex* concept to the sending out of Light because, when you send out Light, you illuminate your *own* vapour trail and you put Light into the matrix of *other* vapour trails around you as you pass through this physical realm. You also spread that Light to other souls who are moving along their own vapour trails, and, from a spiritual point of view, you can see the good that those points of Light do and the improvements that they make to perceived reality.

**It is so important to send Light out.**

Also, it is easier to view your vapour trail if it contains Light within it. There are other aspects to what we are discussing today in that, with your own Akashic Record (i.e. your own universe-in-creation that you are putting together step by step) you can, not only view all your past lives but you can also view the past lives of the people that you have touched as you proceeded through various incarnations. And, in looking at those touching points, you can perceive where souls – angels – have got things brilliantly right, and you can study where they have got things brilliantly wrong!

By going back along your Akashic Record and the Akashic Records of others, you can touch those Light-patterns and experience those points in existence *to consider* what you should and should not put into your own creation when you are creating spheres and planets and universes and working in conjunction with other angels. So, there is a learning process going on and a *wonderful appreciation* that is open to you as you progress spiritually.

What we are talking about this morning is a step beyond the progression through the cleansing spheres. It happens there, too, because you can view the Records within the cleansing spheres, but we are talking with an eye to something *greater* once you have moved back into Infinity. And, so you contemplate and you spend as much 'time' (although we know there is no time) ...you spend as much *experience* as you feel is necessary to contemplate various decisions that have been made emotionally, mentally, spiritually and physically by yourself and by the limitless souls that you have touched through various realities. And, then you consider the best way to proceed in your own creation and the best way to approach others in your creations so that together you can create ever more beautiful areas of creation to glorify and enhance God and to glorify and enhance your own experience.

In the normal course of things, this is a wondrous thing but, of course, there is a 'little hiccup' here on Earth because of the effects of the Fall. So, more concentration is given to the Akashic Records of groups and the individual in the spiritual cleansing spheres than in other spheres, in order to consider in silence and for as long as it takes *what shouldn't be done.*

**The effects of the Fall should not be carried forwards into any form of future creation.**

So, there are many souls who, having escaped the pull of the Earth and the desire to reincarnate, *do* spend much time in the Hall of Records contemplating what went wrong in order to take out of their volition the need to repeat any of those experiences, so that they move forward in a purer way and can much more quickly move on into Infinity – having learnt from the experience of the Fall and learnt not to incorporate *any* of that experience into their future creative ability.

The Hall of Akashic Records is actually an energy field but, as I have said, spirits view it as a hall with a series of books or records or however you want material displayed so that it can be accessed. In this vast hall, there is access to the *entire* history of the Earth back to the Fall *...but then there is a barrier.*

There is a barrier that has been caused by the Fall itself because, if you were to look at the energy trail of an angel that has not incarnated on Earth and so has not been influenced by the Fall, you would find that that point of Light goes back ...and back ... and back through physical existence ...and then back to a 'time' where the angel reunites with itself as an angelic being. **It is a loop.** It is a series of events on a loop, but you cannot do that with the Earth because you go back ...and back ...and back to the point of the Fall ...and there is a block because there you have *a gap in angelic memory.* You have a very visual representation of what happened with the Fall. If you go back far enough in the Akashic Records ...you meet a wall ...you meet darkness ...you meet a lack of Light. You cannot follow the trail any further into your original existence *unless* you are a highly evolved spirit that is looking at those records from an elevated point of view beyond the cleansing spheres.

You meet a wall of darkness and you meet a loss of memory. So, that loss of memory and the fact that you cannot remember who you are until you are reminded is an *actual physical thing* if you look at it in the Records. And, if you do that, then the awesome consequences of the Fall are writ large in front of you because you can *feel* them. You can go back no further. You can happily go back down the lines of Light of yourself ...and the lines of Light of other people who have allowed you to access their records ...and the lines of Light of society ...and the lines of Light of movements ...and the lines of Light of wishes and achievements **and then you hit a dark wall and you can go no further** – not because the trail stops there, but because the trail is blackened, blocked and disengaged from God-reality by the very act of the Fall.

The problem is that those negative vibrations still exist because everything that exists in the Akashic Records *is alive.* So, the Light that we ask you to send out is, not only to alter the present and the future, as you view it, *but is also to repair the past.* It is to be sent down those vapour trails of each of you to reignite the angelic perception that you had before the Fall took place so that

that Light eventually penetrates that blackness of a wall that is in the Akashic Records and lightens it and re-establishes the flow between who you were before the Fall – an angelic being – and who you are now – an angelic being that is working its way out of the effects of the Fall. Once that Light is re-established between who you were on that side of the wall and who you are on this side of the wall, the effects of the Fall disappear. That block in the records disappears and you elevate this world, as we have asked you to do in all the books.

So, in your Light-giving realise that you are not just healing today and tomorrow – you are healing the past. And, also remember in your confined times …in your secluded times …in the times when you feel that you cannot make a difference …in the times when you feel that other people have vast important lives and you have no life at all …in the times when you think that you are only existing – remember that, step by step, you are building a universe within yourself and one day you will build a universe outside of yourself.

And, remember that there is a vast canvas of your existence going back to the time when you were individualised from God and that you are an artist. Even if you have never picked up a paintbrush, *you are an artist and your artistic signature is unique.* There is no other signature like it. And, in your darker times, in your times of pain and in your times when there seems to be lack and loss – remember what is at stake. Remember where you are going. You *will* escape the effects of the Fall. You *will* move through the cleansing spheres. You *will* again become the angelic being in full consciousness that you are now but cannot remember. You *will* go on to higher and higher and higher levels of unending creation and, because you are part of God, you have been given the ability to create as God creates and to bring back to God your 'canvasses' and to exhibit those artistic works in the 'art gallery' that is God's universes …God's unending outpouring of Creation.

I hope I have managed to get across something of this *vast spiritual concept*, as your readers are ready for this. Your readers' concepts of reality need to be challenged, shaken, opened and expanded. And, hopefully, beneath the words of this chapter will be the feeling of glory in creation and the feeling of connection with God, connection with the angelic host and connection with ever-increasing levels of creativity. Hopefully, that feeling will be there and infused into words so that people will, upon reading this chapter, come out of it enlightened and uplifted for the rest of their journey through their physical life.

Are there questions, please?

**Jane:** Joseph, when you gave us the information for **the Fall** book, as you are still in the cleansing spheres (even though you could move on into Infinity but have chosen to stay behind to help mankind), was that information channelled to you from the angelic spheres, because you wouldn't yourself be able to go back far enough to see what happened before the Fall?

**Joseph:** As I have said in various previous addresses, there are people who come to visit us from higher levels and, as I have also said, I am very close to Infinity. If you like, I have one 'foot' in Infinity and one 'foot' in physicality and so, having reached that level, the only reason that I do not put both 'feet' through the 'hatch' and move onwards is because I wish to negate the effects of the Fall. I wish to gather around me the spiritual family that is still suffering on Earth and say: 'This way! …Ahead – through this hatch!'

So, my knowledge is a product of *duality* – as is yours. Your knowledge is a duality of the human frame of mind and the spiritual frame of mind. My knowledge is a duality of the spiritual frame of mind and the angelic frame of mind. So, in contemplation and seeking and in a much more extensive way than you can achieve by meditating on Earth, I have access to my angelic self. And, in those times when I have access to my angelic self as an angel of the universe, rather than an angel of just this area of space, I have access to those other angels – the angelic parents who are so concerned about the effects of the Fall on the angelic children trapped on Earth. So, I have access to that knowledge. Does that make sense?

**Jane:** Yes, thank you.

**Joseph:** Just as you are a dual being, I am a dual being but further along the road. And, yes, there are some areas that are still blanked off to me, but the knowledge that I am sharing today is knowledge that I have had for quite some time. The reason I have chosen this chapter today is to expand minds and to say: 'Look, you feel that you are living in a certain manner and that your life is going in a certain direction and, yes, it is ...but that is only a *small* part of the story. There is so much more ahead for you. There is a glorious existence that you would have now but you cannot get rid of the shackles yet. I want you to get rid of those shackles. Here is what you can do about it and here is where you are going.'

Some of the concepts that I seek to bring through my angelic self are extremely difficult to put across into physical words. Some of them would be so abstract to your mind that I cannot even approach them with you. But, I feel that we have reached a level where it is right to put this chapter in place in the book to *inspire* and to pull people away from the limitations of their everyday physical life, to say: 'Look within and realise what you are, what potential there is and where you will one day be – and rejoice in that.' Also, at this time because that darkness still exists and (as we have said in all the other books) threatens to put a 'bookmark' into your reality again, to say: 'Keep your eye on this bigger picture. Keep your eye on the fact that you are an angelic being and are a creator of worlds and universes. Do not become so petty, so limited or so frightened that you contribute to the viewpoint of mankind that is blinkered and locked in. Be the one who changes! Be the one who illuminates those vapour trails! Be the one who knocks out the "dark bricks" of the Fall and lets the angelic knowledge come back in!' Does that make sense?

**Jane:** Thank you.

**David:** Joseph, just to clear something up for myself – this gap in memory, is that bridged before you go back out into Infinity, or does it occur as a consequence of going out into Infinity, or is it something that happens after you have stepped out into Infinity?

**Joseph:** By 'gap in memory' you mean a reunification of...

**David:** Yes, that bridge when you come up against the black barrier that was the Fall.

**Joseph:** The black barrier can be seen via the Akashic Records in the cleansing spheres. We have access to it in the *higher* spiritual cleansing spheres and access to the reasons for the Fall, but the greater intricacies of how to deal with the Fall come to us as our angelic memory returns.

If I understand the question correctly, you are right in that, as you progress towards Infinity (and this sounds terribly harsh), you are becoming less human and more angelic. That does not mean that you are leaving your humanity behind because the brightest aspects of humanity are angelic. It means that you are leaving behind that limited human viewpoint. The spiritual cleansing spheres, as you progress through them, become learning spheres as well. We have talked about the spheres of contemplation, and in contemplation your memory is restored according to the vibrational rate that you have acquired by cleansing yourself through the spheres. So, as you approach Infinity, you are increasingly reuniting with your angelic viewpoint and your angelic capability. That is not to say that people on Earth cannot access their angelic capability now. They are operating as angels now, but they just do not see it or remember it. What I am talking about is their ability to recognise their angelic aspects and their ability to access creation ...to access communication with other angelic beings ...to access communication with God ...and to access the overall picture of

Creation and of perceived reality. Is that sufficient or have I not answered that?

**David:** Er… I think earlier in a previous book you said that in the rarefied cleansing spheres, souls spend most of their time in contemplation. Is that a process where they are about to go out into Infinity and are bridging that lapse in their memory?

**Joseph:** Once you progress into the spiritual cleansing spheres, the only barrier to your angelic memory is the effects of the Fall. Countless 'years', as you would view it, condition you to think in a certain way, which is why certain spirits reincarnate again and again and again because they cannot get past that small perception of creation. As you progress through the cleansing spheres, you are ridding yourselves of the effects of the Fall. You are ridding yourselves of the small view that you have, and, slowly and gradually as your vibration rises, you are gaining your angelic viewpoint once again. *The angelic viewpoint is vast.* You have, as an individual angel, the ability to create a universe. That is a huge amount of knowledge and it is also a huge amount of confidence. On Earth [*smiling*] sometimes you feel that you cannot create the energy to accomplish anything in a day. So, it is a matter of reintegrating your knowledge of what you are capable of. It is like re-educating a child that has been brought up and conditioned into a wrong way of thinking. You have to unlearn before you can relearn. Do you see?

**David:** Yes.

**Joseph:** You have to let go …and let go …and let go …and let go. And, the more you let go of this limited viewpoint, the more you let in of your greater viewpoint. Your greater viewpoint is vast. Your ability to fully operate as an angel is vastly different from the way that you operate on Earth. It is like trying to pour universes of knowledge and power into a pint pot. So, that pint pot has to be fashioned into a bigger pot …and a bigger pot … and a bigger pot until it says: 'Yes, I can contain this and can appreciate it, and there is more for me. Then, I will pour into a greater reality the contents of my pot and be back into Infinity.' Does that make sense?

**David:** Yes, it does.

**Joseph:** Are you sure?

**David:** Yes, thank you.

**Tony:** Joseph, as I understand it from this chapter, we each have a vapour trail of personal history that goes back through previous lives and also touches other people's vapour trails which, when viewed from an angelic perspective, enables us to gain experience from those points of contact. Do those vapour trails influence us when we are creating in physicality *here*? For example, I was responsible for building the Sanctuary of Healing here in Lancashire, and during that process there was a research and learning phase where I took in information from a lot of other people, but there was also an element of intuition which surprised me because I hadn't planned it in advance. Was that because I was tuning in to the records of wisdom of other people who have done similar projects before me? Does it mean that we have access to those Akashic Records here so we can learn unconsciously or through contemplation how to create?

**Joseph:** There was an interesting phrase in your question where you said that you 'hadn't planned it in advance' ...you *had* planned it in advance! You planned it in advance on an angelic level. So, your plan for the Sanctuary was fully formed before you ever put a brick in place. The problem that you have, and the problem everyone on Earth has, is that you cannot recognise that bigger picture that I talked about this morning.

Once you put something in place as a plan *angelically*, it cannot help but bear fruit and come into being. The only thing that prevents it or slows it down is the limiting effect of the human mind. You were quite right to say 'there was an element of intuition'. *Your intuition is you.* Your intuition is saying: 'Of course, you can do this!' And, your intuition is saying: 'I, as an angel in conjunction with other angels, can accomplish this on behalf of mankind to bring God-Light into a certain area of mankind to elevate them.'

Now, that is a vast concept, and this is back to David's question and back to one of the themes of today – that you cannot pour all that knowledge *that you already have* into the small receptacle of the human mind at this time. And, why is it such a small receptacle? It is a small receptacle because of the Fall. The Fall limits your access to angelic knowledge – to *your* angelic knowledge and to the connection with other angelic knowledge through the Records and through living, breathing angels who are around you all the time.

The Fall has limited *positive* creativity. So, you form a plan and – if it is in the name of advancing angelic knowledge and creativity and advancing the Godhead – that plan is fully formed and then has to trickle down into your consciousness bit by bit. You, as an angel, oversaw every aspect of what happened at the Sanctuary to put that Sanctuary in place. You were already at the point of having the Sanctuary when you thought of it as an angelic being and said: 'Yes, this is what I will do.'

So, you have an example there of what you are capable of and how you operate as an angelic being. It is just that most people do not allow that plan to come into force because they say: 'That can't take place. I can't do that' – whereas you were operating from angelic mind rather than physical mind. Do you see that?

**Tony:** Thank you.

**Joseph:** Does that make sense?

**Tony:** It does. Thank you very much.

Chapter Eleven
# Living Life on the Edge

**Joseph:** *Chapter eleven – Living Life on the Edge.* In the previous chapters of this book, we have explored various aspects of life that are going on seemingly around you, but today I want to explore something that is taking place within you ...or *on your 'extremities'*, as you will see. I want to talk about the ego.

The ego is something that gives you a sense of being *you*, if it is under control, or, if it is out of control, gives you a sense of being the centre of the universe and usually at odds with or seeking to demonstrate power over everybody and everything around you.

The ego that you display, to a lesser or greater extent throughout your life,
is actually not your spiritual ego and is not an expression of the *real* you. It is an expression of you filtered ...dampened ...in fear ...in trepidation ...uncertain ...insecure. The reason for this is because the ego that you express on this level *is actually an extremity of what you really are* – an extremity that is coloured on a material and mind level by the effects of the Fall. You see, you live much of your life here on the outskirts of your being only – in effect, through a shell, through a resistance and through a preconception that has been built up over the millennia, according to the skewed viewpoint of the Earth since the time of the Fall. I had better explain...

At the very centre of you is God (and all these terms are relative, but we have to give you something that you can relate to in material terms). Surrounding that central point of God, there is you the individual ...you the angelic being ...you the creator. Surrounding the angelic you there is then usually – if you are passing through a sphere of influence in order to gain experience – a bubble or sphere of reaction to that experience, reaction to the people who are a part of that experience with you and an inner view of that experience. So, there is a further sphere that contains within it the experiences that you are going through, as you move through a particular sphere of influence in order to learn and in order to contribute your experiences – both *outwards* in the way that you react to those around you and *inwards* to your central God-point. So, you enhance the God-point and you enhance those around you through your interplay with the planets you choose to visit and the experiences that you have with others, who are going through a similar interplay in order to gain experience, that you then take inwards to your central point.

On Earth, you then have another sphere surrounding that sphere of experience. You have a 'hard crust', as it were, of past experience of the Fall that has not been let go of by those visiting the planet and has not been let go of by the planet itself, because it is unable to do so until you change your minds about the situation and bring yourselves out of the Fall.

That outermost sphere or 'hard crust' of experience that surrounds you and is represented by your physicality and by the majority of your thoughts, is where you usually live your life on Earth until you discover more about yourself spiritually and 're-member' who you are. Therefore, in your interactions with your environment, with the people around you and with your life experiences, instead of operating from the God-point within you – *your angelic core* – and colouring your experiences 'outwards', as it were, **you experience from the extremity only**. You judge yourself to be a physical being from the extremity only. You judge yourself to be a mental being from the extremity only – from that shell which is *a shell of fear*. It is a shell of 'I don't have enough to survive.' It is a shell of 'I mistrust people around me.' It is a shell of 'I must rise to the top in order to survive.' It is a shell of 'I must draw power to me in order to survive.' ...Not power from *within* but power from *without*, from the Field of the Fall.

So, instead of operating from your God-point *outwards* and bringing out energy from your angelic point that flavours the experiences you should be having as an angelic being here on Earth, *from the extremity* you bring in fear; you bring in lack and you bring in a vision of insufficiency ...a vision of immobility ...a vision of illness ...a vision of conflict ...and a vision of always needing power, security and stability. Your *true ego*, therefore, is never heard from in normal circumstances because you are expressing yourself from the edge of your being and not from the core of your being.

The secret to changing yourself and to changing this world back to what it was and dissolving the shell of the ego that most people operate from, is *to seek inwards and not outwards in every situation.*

For example, if there is an angry moment between two people, what happens is that angry energy, infused with the negative intentions of the Field, flashes across that outer shell. So, you have anger crackling between two people and that angry energy *consolidates* the ego – that shell of fear and earthly individuality – and makes the situation feed on itself. If you consider then what happens in a war, you have anger crackling between thousands or sometimes millions of people...

To defuse a situation that sparks off between two people who are angry, it takes *at least one person* to understand that that is not really their chosen response but is their response filtered through the effects of the Fall. It takes one of those spirits to step inwards from the anger ...to view it, perhaps, as an experience that is taking place on the outer edge of a 'balloon' surrounding them within which there is the golden Light of angelic and God-energy ...to pull their response to the anger from that outer edge into the heart of their angelic being and, ideally, further still into their God-core ...and to bathe their response within that Light.

And, in doing that, you *completely eradicate* the anger in that situation – not just for yourself but for the other person, because the other person is reacting material-ego-to-material-ego, so is receiving signals from your ego or extremity of being. If you infuse that extremity of being with Light and with angelic intent, then those angelic infusions of energy are detected by the other person, your anger is not sensed and their anger begins to defuse itself as well.

I hope this further explains why the sending out of Light is so important. But, even before you do that, you have to understand that your experiences through life – the times when you have felt wounded; the times when you have felt angry; the times when you have resented people taking against you; the years, perhaps, when you have concentrated on people who have 'done you wrong' – all those times are of a skewed perspective and are not times when you have reacted as you would react as the angelic being that you truly are.

What I am trying to say is that for a *huge* portion of your life, you live your experience from a skewed point of view because, in reality, you are not that angry person. In reality, you are not that resentful person. In reality, you are not that wounded person. In reality, you are not that grieving person. *All* these things are of the material world and of the outermost ego that only exists because of the skewed energies of the Fall. What I am saying is that **you are not yourself** – a popular expression: 'I am not myself today!' You are not yourself on *any day* until you begin to access the angelic vision that you have and that is yours by right and by angelic history within you.

What a waste of life to live life on the edge only, when everything that you need – the comfort, the security, the harmony, the Love towards others, the Love for yourself and the lack of disease – *exists within*.

The ego that you see in many people – the power-seeking, the anger, the arrogance and the self-centring – is not really that at all. It is not a self-centring but *an outermost expression of self* within the circumstances which the spirit, that that person really is, finds itself in on Earth. It is an outermost expression saying, 'I want to protect this outer view' ...not realising that the outer view is *incorrect*. The outer view is not an expression of self at all.

**It is time for you to be truly self-seeking ...*to seek the true self*.**

**And the true self exists within you.**

You will not find your true self in interaction with others on a material level or on a thought level. You will not find your true self in brooding and thinking that life is a terrible lot for you ... in thinking how unfair life is for you ...in thinking that you are damaged or ill or are *owed something*. The 'something' that you are owed is what you truly owe yourself *and that is to know yourself*.

And 'knowing yourself' means retracting for a time each day from the outer shell and visiting *the true you* ...the you that exists within ...the you that has mistakenly chosen to return to this planet and, as a result of that, has found itself embedded within a negative set of circumstances and is only able to express itself very dimly through this thick shell of the past that cannot be erased until the effects of the Fall are transmuted through the transmission of Light and through the realisation that *each of you* is an angelic being.

**What to do in those circumstances?** ...Because, having said what I have said, you will view people *differently*. You will view the person who is arrogant, who is angry or who is manipulative in a different way, and you will say: 'Yes, I understand *why* you are doing these things. You are doing these things because you are operating from the surface only.' And, you will want to change those things. You change those things through the transmission of Light (as we have said in all the books that I have dictated thus far) *but you first begin to change those things by knowing yourself.*

And, in the course of each day (perhaps you work in an office or with many people) when ego raises its ugly head and threatens to hurt you – *step inwards.* When you are tempted to say something from a point of view of ego that would harm someone else – *step inwards.* When there is an atmosphere in the room because certain people feel they should have power and are not finding it – *step inwards.* When there is anger in the room and you can see or sense, at this stage of your spiritual evolution, the crackle of energy that is flashing from outer shell to outer shell of the people involved in that anger – *step inwards.*

**Step inwards and step back.**

Do not become meek but become peaceful. Know when to speak and when not to speak. And, when you do speak, always speak from the point of view of attempting to re-establish spiritual harmony and not from the point of view of the ego. Step inwards. Do not engage in the anger. Do not take on board and add to your shell the hurts. Do not take on board the antagonism and arrogance. Do not take on board the violence that attaches itself to, imprints itself on individual egos ...day ...by day ...by day, because that *does* happen. Not only are you operating, for the most part, from this outermost thick, dense, heavy shell of fear and anger, but pervading your shell and the outermost egos of everyone else *are the inherent vibrations of the Field* ...the anger ...the violence ...the pain ...and all the negative aspects that keep the Field operating in its current state, and **those vibrations attach to *similar* vibrations.**

So, if you are expressing from the outermost aspect of your being only – a need to be secure, a tendency to be angry with people and a resentment because the Earth seems an unjust place – then those signals that flash across the outer shell lock into similar vibrations from the Field and maintain it as it is. I have said in one of my books that you need to take down your walls [*reference to* **Illumination**] and I knew that this point would come in your timescale where 'taking down the walls of your courtyard and letting people in' would mean more than it did at the time that I said it, which I believe was part of a meditation.

You need to take down the walls of your physical ego so that eventually, through living angelically ...day ...after day ...after day, you become a being with no physical ego whatsoever. And, it matters not what people who are not in that position *yet* think of you. What matters is that you are living your life angelically and you are living your life to the full because you will find that, as you disregard and discard that shell around you, life will become more bountiful, more meaningful and more creative for you ...and you will be able to accomplish so much more.

You will also bring yourself *so much more quickly* to the angelic point of view that something is wrong here that needs to be put right. You will bring yourself *so much more quickly* to the point where you, as a vessel for and transmitter of Light, are much more effective in infusing situations with that Light and dissipating the negative and violent effects of the Field. And, you will place yourself *so much more quickly* in a position where you see the world as it is ...you are appalled by what you have formerly thought to be an acceptable way of life ...you seek to change that way of life in the transmission of God-Love and Light ...and, when this particular experience is over for you, you will see absolutely no logical reason (from a spiritual point of view) why you should return here again.

And, *that is a triumph* and is something that we have talked about at great length in all of the books ...**that you do not need to back come here.** What has brought you back here in the past has been the pull of this place and the pull of that shell that has infused you – rather than you infusing it with angelic harmony.

So, you will so much more easily be able to listen to your advisors, return to your spiritual consciousness and move away from the Earth as it is, so that the Earth can be restored to the former glory it had when you, as part of the angelic host and as an angelic child, co-created this planet.

So, I want you to consider carefully your ego and how you react to life and how you view yourself. You are not yourself. You are not as you seem, and the decisions that you have made on an emotional level thus far in your life (if you have not sought spiritual enlightenment) have been based on survival and based on the need, as you have seen it, to be secure, in a position of power and in a position where you cannot be harmed.

You have based much of your viewpoint in life through this incarnation on a false perspective. Hidden within is your *true viewpoint*, and that true viewpoint on life applies to any sphere that you have created as an angelic child. That viewpoint is a desire to move through the sphere of experience that you find yourself in physically (in this case, the Earth) and, as a result of moving through that experience, to enhance yourself and become more than you were when you first visited the sphere. It is a desire to look at that experience via your unique viewpoint as a unique angelic being ...to leave that sphere *the richer* for you having travelled through it ...to leave yourself the richer, more accomplished and able to view creation in an enhanced way because of you having moved through it ...and to take back that unique viewpoint, coloured by your experience in a particular sphere, to the God that is within you, so that the God within you appreciates your unique viewpoint and adds that unique viewpoint to His multi-viewpoint – that is: Himself plus the viewpoints of *all* His angelic children. So, God is enhanced and expanded in terms of what God appreciates and the way in which He views things through you having been in a particular sphere of experience.

**There is no other point to the planets.**

**There is no other point to the stars.**

**There is no other point to the universes.**

Each of those areas of experience (and you created them in the first place) exists for you to experience in different ways so that you can create further experiences and can enhance your viewpoint.

You are not here to be angry. You are not here to be petty. You are not here to be in pain. You are not here to hurt or to be hurt. You are not here to survive. You are not here to build empires of gold. You *are* here to experience what the planet *at spiritual core* has to offer you, which you took part in creating in the first place; and then to take that experience back to the God-within and the angelic host without and to the universe on a material and spiritual level and to other universes.

Now, that is a wonderful, wonderful purpose! That is, I hope, something that dissipates your view of yourself from the viewpoint of the physical ego ...from a small viewpoint ...from a protective viewpoint ...from a reactive viewpoint in a negative way. Yes, you have to work in order to view things from an angelic point of view again because you are immersed in the Fall and things are not as they should be here. But, you can in small ways at first, with 'baby steps', prove to yourself that there is a different way to live ...a more fulfilling way ...a more uplifting way ...a way that doesn't drain you of energy but which enhances your personal energies ...a way that gives you enough energy daily to add to this world *positively* and restore it through the transmission of Light from within.

So much lies ahead for you, but there is so much *now* – even in what you will perceive as a dim and destructive world – that can be experienced and enjoyed whilst you are here. When you start to resonate with yourself again as an angelic being, the aspects of this world that you draw to yourself and give out are of the original intent of this Earth. You will find delights and wonders that you have never seemingly considered or experienced before because you are reconnecting to them and you are reconnecting to that original experience.

So, [*laughing*] not only are you escaping from this world by living angelically, you are also reinforcing the original intent of the Earth. You are ...[*short pause*]... transmuting your own experience and ...[*short pause*]... pulling in the experience that you should have had before the time of the Fall. You are restoring things on all levels. You are using the Earth as it is supposed to be used. You are plotting a path through the Earth that is of original angelic intent. You are doing no harm. You are enhancing the experience and the experience is enhancing you – and that is what was supposed to happen originally. Not only that, but you enhance and expand the experience of everyone else around you because, as a result of you living angelically from the *true ego* at your core, you are enlightening the vibrations of the Earth. You are making it a little less egocentric and a little more angelic-centric, which was its original purpose.

I am sorry that I missed the connection a couple of times there. We are dealing with a depleted Michael at the moment, but I think we have accomplished what I wished to accomplish this morning in getting this message across. Are there questions, please?

**Tony:** Joseph, I have a wife who has spent her life involved in Steiner education, and it seems to me that the lesson today about how we express the ego from the outer shell is something that really should be taught at a very early age, because that ego seems to gain strength in the education system that we operate at the moment, where we appear to be teaching children to be 'strong', whereas in reality we are teaching them to *live on the edge*, as you have said. I think it would be just wonderful to get today's lesson over to very young children.

**Joseph:** There is a flaw, as you say, from the time that people are born because people are living through the extremity of their egos and, built into that extremity, is a need to conform to the view of society and the experience of the Earth with regard to the pull of the Field. That is not what is uppermost in teachers' minds but is, in actuality, what is taking place.

This will not happen for a while, but you need to impress upon children the fact that, whilst being an individual viewpoint of God, *they are also a part of each other*. Rather than the competitiveness that is taught in your schools, there is a great need to underline the harmonics of spirituality and the fact that each child in the class is not alone but is 'family' and that each member of that family needs to be treated with respect ...without anger ...without the individual viewpoints that come in so early ...without the violence ...without the need for one child to be superior to another child ...and without the bullying.

[*Pause in the communication due to Michael having a coughing fit.*]

What I would propose is that there are times for meditation because, in schools at the moment, there is never the time to be still. There is, as you quite rightly say, this ordering of the individual when there should be a *relinquishing* of the individual for a time each day. Children should be allowed to sit in the silence and, without fear, should be made aware of their angelic inheritance and the existence of an intelligence beyond this physical Earth that they can connect to. There should be times where they are taught – gently and in Love and in a communication such as we are enjoying today – that they can meditate, that they can connect to each other in meditation and that, during those times of meditation, they can *become the other person* and then withdraw from them, knowing that that other person is part of them. Imagine what a future generation you then produce – a generation that cannot harm itself; cannot go to war; cannot bully; cannot jostle for prime position because it knows that every other person is part of itself and deserving of exactly the same Love and self-respect that the self enjoys as an angelic being.

It is something that, yes, needs to be expressed today, but I do not see it happening today because the mindset of the teachers needs to change so radically in order for it to happen. Do you concur with that?

**Tony:** Absolutely!

**Joseph:** It is a *huge* necessity, and it would be wonderful if there were enough like-minded souls to form schools where children are made aware of their spiritual inheritance from the time that they go to school. Of course, *ideally* we want children to be *kept aware* of their spiritual identity from the moment that they can understand that they *have* a spiritual identity. Then, they are not forced down one path or another in order to conform to a perceived societal position that their parents desire of them ... but, rather, are treated as an angel from the time that they incarnate here and are given spiritual teaching, are taught the importance of the need for silence and are taught how to interact with others from the point of view of spiritual family and respect. It is a vast task, which is why I ask you to send out the Light; and, if you are a parent reading this, to consider that it is *more important* to educate your child as to who and what they really are than to solely prepare them for the exams they must pass in order to take up a position in society that leads them into an unhappy life. Is that a sufficient answer?

**Tony:** Thank you so much, Joseph.

**David:** It is not so much a question as an analogy that has crossed my mind. It has snowed today which leaves a crust of ice on the ground, and that crust is melted and taken away by sunlight, which is a physical metaphor for what you are saying – that, in order to break up the crust of the ego, we need to bring in Light.

**Joseph:** It is a lovely analogy, David, and that is *exactly* what we are saying. You see, the ego seeks from *without*, but the angel seeks from *within*. So, the Light that people mistakenly look for ...you have just had a 'sale day' [*reference to Black Friday*] where people have looked for 'Light' in all the wrong places and felt that certain things that they *simply must have* will bring them happiness... all those things are outside. The shell promotes the seeking of comfort from outside when the angelic being, in full consciousness, knows that everything is in here [*pointing to the heart-centre*] and that everything radiates outwards from within. So, that 'sunshine' needed to melt the ego is always there within and, in the darkest times of year and in the darkest night, can be brought into play at any time from within. There is that inner 'sun' that can banish all upset at any time of year ...all illness at any time of year ...all conflict at any time of year; and it is an endless, *endless* supply because God is endless supply, infinite supply and perfect supply.

So, yes, a wonderful analogy and also an opportunity to say to people that you will discover everything that you need, in every situation as you walk through this physical life, *within* and not outside ...not in the salesroom ...not, ultimately, in travelling the world ...not in gleaming metal ...not in new material-construction projects. All these things are, yes, expressions of angelic intent because everything is *at core*; but, when you bring out the 'sun' from within on a daily basis, the things that you construct *change* because your viewpoint of what you should be taking from the Earth and each other changes.

So, the buildings become more spiritually designed and the means of transport becomes more ethical, and you find that you evolve away from these things – rather than consolidating them so that they become more brutal and more entrenched with each successive generation. You might think that the buildings you have are beautiful, but there is an element of the brutal in them and an element of the expression of: 'This is what we are, and we exist and are the supreme expression of God here.' And, if you look at them with spiritual eyes, you will see that becoming more and more inherent. The cars that you drive and the aeroplanes that you build are becoming heavier and bigger, are becoming greater expressions of man's celebration of man rather than an angelic celebration of God. Does that make sense?

**David:** Yes, thank you.

**Jane:** Joseph, I don't have a question but just an observation about anger and the stepping away from anger. When we are angry, we have to expend a lot of energy in fuelling a resentment that can last hours, days or years – whereas, if we *do* step away from anger, it can save us a lot of personal angst and energy-loss. Another thing is that, in a confrontational situation, if we *do* decide not to respond in anger – not only are we controlling ourselves, but in a way we are also controlling the other person's reaction because, as the situation defuses, they become more balanced and peaceful as well.

**Joseph:** You can ignite points on the 'shell' of the ego in different ways, and they connect point-to-point to areas of a similar vibration. If you were to see the shell of the ego igniting in anger, you would see this flare-up of energy and would see angry lines of vicious red energy across the sphere with a swirling of darker energies around those red lines. Then, you would see red energy flashing out from that shell of ego to a point on another person's ego, which then begins to ignite their red lines and whirling grey clouds …and attracted to the ego you would see further red lines and further darker energy *from the atmosphere that then consolidate that situation.*

And, because you are used to living life on the edge rather than from your source of energy within, that is how you perceive your life force and that is where you direct your life force to. Instead of conserving it and going within to replenish it daily, you expend your life force on the surface and it is burnt up in this storm of negative energy. So, you become old; you become frail; you become infirm; you become diseased, because you are living life from the extremity only. And, then [*smiling*] you are donating that lack of energy and that frailty and disease as an image to other people. So, they expect the same via their outermost shell and begin to live their life as a mimicry of what they have seen take place around them via the lives of other people.

There is so much of benefit in putting out Light, in refraining from anger and in changing the outer scenery by connecting, once again, with the inner viewpoint. Does that make sense?

**Jane:** Yes, it is another thing that should be taught at junior school.

**Joseph:** You cannot change society at present by material means, as we have said in the other books. You have to change society from within. You have to place, in that outer shell and within each person, the knowledge of Light. The knowledge of Light then flashes from angelic ego to angelic ego and creates enough positive Light-energy for people to consider themselves differently. And, in considering themselves differently, they then *inevitably* have to consider society differently ...the set up of society differently ...their children differently ...their relationships differently ...their attitudes to others differently.

It all begins with being still and knowing who you are; that the answers to everything lie within; that your true self lies within; and the 'you' *that you really are* is not the outer personality, for the most part, that you see and have become accustomed to in your life. Does that make sense?

**Jane:** Thank you.

## Chapter Twelve
## Once upon a Time

**Joseph:** Chapter twelve – *Once upon a Time*. In this book thus far, it has been my intention to open your eyes to new possibilities; to look at various aspects of this Earth to help you discover new things about them; to help you understand that you are not the only intelligence at work around this globe; and to help you understand that you are living in *unseen harmony* and *unseen disharmony* with other forms of angelic life.

We talked in a previous chapter about the devas – those magnificent spirits that provide the backdrop against which you can act out your potential whilst you are here in physical form. The devas are angelic beings – as you are angelic beings – and in one of the previous books [*reference to **the Fall***] I described the mechanism by which angelic beings 'give birth', as it were, to angelic children by extending part of their being into planetary spheres. That is a constant throughout the universes. That is a constant way of *God becoming more God* – of God's experience allowing more experience to be appreciated. In other words, the angels project part of their being into the planetary spheres that they have created in order to experience new things. That experience then takes on an intelligence and independence of its own, although it is still linked to the angelic parent, and eventually becomes an angelic 'shard of God' in its own right.

The same is true for devas, but the situation on Earth is slightly different than throughout the rest of the universe. In the rest of

185

the universe, a deva, as an angelic being, projects itself into the creation of the landscapes of spheres and into the creation of physical manifestations to house those angelic children that wish to experience on those particular spheres. It projects itself from outside of the sphere into the sphere and, by doing so, pushes a part of itself out that eventually becomes another deva … eventually becomes a 'deva child', if you will. That is in the normal course of things.

In the case of the Earth, the devas (as we have spoken about previously) are somewhat trapped by the effects of the Fall and have chosen *through volition* to remain here to provide a backdrop against which the souls that were involved in the Fall can work out their experiences until such time as they are brought out into the Light. The devas are encapsulated within the sphere of the Earth; but, nevertheless, the process of angelic birth – the process of projecting angelic children from oneself that originates as a desire to push out part of oneself in order to experience – that process actually goes on within the devas that are trapped here and are maintaining the landscape against which you can move and have your experiences.

Those projections of consciousness and that universal God-urge to expand and create more of Himself/Itself/Herself that flows through the deva results in *a partial manifestation of deva children*. That partial manifestation of deva children begins as a need by each individual deva to manifest a means of maintaining the area of creation under its jurisdiction. For example, if a deva is concerned with an area that is wooded, then those trees and plants within that area have to be maintained. Energy has to be sent to them. There has to be a constant check as to whether each tree is healthy …whether the energy from the tree needs to be returned to the deva …whether the animal forms within that area of woodland are healthy …are located in the right areas …have the right amounts of energy …are bringing back experience to the deva …are fulfilling their purpose in integration with the rest of the sphere. And, in order to manage the area under its jurisdiction, the deva sends out 'tendrils of energy' – that is the closest description I can give you. It sends out extensions of itself, which are also part of the angelic birth process, but those angelic energy tendrils manifest themselves in whatever way the deva is most allied with.

For example, if the deva feels most comfortable with the universally accepted (with variations) human physical form, then the tendrils that are sent out, in order to work with the landscape under the deva's creative jurisdiction, manifest themselves as a replica of that human form. So, if a deva allies with the head, torso, arms and legs assembly that is universally accepted as being *one of the most practical on a physical level*, the tendrils – as potential deva children and as part of the deva's manifestation of itself sent out to police and maintain the area of creation under its jurisdiction – manifest themselves as replicas in miniature of the deva.

And [*laughing*] you will see that I am leading very subtly to something that will perhaps shake many of your readers and will perhaps delight others, because there have been manifestations of tiny figures and myths and legends surrounding tiny figures for centuries ...and the word that is the most controversial that I will use in this chapter is ...**FAIRIES**.

Now, at this point, you are instantly taken back to childhood and taken back to the *Once upon a Time* that I mentioned as the chapter heading, but I am perfectly serious. You can describe these spirits, these manifestations of the deva, these tendrils as whatever you want to. You can call them 'fairies'; you can call them 'energy tendrils'; you can call them 'potential deva children' ...but *I am telling you* (not asking you to believe, but telling you) that the tiny nature spirits, which have been talked about in various cultures but have receded into the distance and into fiction, *do actually exist*. **Do actually exist!**

You could call them the 'living toolbox' of the deva, and these 'living tools' are necessary to maintain order, to maintain the correct energy-flow and to maintain the correct sequence of birth

...life ...and retreat from life in the many forms that are under the deva's particular jurisdiction.

The point with these fairy forms or energy tendrils from the deva is that *they cannot manifest fully* as they would if they were operating in another sphere of creation, and this is because of the Fall. In other words, in the normal course of things, the deva would 'give birth' and would create another deva. But, because of the limited, oppressive and restrictive energy of the Fall that surrounds and interpenetrates this sphere, the deva can only *partially* extend from itself that expression which, in the normal course of things, would eventually become another deva – a separate and, yet, connected entity to the deva parent.

So, these little expressions of the deva – these miniature life forms (as you would see them but not miniature according to the deva) that tend the natural order of things on behalf of the deva – do not fully form into the complete deva that their parent is. They cannot do so because there isn't the energy. The deva cannot retreat from the sphere to gather more energy from the surrounding universe, and so can only *partially* manifest a copy, a child, a further progression of itself. These tiny life forms that are linked back to the deva (in the way that we, as angelic spirits, are linked back to the Godhead) are projected but then cannot be fully formed and, so, have a limited sentience and a sentience that is brought back along those energy tendrils to the deva and which is, ultimately, reabsorbed and then further tendrils are sent out.

This means (which is another shocking realisation, I hope, for you) that the devas – these beautiful, wonderful spirits that create your surroundings – are not able to create and exist and expand as they are supposed to and *do* in the rest of the universe. In other words, they are limited as though a restriction is placed on them and they can only go so far in their natural creative abilities. So, they can only bring back information to *themselves* via the tendrils that they put out. They cannot bring back information to God via another deva that they put out that is fully formed.

And, this is a sadness that I want you to consider when you are walking in nature looking at the skies, and the trees, and the waterfalls and the streams. Because of the experiment that went wrong that you were a part of (the Fall that we have spoken about in great detail in other books) you are, not only restricting yourselves as spirits, **you are restricting those spirits that selflessly enable you to live on this planet.**

The fairy forms that I have been talking about can also take *other* forms. If the deva is, for example, involved in insect life or in the creation of a particular type of animal then, at times, that deva is so associated with that manifestation of energy that it takes on the appearance of a 'super-being' in the form of the life form that it is projecting outwards. It is far more complicated than this but, as a limited example, you might have a deva that is connected with the fox and another deva that is connected with the wasp, producing the physical vehicles to house those types of life and producing the spirit *itself* that inhabits and animates those types of life. In those cases, the tendrils of energy that are sent out from the deva in order to maintain, watch over and protect those forms of life (to the extent that they are able to) manifest as tiny forms of the respective type of animal. So, you would have a nature form that resembles a tiny fox or resembles a wasp or the myriad of other life forms that exhibit themselves around the globe.

In times past when you were not as steeped in materialism as you are today, in your quiet times away from the major human centres, you were able to grasp glimpses of the fairies at work … glimpses of these 'tools' being applied. But, as with your knowledge of demons and knowledge of devas, as time has progressed and you find yourselves edging further towards a collapse of society (if you do not change your thoughts and imbue the sphere with Light) you have forgotten how to see, appreciate, acknowledge and respect other forms of angelic life around you. And, indeed, the term 'fairy' is one of derision and is something just for children.

189

Have you ever considered, Reader, why fairies are associated with children? And, have you ever considered, Reader, why in many legends and fairy tales it is said that only children can see fairies? Consider that statement: *only children can see fairies*. The core meaning of that statement that has been lost is that **only through the simplicity of the spirit and the shedding of the complexities of the Earth-life under the effects of the Fall, can you connect with and appreciate the other angelic forms that are around you.**

So, if I were to suggest that there were, indeed, fairies at the bottom of your garden – how would you react? I hope you would react in the way that I hoped you would react to the earlier chapters describing demons and devas. I hope to take away the scales from your eyes, and I hope to convince you that each day of your life should be a day of *respect*. When you are walking in the countryside, there should be respect for the countryside. When you are in town, there should be respect for the town. When you are in your house, you are never alone with regard to angelic spirits that are similar to you (as we have said in other books), but you are also never alone because your path criss-crosses and intermingles with the path of the devas. There are the devas' angelic tools around you all the time tending to the natural aspects of your world, tending to your plants and tending to your garden.

Yes, you can grow your flowers with Love and with Light and that is an excellent way to do things, but you also have to appreciate and acknowledge that there are *other forces at work*. When you look at the complexity of a plant, when you look at the beauty of a flower and when you look at the intricate patterns and systems in living organisms – how can you feel that you are in charge of those things? You can add to the wellbeing of those things, but you do not create them. And, those things are more attuned to the God-within that you are at this moment.

My point in talking of fairy spirits and in talking about the extensions from the deva of further deva creative energy is to devolve you from your complexity, is to make you aware and to make you consider that there are other forms of life around you which command and *demand* your respect.

## A Meditation

As an exercise I would like you to become still. I would like you to descend into the heart-centre (as I have instructed you to do in previous books) and I would like you to take into your visualisation an area of your life that is composed more of *natural* creation than man-made creation. It can be your garden ...it can be an area of woodland ...it can be the seashore – whatever natural vista you want to visualise that you are totally familiar with and can bring to mind with some conviction through your imagination.

And, I want you to take it into your 'inner viewing room' and I want you to ask to be shown the patterns of energy within that landscape. I want you to ask to be shown the pulses of Light that extend from the ground upwards through the trees and into their leaves. I want you to ask to be shown the intricate movement of energy that takes place within an animal's body and the Light that particularly surrounds their face and crown chakra. I want you to ask to be shown the criss-cross of energy that laces through the ground beneath your feet – be it the beach or the forest area or the garden of your chosen view.

I want you to see those pulses of Light, and then I want you to ask to be shown the fairy influence that tends, on behalf of the deva, those aspects of the landscape that you are bringing to mind. Perhaps you will see them as figures, or perhaps you will see them as brilliant points of Light, but observe in your meditation *where* those points of Light are. Observe that they go to the pulse points of the tree ...to the chakras of the animal ...to the intersection of ley lines of the Earth. Watch, observe and ask to be shown the energy that goes into the landscape through those extensions of the deva that you would describe, according to legend, as 'fairies'.

If you are *really* lucky, and you do this on a number of occasions, you will find during one visualisation that some of those tiny spirits will turn ...**and will look at *you*.**

And, then you will have one of two reactions: either you will be *amazed and uplifted* or you will be *very afraid* because, looking at one of those forms looking back at you ...reminds you of how far out from the God-centre you have travelled ...reminds you that there is energy *far more powerful* than your supposed energy and power ...reminds you that all the constructs in your world are 'matchwood' and can be levelled with a gust of wind ...and reminds you that the only *true power* in your life comes from reconnecting to the God-within – something that the devas have absolutely no problem in doing.

Are there questions, please?

**David:** On past occasions you have said that the devas voluntarily entered into the Fall, not that they had a part in it but volunteered to 'stay behind' as it were.

**Joseph:** Yes.

**David:** That is quite an amazing thing really when I think about it, because it does show that they have a Love for us even though we don't acknowledge them at all.

**Joseph:** Yes, outside of your encapsulated lives, there is the biggest family and the biggest unison of spiritual energy that you could ever imagine. There is a connection to every other angel and to every other angelic form – both in this physical universe and in other physical universes and, also, in non-physical universes. There is a thread that you have touched upon in that question (and I applaud you for that) and that thread is *Love and dedication*. It is the same dedication that we draw on ...or 'draws on us' is a better expression... to attempt to remove you from the effects of the Fall and to attempt to re-illuminate you. That Love is not something we see as 'sacrifice' – it is something that we see as *the norm*. It is something we see as *how else could we possibly act* when members of our family are mistaken and are 'washed ashore on a foreign land'. It is the only choice we have because there is no choice ...*the only option we have is to get you out.*

At the time of the Fall, information from the Godhead was given to the deva spirits that, if they withdrew from the background theatre, there would be no structure against which the souls in stasis could measure themselves and, so, the souls in stasis would have to remain there until such time as *another physical landscape* (obviously formed by spiritual means) could be created for them. So, the choice was given to the devas to either abandon the sphere (which would have been *their right* if they had chosen it because free will is a universal constant) or, in Love, to aid the souls who are lost because of the effects of the Fall. At that point, having been given the choice, the devas decided that *there was no choice*. What other choice could they make?

**And they continue to make that choice on a daily basis.**

Their creations, which are works of art, are damaged on a daily basis. The planet, which is an interlacing of deva activity within a sphere of angelic intent, is damaged and brutalised on a daily basis ...*the concept of which is completely alien to angelic minds, to our minds and to deva minds*. So, there has to be constant repair by the devas of the Earth to bring it back to a state that can still maintain the angelic children in human form. That constant repair is not the effortless task that it is in other spheres of creation, because *the devas are working within limited energy*.

As I explained earlier in the chapter, in the normal course of things, you would have a deva that was connected to the planet ...that would have projected a further deva ...that would then project a further deva. So, you would have this coming and going of deva activity and a freedom that allows *new* energies in. But, because the devas are encapsulated within the effects of the Fall, there is only limited energy available to them and it is a different source of energy. It is still God-energy but, because they are creating from within, they have to filter that energy in through a very dark, draining and debilitating sphere.

So, they repair at *great energetic cost*, and I hope that goes some way in allowing readers to understand why in Michael's experience, for example, there is seemingly a harshness to any intrusion into areas of deva activity where devas choose to have their being*. There is not a resentment but a need to push out the human forms so that they can get on with the already demanding task of creating using diminished energy and repairing expressions of form that are being attacked and degenerated by the Field.

There is no reason why a tree should die except when a deva decides that, at a certain point in the tree's existence, that tree has had all the experience it can possibly bring to the deva and to the inhabitants of that particular sphere. So, the energy is withdrawn; the construct is collapsed; and a new construct is made. Not so on Earth where the deva is constantly having to combat the surrounding decay placed upon all living objects by the effects of the Field ...which are fuelled by the thoughts of mankind.

So, the deva, as you quite rightly say, is selflessly working for mankind and, yet, mankind is working all the time – be it subconsciously – to undermine and destroy the creations of the deva that are there in order that mankind can escape the effects of the Fall. Great Love! *Great irony*!

Does that answer your question?

**David:** It certainly does.

**Jane:** Joseph, not only are the devas restricted in what they can do but isn't there also an element of *suffering between devas* arising from the competition for survival between the life forms as a result of Fall? For example, the deva of a fox 'benefits' from the killing of a rabbit for food, whereas the deva of that rabbit must surely feel the suffering that that action entails?

**Joseph:** There are degrees of sentience, and the degree of sentience within animal forms is God-centred more than material-centred. So, the animal's core expression is based on God-energy with the suffering taking place further away from the core, but that is only an analogy. With the human spirit, the suffering takes place *at core* because the human spirit only acknowledges the material aspects of life. With the animal, it is more of a peripheral suffering ...*but suffering nonetheless.* And, there is constant work with the tendrils of energy that the deva puts out (and I want you to imagine the complexity of this) to extract, at the moment of death with a minimal amount of suffering, the deva energies that have constituted the animal, so that the animal's spirit returns to the deva with the least amount of suffering. Do you understand what I am saying?

**Jane:** Yes.

**Joseph:** Just as the tendrils of energy or fairies (or whatever you want to call them) are tending to all aspects of creation to *maintain* that creation around the sphere, there is *an extraction process* as well to make sure that when one animal attacks another (which is as a result of the Fall, as I have said in previous books) that animal is extracted at the moment of physical death with the minimum amount of suffering. But, suffering does take place and it is a different expression of the same suffering that the deva undergoes because it cannot fully manifest.

So, the devas are suffering *on many levels* and have to integrate and interweave in order to maintain their levels of energy and maintain the landscape and animal forms for us. It is completely selfless.

...But, there comes a point – if society degrades itself to the extent that it has to go back into stasis – where *the devas still do not leave* but are freed in peace from the pollution of humankind for a considerable amount of time, as you would measure it, to create as they wish to create ...to replenish their energies ...to be in touch with other angelic expressions of deva activity from beyond this sphere ...to recreate, as is their wish, the paradise that this Earth was. And, *if* it is necessary for the souls, who have not escaped into the spiritual cleansing spheres but have gone into stasis, to come back then the process begins again ...and the suffering begins again.

Do you see that?

**Jane:** Yes, thank you.

**Tony:** Joseph, fairies at the bottom of the garden ...when we moved into our house twenty-odd years ago, it was a field and we let it become organic over a period of time. We started growing vegetables and then one year we thought: 'Ah ha – the nature spirits have arrived!' We could feel and sense them, and it is the same in some beautiful gardens in the country. So, is there not a connection there with those fairies and nature spirits?

**Joseph:** Yes, in the normal course of things in other physical spheres, there would be a natural and established connection with deva and fairy activity. From the viewpoint of the Fall and from where you are now, you have to re-establish that link. You have to ask for that link to be *consciously appreciated*, and so few people know how to do that. The reason that you acknowledged and were aware of that reconnection with fairy activity was because your perspective was correct. You didn't intend to do any harm to the landscape. You intended for the produce from your land to be the best it possibly could be and to have the most energy in it. That, then, aligns you with the intents of the deva …to harm nothing, to love everything and to appreciate creation.

It is a very good question because, in approaching nature spirits and in wanting to see them (and, again, it goes back to fairy tales which have a basis in understanding that has been written down but is now regarded as fiction) you have to approach the fairies with innocence and with an intention, *at least,* not to harm and, *at best,* to co-create with them. Do you see that?

**Tony:** I do, thank you.

**Joseph:** The energy has almost gone, but I feel it important to comment this morning very briefly on the insanity of the violence in your world [*reference to the missile attacks on Syria carried out that day by US, French and British forces*]. It is appropriate and no coincidence that I have spoken today about the connection that needs to be made through Love. And, I would simply say to all of you reading this at whatever time and in whatever country: your reconnection to God, your reconnection to each other and your reconnection to joy, to bliss, to healing and to harmony comes from Love and comes from Light, and (as we have said in all the other books) the two are interchangeable and are the *same* thing.

You cannot ever, ever, *ever* through violence produce Love. The two are opposite concepts. You cannot hope to create Love as an end result of violence. **NEVER, EVER, *EVER*!** To us and to you, at core, that is such a simple equation. You could give that equation to a child that has not been brought up against a violent backdrop and instantly that child would recognise the sense of that equation. It is a *simple equation* – you do not have to be a professor of mathematics to understand it.

**Please, please, *please* study that equation!**

**If you do not, it will once again be too late.**

---

\* Michael: On more than one occasion I have spoken with devas, having intruded unknowingly into an area that they wish to keep 'untouched' by the pollution of human influence, and have been told in no uncertain terms that I should leave immediately.

Chapter Thirteen
## Starlight Signature, Planetary Evolution
## and the History Dam

**Joseph:** Chapter thirteen – *Starlight Signature, Planetary Evolution and the History Dam.* We have so much to cover this morning, and you will see that the three phrases I have just used are interlinked.

I want to talk initially about planetary evolution and the way that planets are *meant* to evolve in the normal course of things on a spiritual and also a physical level. Planets, of course, are in reality spheres of angelic influence – energy parcelled together for a period of time so that members of the angelic host can visit those spheres in order to experience and to grow. And, so (as I have detailed in some of the other books) certain members of the angelic host decide that a sphere of influence with *specific* properties would be a good idea for the benefit of other members of the angelic host and for their angelic children. So, they band together to create a planet with particular characteristics in order that those travelling across that landscape can experience certain things that will add to their own personal spiritual evolution and to the evolution of the angelic group they have originated from. Eventually that experience is then shared with the whole of the angelic host and is taken back to God.

A planetary sphere can initially be created as one set of circumstances and then evolve into a refined set of circumstances via the angelic children travelling through it. In other words, the original intention of the planet is not fixed but, as with everything else spiritually, is able to evolve. And, it evolves via the angelic children passing through its landscape and discovering things from that experience that are of benefit to the other members of the angelic host and also to the matrix of the planet *itself*.

If certain trends become apparent that are of value to that sphere and, therefore, offer *further* opportunities for those who have yet to come and travel through that landscape then, after discussion and with consensus, they can be added to that sphere. It is a difficult thing to try to explain, but if there are beneficial spiritual concepts that arise from members of the angelic children travelling through a certain planetary experience then those aspects are added to what the planet can offer.

So, a planet begins as a perfect sphere of Light that offers certain experiences that have been embedded into its matrix by the members of the angelic host that wish to make that planet available as a theatre of experience to their own section of the angelic host. Then, as a result of members of the angelic children travelling through that sphere and gaining experience, *further* opportunities to experience and to grow can be added to those that the planet provides. If a number of angelic children moving through that sphere have similar experiences then those experiences *cluster* together. And, if it is decided by that section of the angelic host that the opportunities to experience in that way are a good idea, then they are incorporated into the sphere so that the sphere offers more enhanced opportunities for spiritual growth than it did when it was first created. Any aspects of that sphere that do not present something new, something of interest or something of enhanced spiritual evolution are discarded and let go of by the angelic child when it leaves that particular sphere and returns to the angelic host. What the angelic child retains are those experiences that *enhance* the host.

So, in the normal course of things, *planets evolve too* because it is a natural thing that *every* aspect of spirituality evolves and becomes more than it was when it was first created.

Now, the Light that a planet gives off is a 'signature'. When you look up into the night sky, the pinpoints of starlight that you see represent a pretty picture of silver lights in the sky, but to the angelic host that Light is a signature from each planet and that signature says: 'Here I am! This is what I have to offer you if you come to visit me.' The opportunities that a sphere can offer an angelic child are initially made available to that section of the angelic host that created the sphere and to their children, but then that sphere, *operating for the glory of God*, is opened up to other sections of the angelic host that might wish to visit it to experience the *unique* properties of that planet in order to grow. That unique experience is able to be read via the vibration of Light that the planet gives off.

With *each* sphere the angelic host, looking on a spiritual level across the universes, can see and consider what that sphere is able to provide and whether they would like to visit it to enhance themselves and have adventures that bring greater glory to God and greater experience to the angelic host and to the individuals within the angelic host, because that is the nature of existence … to have adventures and to become more, to evolve and to grow.

So, on an angelic level, the opportunities that each sphere presents can be read, interpreted and considered by the angelic host. Now, in normal space that also operates *on a physical level* with regard to what you would describe as 'alien life' or 'visitors from other planets'. I want to touch for a moment on something I said in an earlier book about the Earth being *quarantined*, which is why you do not have flying saucers hovering over your cities and saying: 'We wish to make contact with you.' That statement is absolutely true and I stand by it.

What I also want you to understand is that there are expressions of life within the *physical* universes that are advanced enough spiritually to be able to see instantly (just as the angelic host can see instantly) what a planet is able to offer them. The signature of each planet shows them whether that world *should* be connected with and visited and whether that world is ready to harmonise with physical beings from another sphere and would benefit from such a visit. ...And, looking at the Earth that quarantine is instantly recognisable because the vibration of Light that the Earth gives off is nowhere near as brilliant as the vibration of Light that the other spheres give off.

**The starlight signature of this planet reflects its inability to operate correctly at this time ...*due to the effects of the Fall.***

'The effects of the Fall' is a phrase I have used on numerous occasions and brings me around to the third aspect of today's discussion, which is *the history dam*. Now, what do I mean by 'the history dam'? You have dams in your physical world that are built to hold back water to ensure that it is stored and can only escape in controlled circumstances. As I have explained, this sphere was originally created like all other spheres in order that the angelic children could move through it and, as a result of that, could gain experience and then take that experience back to the angelic host and, ultimately, back to God.

Because of the effects of the Fall and that speeding up of matter, the sphere became locked with regard to dispersing with experience. In the normal course of things, as the angelic child returns to the angelic host at the end of its journey, any experience that is not required is dissipated and only experience that is seen to be *of value* is taken in by the individual, is taken in by the angelic host and is folded into the matrix of the planet so that the planet can offer further positive and evolutionary spiritual experience.

**That doesn't occur on Earth.**

You are still angelic children travelling through a physical and spiritual world. You are still angelic children gaining experience.

At angelic core, your reason for being here (no matter what you believe) is to go through an experience in order to become more than you were before you visited here.

Unfortunately, because of the effects of the Fall, when you decide to reincarnate here you are reconnecting with a *loop* of experience. As you travel through the physical plane of the Earth – you gain experience, you interact with people and you create history which, because of the effects of the Fall, cannot be relinquished *fully* and dissipated at the end of your experience because mankind altered the way in which matter expresses itself.

**And so, on this physical plane, you *layer* history.**

From the first time that you awoke and became sentient following the Fall, you began to experience and that experience became like the building bricks of a dam around you because you could not get rid of that history. So, as you move through the experience of this planet during a lifetime here, all your experiences are expressed (as *all* angelic experiences are expressed) both *within* you and *around* you but cannot be dissipated. You cannot come to the end of your journey on Earth and *instantly* relinquish those vibrations that you have expressed around you, which is one of the reasons why the cleansing spheres exist, in order to rid you of the spiritual history that you have accumulated whilst you are here.

Further to that, as an angelic being, because you express *outside* of yourself – *you create*. Whilst you are here you are creating circumstances that cannot be fully dissipated. You are creating your own history; you are contributing to societal history; and you are contributing to planetary history. Due to the effects of the Fall, that history continues to exist as a vibration, so aspects of that history build up layer ...upon layer ...upon layer ...upon layer and encapsulate the further experience and viewpoint that souls travelling through this planet create whilst they are here ... *layer upon layer of history*!

In visiting your sphere and in communicating with you, if I reach out my hand into the ether of the planet, I am experiencing – not what I should experience in visiting a planetary sphere as an angelic being, but I can feel the mist, the roughness and the coarseness of layer upon layer of creative thoughts that haven't dissipated. And, if I choose to, I can reach back through the centuries and select various experiences from what you see as the 'past' that *are still present* ...ghosts, if you like. In amongst this mist of confusion and these layers that press upon the planet and degrade it (and degrade you, which is one of the reasons why you age so quickly) I can also see angelic children who are so connected to that history and who have invested so much of their consciousness into it throughout their lives on Earth *that they cannot escape from it.*

So, in addition to spirits who come back to the cleansing spheres but feel drawn back to the Earth and have to be counselled that it is not a wise decision to return to the Earth (at least they have escaped to the start point of the spheres of cleansing) you also have spirits who are so invested in the history of the Earth, so steeped in the view that *this is all there is* and so connected to those vibrations that cannot be dissipated yet ... that initially they cannot leave here at all. So, in their spiritual form, they are lost in the 'soup of history' until such time as teams from the cleansing spheres aided by the angelic host can minister to them, can explain that they should be somewhere else and can extricate them from that layered dam of history so that they can start their journey through the cleansing spheres and out into Infinity.

To observe and interact with your Earth is draining. I hope what I have said today explains why we often say that it is so terrible for us to visit this level of consciousness and why we can only maintain communication for a relatively short amount of time because, in coming back to this level, we are steeped once again in this sticky vibration and 'glue' of undispersed experience that pulls at us ...but this experience also pulls at *you.*

And now [*laughing*], to return to a subject that I have not touched upon much in this particular book because there were other pieces of information that needed to come through first ... **dissipation of this dam of history is down to the transmission of Light.**

Dissipation of your *personal* history here is down to the transmission of Light. If you immerse yourself daily in the God-Light that comes from your centre, you lighten your personal load of expressed history. If you then encapsulate yourself within a bubble of Light, you push back the history that is around you and you limit the effects of that history upon your physical body and your mental faculties. If you then transmit that Light out into the world and into the hearts and minds of others – with a wish that they evolve in the right way and remember their spiritual heritage – then you begin to dissipate and push back their history a little so that they can start to examine spiritual concepts, which otherwise they would not consider because of the weight of undispersed vibration that is within and around them.

Looking at the planet from the perspective of the angelic host, the Earth seems condensed ...seems crushed ...seems bursting with heavy matter ...seems to be folded in on itself, and the amount of Light that it displays is, unfortunately, pitifully small.

I also want to mention that this dam of history around you affects the decisions that you make with regard to the planet because you are not reaching *within* to make decisions from your spiritual core. In other words: **you continue to pollute the planet because it is what you have *always* done since the time of the Fall.** If you are purely operating on a mental and earthly level, then you are influenced by the vibrations around you that resonate with what you have done as angelic children since the Fall ...and you have plundered the planet time and again, acting within the loop of skewed causality you have created. You will not stop plundering the planet and you will not stop harming each other until you bring enough Light into your souls so that you can see clearly past the influence of the heavier vibrations of history that you have created and which at present cannot be dispersed.

So, most of your negative actions are based on your skewed viewpoint because of the Fall but are also reinforced by the history of what you have done thus far, which is a *trapped* vibration that you link into if you operate solely from a mental and physical perspective.

I hope that this short illustration of a vast subject illuminates the need for Light on this level (as I have tried to emphasise in all the other books) but here is *another* practical reason why you should be transmitting Light …**that history needs to be dispersed.** In the normal course of things, in travelling through other angelic spheres, you would not be creating such negative experiences as you do on this sphere, and anything that is 'not needed on journey' is simply let go of and dissipated – leaving only the 'jewel' at your centre …the 'jewel' that is brought back to the angelic host and to God …and the 'jewel' that can be added as a benefit to the sphere so that other angelic children moving through that sphere can gain further, richer experiences. This doesn't happen on Earth.

However, this dam of history *can* be dissipated by praying for it to be dispersed and by seeing the planet in a state that is beyond pollution, beyond degradation and beyond ruination. So, as part of your sending out of the Light, you have to acknowledge the planet as it is *at its core* – unpolluted, unsullied, unharmed – and, in doing that, you also begin to dissipate the history that is around you.

It is little wonder [*laughing*] that you feel you see Roman legions on occasions marching across your cities or see people in various costumes from the past that you perceive of as ghosts and spirits. And, sometimes they *are* ghosts and spirits, but your recording of history from the time that you became sentient here following the Fall is locked into the matrix of the planet and is *still* here ...everything that you have ever thought and everything that you have ever done! And, because of the effects of the Fall, the predominance of vibrations within this planet are negative and diminish the nobler aspects of journeying through this world *unless* you put Light into them.

I hope you can see the struggle you have, and I hope you can see the *need* for Light because Light dissipates *all*. In your Light-projection, you can look at the concepts of negativity around your world. For example with war, if you link into the God-within and visualise war *as a concept* dissipating, then you affect all those memories and vibrations of war and bloodshed that are still there, and you make them lighter and you dispel them. You can concentrate on violence within individuals and see that violence lightening and those individuals becoming calmer, more God-like and putting aside their violent ways. Or, you can look at violence throughout history (but only if you are strong enough) and lighten those periods of history by visualising Light streaming into the aspects of the past that are detrimental to the future of this planet and to the angelic children visiting it. Visualise the past being flooded with Light and see those molecules of violence, war and disharmony dissolving away.

I think I have covered the subject I wanted to cover. It is a complex, *complex* subject, and I think I have also demonstrated, once again, the need for Light. If you are reading this book and haven't read the others in the series, I must just quickly say that *as an angelic child* (and I refer you to the other books) you are a vessel for Light. You are a beacon for Light and, as the recipient of Light from the Godhead and from the angelic host, you are able to channel that Light for the good of mankind and for the good of the planet.

**You *need* to do it.**

The objective of this book is to show you that there are other aspects of life that you will not have considered before, but it is also to say to you that *it is time for action*. It is time for you to do something if you wish to change this world and if you wish to elevate yourself and the people around you.

Are there questions, please?

**Tony:** Joseph, as individual souls should we be reflecting on our own particular dam of history, and I don't mean just from this lifetime because I know there are shamanic practitioners that can regress people back through past lives. On a personal level, is it useful to reflect upon and put Light into our own personal history?

**Joseph:** There is a benefit and a danger in that. I have explained previously how, once you return here, you reactivate the karma around you, and I hope that today's discussion illustrates why that happens. As an angelic being revisiting this sphere, you are dipping back into a vibration with an energy-signature that reconnects you to the aspects of your past lives that are detrimental to you. They chip away at you, much as a little dog would yap at you to say: 'I'm here! ...I'm here! ...I'm here ...I need to be taken notice of!' They attack you until you do something about them by becoming more *illumined* than them.

You have to be aware of the patterns in your life, but what I would caution against is the *glorification*, as it were, of examining past lives in order to understand more about yourself. And, by 'glorification' I mean that, in examining past lives, you can come to the point where it becomes a fascination because aspects of those past lives become something that you treasure rather than something that you should dissipate.

So, I prefer souls here to understand that they have had past lives but to regularly look at their *present* life and to lightly examine those aspects of this life (because they are a reflection in part of what has happened in past lives too) that they are now superior to and no longer have a need for and to inject Light into those areas of their life until they are dissipated. There is a great need for personal forgiveness in a life and a great need to forgive others ...to let go of grudges ...to let go of anger ...to let go of resentment because these are the things that connect you to the 'little devils' of your past lives that are still around you in terms of vibration and which drain you, age you and fuel you to commit more acts of the *same* vibration. Does that make any sense?

**Tony:** Thank you, Joseph.

**Jane:** Joseph, I am a bit confused with you saying that at the end of our life we should dissipate certain experiences and let go of them, and I wondered how that relates to a previous chapter about the vapour trails and the Akashic Records where everything we have ever done since we were first created as an angelic child is recorded and retained. I just wondered how the two concepts fit together.

**Joseph:** Yes, with the Akashic Records everything you have done *is* recorded, but everything you do here also has an *emotional charge*. If you are reading a biography about someone else's life, you can read about the things that person has done for good and not so good, but you are not emotionally connected to those things. You are not reigniting them. The difference is (and I must not have made myself clear) that you need, at the end of this life, to disengage yourself from those emotions that pull you back because those emotions are linked to the experiences that you have had in the past. Do you see that?

**Jane:** Yes.

**Joseph:** Now, there have to be Akashic Records – there can't be anything else because you create your record as part of yourself and, from your point of view on Earth, you might think that is delving back into the 'past' but, from our perspective, we are looking at different viewpoints of the 'present' along that eternal existence of an angelic being. The Akashic Records can to be viewed to enable decisions to be made regarding the future evolution of an individual soul but also so that the experiences and challenges that angelic beings have gone through can be of help to other souls seeking to free themselves from similar challenges or wanting to look at someone else's experience in order to enhance their own viewpoint. Again, does that make sense?

**Jane:** Yes.

**Joseph:** It is a complex subject, but please don't misunderstand me – *everything that you are is recorded because you are the recorder*. Your experience is retained and that experience is used on an angelic level in order to illustrate a particular point of view and to enhance the lives of other members of the angelic host. On Earth with its layered history, you have skewed emotional charges because of the effects of the Fall and, unless you are spiritually elevated in consciousness, when you leave this sphere you pull many of those vibrations into the initial cleansing spheres – which is why they elevate gradually to cleanse you from those experiences. It is the emotional charge and investment in mistaken viewpoints that have to be refined out of the spirit, but the angelic history is always there. Have I explained myself sufficiently?

**Jane:** Yes, you have. Thank you.

**David:** Joseph, I suppose a lot of people think that they lead quite humdrum lives where opportunities don't come their way and life doesn't seem to go as they would desire – is that because they wrap so much energy up in maintaining their personal history? In other words, they can't release themselves from the past to face the future in a new way.

**Joseph:** Yes, and also because they view themselves in a certain way with too much emphasis on the physical personality, which as we know is only a shell. So, as their life unfolds they have various expectations based on the history of what this planet has to offer, which they compare themselves against and say: 'I am not rich enough. I am not powerful enough. I am not in the position with regard to other people that I wish to be in at this point in my life.' And, it is always ...*I'm not ...I'm not ...I'm not* because they are drawing on the negative vibrations of history from the time of the Fall that emphasise the perceived lack on Earth. It is an illusory lack (as we have demonstrated in the other books) existing only on the surface and in how we view ourselves with regard to others.

Isn't it true that, from an earthly viewpoint, most of us measure ourselves against *what others have* compared to what we have or have not? You don't get up in a morning and say: 'I have everything today. I am an eternal, infinite spirit because I cannot be anything other than an eternal, infinite spirit ...loved ... healthy ...full of purpose ...able to add to my experiences today in a positive way because I am here in this beautiful sphere that I can interact with in order to enhance myself and also to enhance my brothers and sisters in the angelic host.' That is never (or hardly ever) the viewpoint of souls on Earth.

The viewpoint of souls on Earth as they get up in the morning is: 'I don't have enough money. I don't have a big enough house. I don't have a big enough car. I am not living in the right area. My relatives don't understand me. I don't feel as healthy as I should do. I am not where I am supposed to be.' And, by looking at the world from that viewpoint, it connects to and harmonises with similar vibrations and draws them to you so that you feel less wealthy, less healthy and less empowered.

It is that little self that is consolidated and made more and more 'real' by the vibrations of history on this planet. The key to overcoming that is to look at life from the viewpoint of the higher self and to say: 'Today, I am not this small envelope of flesh – that is just my recognition point on Earth. Today, I am an angelic being. Today, I am able to make a difference. Today, I am able to enhance the lives of my brothers and sisters who are suffering here because they are looking at life from a viewpoint that I no longer have.'

And, I suppose the end of this question is to consider whether you are prepared (not you, David, but the reader) to be selfless. **Are you prepared to discover the *joy* of being selfless?** And, by 'selfless' I mean discarding the small self and working for the Light ...for the good of you ...for the good of everyone else on the planet ...for the good of the angelic host that you are connected to ...and for the good of God.

**When you lose the self and the earthly polluted viewpoint – you gain *everything*.**

Does that answer the question?

**David:** It certainly does.

Chapter Fourteen
## You Unbound: Builder of Worlds, Creator of Universes

**Joseph:** Chapter fourteen – *You Unbound: Builder of Worlds, Creator of Universes.* Thus far in this book, I hope I have filled in some of the gaps and demonstrated that there is far more going on *around you* than you have perhaps considered before; but there is also far more going on *within you.* You are not what you appear to be and, of course, in the previous books I have explained that you have angelic origins – that you were once an angel and that you are *still* an angel but have forgotten that fact. However, I want to concentrate today on the way that you perceive your universe and the way that you perceive your world whilst you are on Earth.

You look at the world and feel that you are positioned on it. You feel that you are looking out on different expressions of life and different aspects of society, and you feel that everything happens to you *externally* – with an impact on you physically and an impact on you mentally – but that everything is happening *around* you and *to* you ...not so!

**Not so!**

Many years ago in the first of the books [*reference to* **Revelation**], I gave the symbol of the dot within the circle as a representation of God in man's attempt to encapsulate God into a rune – with God being circular in nature, as I have said, and everything happening within that circle ...coming out from the dot at the centre to the edge of the circle and then bringing experience back to that central dot ...so that the pulse can be renewed and the pattern repeated to bring back *more* experience to the Whole.

You are an expression of God and, just as everything is contained within God, **everything is contained within you.** Your *true* form is not that of the human being ...with head, torso, arms, legs, hands, feet, fingers and toes... but is circular in nature. You are the expression within a sphere of energy. That sphere of vibration is described in esoteric circles as the 'aura' which, according to those spiritual groups, is *around* you; but that aura is not only around you, it is *through* you and is *part* of you ...and is in miniature what God is. You are a dot within a circle and from that core of motivation (which is what you truly are) extends the circle of your sphere of influence or aura.

As you progress from 'angelic birth' or detachment from God in consciousness ...everything that you experience ...everything that you do ...everything that you become ...everything that you *think* is externalised around you, is *in reality* contained within that expression of energy with you as the dot or point of motivation at the centre. As an angelic being, as you move in consciousness through various worlds and through various challenges and scenarios, you gather everything that has happened to you into your aura or 'mini-universe' – that sphere of Light which you influence *that is you.*

When you leave the Earth, you carry with you into the next spheres of being *all* the experiences that you have had thus far as the dot or motivator at the centre of that aura. That energy field has been with you through various lifetimes because it is the true expression of you as an angelic being. So, contained within your aura *now* is, not only the experience of *this* life – but the experience of *all the other physical lives* that you have had on Earth. In the normal course of things, beyond the experience of the effects of the Fall, your aura also contains the sum of your experiences on *all the other worlds* that you have passed through in order to grow and become more Godlike.

So, you take with you from this world into the spiritual cleansing spheres, not only yourself – that dot of motivation that you truly are – but the aura that contains within it all the experiences on various planes of reality up to that point. And, you continue to express, to absorb and to contain within that aura the *new* experiences that you gain whilst you are passing through the cleansing spheres towards Infinity.

As you progress through the spiritual spheres, in the higher spheres you begin to understand how much you influence the landscape around you and how much you are able to influence and create within that sphere which is essentially a part of you. As you grow back into angelic consciousness and nearer to that 'trapdoor' that takes you out into Infinity, you become interested *once again* in creating worlds through the joining together of the angelic host to create planets that other members of the angelic host can visit in order to pass through them, experience and add to their auras or spheres of influence.

You are a *creator* and that is expressed before you reach that 'trapdoor' to Infinity by your wish to join together with other souls to create the landscape around you, as I have described in another book [*reference to* **Your Life After Death**]. As you progress through the cleansing spheres you become more creative, more aware of your ability to influence the landscape and more aware of the fact that the landscape is not outside of you at all but is *within you* – within that sphere of influence. As you move up through the spiritual spheres and join with other souls who are also interested in creating a certain type of landscape or undertaking a specific project – your 'aura' (if you still want to call it that at that stage) touches their auras so that you blend together your experiences to create the landscape that you live in or to undertake the projects you want to participate in as advancing and evolving spiritual beings. But, you can also move away from those souls that you are a part of *whenever* you wish to in order to experience your *own* creative mini-universe that you have built thus far through adding to your knowledge and experiences since you became individualised as a facet of God.

Your *destiny* as an angelic being, once you have moved through that 'trapdoor' into Infinity, is to *once again* create worlds. And, in the same way that you operate as a group soul, you create worlds by coming together as a host of angelic beings to share your individual perspectives and, based on the experiences from your individual perspectives, you decide on the type of worlds you want to build that would be good for the rest of the angelic host to pass through so that they can absorb the experiences and challenges of those worlds, built as a result of your individual experiences.

I hope I am explaining this sufficiently. The worlds that you see in the night sky *each* have a unique signature and set of specific challenges and experiences and have been formed through angelic beings coming together, reviewing their individual experiences and a certain type of world being built as a result.

So, as you read or listen to this and consider these words, your destiny is not to just sit in your chair or be part of a life that is limited. **You are limitless.** Once you free yourself from the effects of the Fall, you begin to understand your creative potential and your ability to eventually create worlds. As an *unbound* angelic being, freed from the effects of the Fall, not only do you create worlds – but eventually those circles of experience continue to draw themselves together in order to create solar systems, in order to create galaxies and, ultimately, in order to create *universes* …which in themselves are theatres of experience for countless hordes of angelic beings, with specific universes having specific tasks in bringing specific challenges and sets of experiences to specific areas of the angelic host.

So, from you listening to or reading this book today and feeling that you are here for a number of years, I *guarantee* that you will eventually grow to be a builder of worlds and a builder of universes *because it is God's intention that you evolve*. It is God's intention that you become more. It is God's intention that that part of Him that He has pushed out becomes more like Him and understands that it *is* Him. And, just as God contains everything and creates everything through Himself, through the angelic host and through you – eventually you will create and *be of similar status to God*. ...But, by that time, God will have evolved because of the worlds, universes and experiences that you have created and have brought back to Him so that He becomes more. There is an evolutionary process going on constantly and you, seemingly this being of flesh and bone and physical mind, will eventually become so much more – *are* so much more – than that.

I want you to understand at this point (which must seem a million miles away from you being able to create worlds) that you are not experiencing an *external* Earth. You are not experiencing an external journey but an *internal* one and, more importantly, that internal journey always prepares you for the *next* stage of your journey after this life. Because you contain within you everything that you have experienced – if your vibrations are earthbound, if your vibrations are low, if your vibrations are based on power-seeking, monetary comfort or the manipulation of others – then *that* is what you build into your aura. In the cleansing spheres that lower vibration can only resonate with and touch *similar* vibrations, so you cluster together your mini-universe with the mini-universes of souls who are exactly like you. So, if you have been a power-seeking, manipulative soul, you link to other power-seeking, manipulative souls and by combining together cannot generate the energy that you need in order to create on a higher vibration. In other words, your journey to become a builder of worlds and universes is slowed down, anchored and fettered because of the way that you look at life.

My intention today is to expand your view of life and to say: 'You are so much bigger than this. You are so much better than this. There is so much more potential than this.' But, that potential is only attainable if you let go of the lesser vibrations, if you realise your place in the universe and if you realise your destiny and work towards it. ...And, you work towards it by being the best, highest and most refined personal universe that you possibly can be. You do that by elevating your vibrations through living in harmony with all things and by realising that this Earth that you are journeying across was placed here originally *by you* and by others in the angelic host with a *specific* purpose. That purpose is not to manipulate others ...that purpose is not to centre yourself on monetary gain ...that purpose is not to invest yourself in the material aspects of this planet to the extent that you lose sight of who you are.

**This Earth was made originally by you in order to *elevate* you.**

It has fallen from grace because of the Fall (which is, of course, explained in a previous book) but the core intent of the Earth – *placed there by you* – was to be in harmony with you and with all the other souls making this same journey so that, by the time you exited this journey and returned to the higher vibrations of reality, you would have taken on board experiences which allowed you to become more creative ...which allowed you to invest in creative projects to build other worlds ...and which allowed you to see yourself as part of God in an elevated way for the good of yourself, for the good of the souls around you and for the good of the whole of the angelic host.

This is a far cry from how most people live their lives. This is probably a far cry from how you have viewed your life thus far, particularly if you feel that you are nine-to-five ...if you are part of a small family unit and feel you have to work to provide finances ...or if you feel that you have a particular goal in mind but that goal is nothing more than retirement and comfort prior to eventual death. None of this is what is really going on with you and *this is where the biggest 'space between' occurs* ...a space between what you actually are and what you perceive yourself to be.

This is a *huge* concept but start to contemplate the fact that you are not at the mercy of what appears to be going on around you. What appears to be going on around you is actually going on *within you* – with you at the centre of that energy-bubble manipulating it. And, you will say: 'I am not manipulating my life. My life is terrible and I don't want these awful things to happen to me.' But, you *are* manipulating that bubble of reality or mini-universe because you have taken that perception on board. You believe life to be bad. You believe there to be lack. You believe life to be limiting. You believe there to be pain. And, as a result, you build *all* those things internally within your aura and you move forwards through this life harmonising with similar vibrations and so your low vibrations are *enhanced*. Your sense of insecurity is enhanced; your sense of ill health is enhanced and your sense of lack is enhanced because you are the creator, creating it day ...after day ...after day ...after day.

**You are not at the whim of external forces – *you are the force*.**

You are the motivating force in your life that will eventually create worlds and stars and universes and beauty and experience for countless, *countless* billions of angelic souls ...YOU! That is what you are capable of. There is much said in spiritual books about 'waking up' and ascension – I wish you to 'wake up' in the right way. I wish you to contemplate what has been said today so that you view yourself in a far different way than you have done thus far and become energised by the prospect of accomplishing *so much* ...of never dying ...of never coming to an end ...of becoming more and more and more ...of becoming more consciously integrated with God-intent and evolution as 'time' goes on because of the experiences that you donate to the Whole.

A good start to expanding your consciousness would be to become quiet and to contemplate your aura. Imagine yourself sitting in a sphere of energy. There are many programmes in science fiction these days that show 'force fields' – imagine that there is a force field around you (because there *is*) or that you are sat in the middle of a glass sphere perhaps, or a sphere of colour – and you can choose the colour that you wish to be in the centre of. Then, look at the experiences of your life. Consider the memories that come to you as you sit within the confines of your personal universe ...asking that, for the time that you are meditating thus, all thoughts from other souls are barred and that you are alone within your own sphere of influence. Look at the memories that come to you and consider that those memories, which seem to involve other people and seem to be outside of yourself, *are alive within that aura.*

You are a creator *now*, and those experiences that are skewed because of the Fall are, nevertheless, creative experiences that work in the same way as you will operate when you pass beyond the cleansing spheres into Infinity. You are creating your own universe and your own perception of the past *now*, and it is not outside of you. It is alive within you – within that sphere with you, as the motivator at the centre, keeping it alive. You have chosen to keep it alive. You select the memories that are important to you. You select their influence on you. You select how you view the past. You select how you connect to the past. You select them ...and, therefore, determine how the past creates the future for you and how you maintain *today* the universe that you are creating *tomorrow* by your memories of the past.

Look at those memories and, if they are sorrowful for you, reread this chapter, consider what wonders lie ahead for you and, within that force field and sphere of colour, fill those memories with Light. Bathe them in Light. Thank them for being a part of you, transmute them with Light and file them away within that sphere of influence as something that has been beneficial to you and something that has allowed you to progress. Free yourself by charging with Light those aspects of the memories that cause you pain. Every time a painful memory comes to you, fill it with Light and say: 'I am so much more than this. Thank you for teaching me. Thank you for being part of my experience. Thank you for allowing me to eventually build worlds because that is what I am going to do. That is what I am capable of, and you by comparison – the hurt that you have caused me – is *so small* that I can instantly transmute it just by shining Light into the dark corners of those memories.' …And, you will begin to progress and you will begin to evolve.

Finally, I have to talk to you about your motivation here. If you have not had spiritual thoughts before, or if you have been dictated to by religion, or if you have been confined in thought – it is very difficult to view this world in any other way than the way that most people see it …as a finite experience, as a means to survive and as an experience that requires you to strive to become as comfortable and as secure as possible. Look past those thoughts – that is not what you are about. Start to view this world in a different way because that is not what the world is for. And, you will say: 'Well, yes, it is! My newspapers and my news programmes tell me that constantly.' They tell you that constantly because they are enmeshed in the effects of the Fall and have taken into *their* personal universes that belief that the world is as you see it today.

As a creator, you are capable of changing your personal world and radiating outwards from that sphere of influence to change the outer world – to change the 'stage set' that your adventures take place in and on. So, you have to say: 'I shake myself loose of my reliance on materialism and my reliance on power-seeking. I shake myself loose from that, and I replace it with Light …Light that illuminates my personal universe and radiates out from me to change the global world and to change the perception of other souls to create enough Light around them so that they can begin to absorb Light into *their* personal universes.'

**You are capable of doing that.**

*Each* of you is capable of doing that, and there is a *great need* at this time to do it because energy-wise your world is collapsing. The world around you is collapsing because, due the effects of the Fall, the angelic beings that live on it are not adding the Light, experience and energy from their personal universes needed to maintain the world in the setting that it was originally created.

You see, the world also has an aura around it and that aura, with the spirit of the planet as the motivator or the dot at the centre of the world, is restricted – not by its own belief but by the belief imposed upon it by billions of souls over countless, *countless* ages believing that the world is as it is ...that there is lack ...that there is hurt ...that there is pain ...that there is suffering. Those beliefs, via the personal universe of each soul, have been placed within the greater aura of the planet so that the aura of the planet is polluted and the aura of the planet presses down on the motivator – the point of expression that is *the spirit* of the planet – to such an extent that the planet cannot reinstate its original purpose by itself. You have to help it. You are 'farmers' of the planet as well. You have to help the planet, not remember who it is – but to have the energy, via each of you joining together in Light, to regenerate itself ...to expel from *its* personal universe those damning dark vibrations since the time of the Fall ...and to re-establish itself as the sphere of experience it originally was – and *still is at core* – that you created.

**It is *your* responsibility to change you, to change others and to change the planet.**

**As a creator of worlds and universes, surely that should not be a problem for you.**

Are there questions, please?

**David:** Joseph, in previous addresses you talked about how an angel would be able to 'give birth' to an angelic child by projecting itself into a world and then that angel would grow – how does that fit in with this process of creating universes?

**Joseph:** It is a good point because we have seen through some of the misadventures in previous chapters that you are capable of creating all manner of half-formed spiritual beings. You *do* continue to create your own angelic children – not the physical children you see around you (that is entirely another process on a material and spiritual level, as we have explained in other books). That desire and mechanism for the creation of a further angelic generation is there with you all the time, and is something you do subconsciously – just as you add to your own individual universe subconsciously. Unfortunately, because of the effects of the Fall (again an expression that I use *ad infinitum*) you only 'half-create' and you create based on your perception of the world, which for many, many people is a world of darkness because, no matter what they say ...they are afraid of life ...they are afraid of death ...they are afraid of running out of time ... they are afraid of running out of money ...and they perceive the world as being a violent and dark place. Also, until you transmute your personal universes, you do not have the energies to invest in the next generation with the right 'spark'. Does that make sense?

**David:** Yes.

**Joseph:** First of all, you do not realise that you are creating a next generation and, secondly, you do not have the right spark of energy to create that next generation *perfectly* – as you are supposed to do as the angelic being that you really are. So, you half-create, which is, again, this folding-in of dark vibration that exists within the sphere of the Earth and within your individual spheres because of the experiment that went wrong so long ago. Is that making sense to you?

**David:** Yes, so we continue to create but just don't realise we are doing it – in the same way that we don't realise we are creating the world around us.

**Joseph:** Yes, and you fill the dark corners with more dark corners. You continue to fill the Earth and the spaces between each of you with more darkness because that is your perception. You have lost the view of yourself as a creator, as an angelic child, as a potential angelic parent and as a creator of worlds and of beauty. You have lost that view, and you only see the externalisation of your thoughts *en masse* that exists within the sphere of influence of the planet. It is like pouring a dark liquid into a bowl and that dark liquid cannot escape and cannot be lightened until you add other ingredients ...and the ingredients that are missing are: the realisation of who you are and the Light that you need to pour into that bowl to lighten that dark liquid.

You have to have access to the Light, but in order to have access to the Light you have to broaden your vision, you have to remember who you are and you have to acknowledge then push away the darkness that is around you because of the choices that you made millennia ago. It sounds like an impossible task, but it is only an impossible task from the earthly point of view. From a spiritual point of view, it shouldn't present any problem whatsoever. The big task we have is getting you to change your mind and to broaden your horizon – not the horizon that takes you to a foreign country but the horizon that takes you back to your spiritual roots. Then the Light goes on within your personal universe and you can expand that Light out to be a breeding ground for the personal universes of others within which Light can be appreciated and not the darkness. Has all that made sense?

**David:** Yes, thank you.

**Tony:** Joseph, just personalising what you were saying about contemplating our aura – recently thoughts have been bubbling up from my past ...some of which I wasn't even aware of ...some of which I am not at all proud of ...and some of which were from a different 'me' thinking and acting on them at that particular time. So, are you saying that – no matter what those thoughts are – we should simply be putting Light into them without being guilty about a part of our past or something we did to somebody? Is it about putting Light into those thoughts and distancing them from our aura?

**Joseph:** First of all, *universally there is no judgement* (and by 'universally' I mean 'multiversally' and on every level of God-existence). The God within you, the God around you, the God that permeates you *never* says: 'You have been a naughty child! You shouldn't have done that. How could you have acted in that way?' There is *never* that kind of judgement from God, and this is one of the great problems of religion because religion supposes there *is* that type of judgement from God. So, there is no judgement, and the *illumination* that comes from connecting to God is there to allow you to view your experiences and to decide whether those experiences have been beneficial to you and to the others whose lives you have touched, and to then to decide – *as a result of the judgement that YOU make* – whether you need to make changes today and in the future to elevate those approaches to life in some way so that you can further benefit yourself and others.

Secondly, you cannot push away the experiences that you have had because, contained within your aura, is everything that you have ever done, and [*laughing*] I am reminding myself at this point that I must just briefly mention the Akashic Records. This is only an analogy, but the Akashic Records are like having a flex and plug extending from each soul with that plug connecting to the Hall of Records. So, *with permission* if they have reached a certain vibration of understanding, someone can go into the Hall of Records and by 'flicking a switch' can obtain access, in the equivalent of a book, *to everything that you have done*. God is open, as I have said in previous books, and there are no secrets. The reason you would allow access to someone else is so that they can benefit from your experiences – from what you see as the 'good' experiences and also what you see as the 'bad' experiences. Do you see that?

The Akashic Records exist so that souls can think: 'Gosh, that was an interesting experience!' …Or: 'I don't think I would like to act in that way.' …Or: 'I see the connection of 'dots' along this particular challenge. I understand what that soul has gone through. I understand what they have achieved. I understand what to avoid. I understand what to take on board. I understand how to act in future. Thank you so much, Dear Soul, for lending that experience to me so that I can understand more.'

So, the experiences that you have within your personal universe are not to be chased away – *they are to be illuminated*. In illuminating your experiences, you see them in the right way and you are already doing that. You have said to me that you look at some experiences and think that you acted badly. You didn't act badly – you acted *ignorantly*, and by 'ignorantly' I mean that you acted without the knowledge that you now have, which – had you had that knowledge at that point – you wouldn't have acted in that way. So, you have moved on and have proved that you have moved on by the fact that you can look at your past experiences in that way. Illuminate them! Embrace them! They are a part of you. And, if they are difficult for you, put Light into them and say: 'They might be difficult for me, but I embrace them and bless them because some other soul at some point can view them and can benefit and learn from them. Does that help?

**Tony:** Thank you, Joseph.

**Joseph:** I wish to help you in the way that you view your past experiences, not to have guilt over them – but to see them as being of benefit to you and of benefit to others. Remember that there are many, many souls around this Earth that have not yet reached the point where they can view certain past experiences and say: 'I acted badly. I now want to act differently.' If you are at the point where you want to act *differently* – congratulations! You have illuminated yourself to that point where you can see things in a different way. So, thank God for those past experiences and thank *yourself*. You have allowed yourself to learn and evolve by going through them and, because you have added spiritually to the sum of your experiences, you can now see them in a different way. Is that clear?

**Tony:** Does our subconscious mind present these to us consciously at a particular time so that we can put that Light into them? Is there an inner process going on?

**Joseph:** Yes, it is almost as though you are putting slides into a projector. If you join the 'dots' correctly from the thoughts that come to mind, you will see patterns that are relevant to helping you to move on and evolve from those situations. Then you can turn off that particular 'projector' and say: 'Thank you, that is now illuminated. I can move on and do something else.' However, you cannot eject the 'slides' because they are a part of you. You can view them, transmute them and value them, but you cannot push them out from you because they are part of your personal universe.

Every angel's personal universe has stages in it. If you were to view an angelic being from outside of the Fall experiment, you would see that there are *certain* experiences ...that have led to *other* experiences ...that have led to *other* experiences ...that have led to *other* experiences. Some experiences have been put aside and 'filed' and other experiences have been used to expand upon in order to create in better ways. You are the sum of your experiences and they are something to be proud of having travelled through. Do you see that?

**Tony:** Thank you, Joseph.

**Jane:** Joseph, in the normal course of things worlds are created and the resultant experiences are then taken back to the Godhead and God is thereby enhanced. You have said in the past that because of the Fall the experiences of the Earth have never been taken back to the Godhead (which, I suppose, is quite fortunate for God) and I wondered why that was. Does a world have to have concluded for the experiences to go back to God?

**Joseph:** How can I put this? There is a feedback system from a planet but you also have to understand there is a *purpose* in mind for each planet. A planet has to evolve and has to present its travellers with a certain set of circumstances. They then add to their own personal experiences, the experiences of the angelic host and the experiences of the sphere, which again evolves because of the added experiences of the travellers that are going through it. Do you understand it so far?

**Jane:** Yes.

**Joseph:** Now, that process was halted at a certain point due to the Fall. It is like drawing a shutter across a searchlight or like draping dark curtaining-material around a sphere. I have said before that the Earth is quarantined and that other souls are not (if they know what is good for them) allowed to visit this sphere because it would be detrimental to their evolution, and so there is the equivalent of a 'keep off' sign. Do you understand that so far?

**Jane:** Yes.

**Joseph:** Because of the Fall (which we are desperately trying to work you out of) that encapsulation of the Earth has been there for millennia. Now, of course, God is aware of the Earth, its original purpose and what it is trying to achieve; but that awareness is of something that is of such a base, low level at present that there is really nothing that can be obtained by the Whole from absorbing those vibrations and pondering them ... except to contemplate how so many souls have encapsulated themselves and that it should not be repeated anywhere else in the multiverses. Do you see that?

**Jane:** Yes, so the term 'taking experiences back to the Godhead' refers to the positive experiences that can be built upon for the good of others – whereas the Fall experience is something that should just be avoided.

**Joseph:** It is still something that automatically goes back to the Godhead as *information*, but that information is not progress for the evolution of God. Therefore, it is acknowledged and is felt because there is God in everything, but it is not something that can be promoted or expanded upon until Light is put back into the planet. The Earth is cut off in a way, but the information still goes back to God because information from each soul goes back to God constantly because God *is* each soul. Does that make sense?

**Jane:** Yes, thank you.

**Joseph:** You're sure you understand?

**Jane:** Yes.

Chapter Fifteen
# The Forgotten 'You' Times Two

**Joseph:** Chapter fifteen – *The Forgotten 'You' Times Two*. There is much said in spiritual circles and in spiritual literature about the higher self and the greater self, but what do we mean by the 'higher self' and the 'greater self'? Is it that you, in your earthly form, are merely a puppet or an extension of a greater being? ... Well, yes and no.

I should first explain that every experience that you have ever had during your earthly lifetimes is yours. Your memories *cannot* be taken away. They are yours by right and by history. So, where do they go when you incarnate, and why can't you access them? Well, we know, of course, because of the Fall, that you are encapsulated and restricted when you elect to come back to the Earth and experience an earthly life again. But, you *still* have access to those memories *if you bridge the space between.*

...The space between *what*?

**Between your earthly self and your higher self.**

The higher self is not a separate being. It is you, but it is you fulfilled ...you restored ...you with access to all your memories from past lives ...you with access to all the experiences that you have gone through ...and, most importantly, you with all the *wisdom* that you have as a spirit who has incarnated many, many times and undergone different karmic situations and *learned* as a result of them.

So, there is the space between you as you are now and you as your greater self, but *where is* your greater self? Your greater self is an expression of you that cannot be given form unless you seek out its wisdom. Your greater self exists apart from you ...but only because you have chosen to become apart from it in the way that you view your consciousness. Your greater self pervades, surrounds and infuses you, but your greater self can only be reached in times when you push aside the illusion of the Earth, you reach beyond your illusion of individualisation and, in silence and in contemplation, you seek out your greater wisdom. So, in silence, in meditation and in seeking, you raise your vibration ...**and at a higher vibration you find the rest of you.**

And, you find that the rest of you is able and willing **to guide you in any situation** because, once you connect with the rest of you, you see the Earth as it is, you see your present life as it is and you see the way through, past and round any situation that comes to you. You have access to ultimate healing. You have access to greater spiritual knowledge. You have access to the words that you should say in any situation, the attitude that you should take in any situation and the way through any situation that is not of God and not of your higher self.

And, so there is a space between yourself and your higher self. You are, in a way, suffering from 'memory loss', but repeated meditation and application of spiritual techniques to calm yourself in order to move inwards to the heart-mind gives you access to your greater self. You are not being manipulated by your greater self as many spiritual books would tell you. The greater self – *which is you* – exists to guide you.

**You, ultimately, are your own spiritual guide.**

You have not been pushed out to Earth by the greater self, with the greater self residing as a personality in a higher vibration.

What is happening is that part of *you* is residing in a higher vibration *as a consciousness*. So, you cannot, for example, on the lower spiritual levels walk to a certain house in a certain street, knock on the door, open it and there is your greater self waiting to meet you! Your greater self exists as an expression of yourself that is not being inhabited fully at this time. On the higher spiritual levels, your greater self is given greater form but is 'sleeping' and is not conscious of its surroundings on those higher levels. It is conscious of your plight, and is *always* conscious of your plight *because it is you.*

So, the key to connecting with the higher self and the key to receiving ultimate guidance in your life is to acknowledge that you are (and forgive the expression) 'not all there'. Even in your diminished earthly form, you are not all here. You are an expression of energy that has a point of contact that others can relate to, but you are not just that point of recognition. Expressed through your sphere of influence or aura, you are far more than just the body that you appear to be as a human being. And, so it is with the higher self, where your vibration is more integrated with the whole but, just as you have a point of contact on Earth that people identify you by, you also have a point of contact on the higher levels ...and you have to connect *both* points of contact to be operating as a *complete being.*

So, you can guide yourself, and this is what I want to say initially this morning. You guide yourself by reaching inwards and discovering, permeating and pulling in more of what you are into that individualisation of yourself that you perceive yourself to be at this point. The more that you contact the higher self – the more your vibration is raised and the more your higher self permeates your lower self to give you guidance, to reinvest your body with energy, to give you vision in all challenges so that you know what to do and, ultimately, to give you a different view of the Earth that makes you 'retreat' from it, in a way, and realise that: *one* – it is an illusion; *two* [*laughing*] – that you really shouldn't be in it; and *three* – that there is a greater perspective to you that is calling to you.

So, you have a greater self and you have a gap in your memory as a spirit being between what you are now and what you are in totality – part of which is funnelled into your earthly being. **But there is a *further* gap.** We must not forget (having mentioned it in all the other books previously) that you are an angelic being and, just as you have access to those memories that you have created during your incarnations on Earth since the Fall, you also have angelic memories from *before* the Fall. You are a divided being. You are a nested being. You are a being that appears to be an individual on Earth ...then there is a space between you and your greater self ...then there is a space between your greater self and your angelic self.

**Remember that you are an angel!** And, the key to that sentence is the word *'re-member'* ...reconnect... because, beyond the greater self that deals with your incarnations on Earth and with your experiences in the cleansing spheres, is also the *angelic self* that is waiting for you when you move through that 'hatch' out into Infinity. But, your angelic self is waiting for you in flashes of inspiration *now* because, just as you get flashes from your greater self to your earthly personality, when you connect with your greater self – you get inspiration from your angelic personality; and the greater self then 'channels down', as it were, those flashes of angelic insight that are yours *by right* (because, ultimately, they *are* you) into your individual expression on Earth.

The more that you connect with your higher self, which you are *reunited* with when you exit this world and go to the spirit worlds (but I will talk more on that in a moment) and the more you elevate your higher self – the greater the inspiration from your angelic self. Once you have finally left this Earth behind, the higher that you and your greater self elevate through the cleansing spheres, the greater the connection with your angelic self before you emerge into Infinity once again. So, one of the processes as you move through the cleansing spheres is to reconnect – not totally but slowly and inspirationally – with your angelic memories [*laughing*], so we have to remove those *two* spaces between.

To return to what I was saying earlier, when you move from the earthly sphere into the cleansing spheres – are you then reunited with your greater self? ...To *an extent* and that extent depends on you and your acceptance of or resistance to your greater memories. How you recognise yourself when you go to the initial realms in the cleansing spheres is dependent on: ...how your spirit memories come back to you ...what your mission on Earth has been ...and how you process the life review that is outlined in an earlier book [*reference to* **Your Life After Death**].

So, *initially*, you can still be in a similar situation in the cleansing spheres of not recognising that you have a greater self. You will feel that you are more than you were on Earth, but there can be resistance to that because of your desire for life to continue as it has been doing up to that point – either by you returning to Earth for another incarnation or by you expressing yourself in one of the initial spheres as someone very similar to who you were on Earth. So, there is a resistance and many spirits put a 'wall' up from a fear that, if you recognise those greater feelings, you will lose yourself. And, that is very sad because you do not lose yourself – you *reunite* yourself.

The point of the whole process of earthly incarnation, of moving through the cleansing spheres and out into Infinity **is to reunite you with who you were before the Fall took place** ... initially to reunite you with the sum of your experiences ...then to reunite you with your angelic memories ...and then to move you back out into Infinity, where you are a whole angelic being again and can review your earthly self and your greater self pertaining to your earthly incarnations as just a period in your infinite experiences and not the be-all and end-all. ...And, you are restored to angelic knowledge and to angelic creativity and can take your place once again in Infinity as an individual, as part of a group and as part of the various group-projects that you undertake as an angelic being in order to create worlds and scenarios that advance you, advance the angelic host and advance God.

It is very difficult for us to see so many spirits coming across who are so invested in the earthly personality that, even if they do not decide to reincarnate, they spend much of their time as that individual personality – restricting themselves and putting a barrier between themselves and *themselves*.

On the other hand, there *are* spirits who have prepared for their transition, who have investigated spiritual values and have seen which ones resonate and are right for them. It is a pleasure to see such spirits come across and *instantly* recognise who they *have been* as well as who they are at that point. And, in instantly recognising who they have been, they take on the persona in the spiritual realms of who they were *before* they incarnated on Earth.

For example, if they are a spirit that lives in a certain elevated sphere as part of a soul group, then that memory is restored to them. But, they do not lose themselves with regard to the earthly personality they have just lived – they *absorb* that earthly personality into their greater personality and are the *two* beings at the same time ...the two are *one* being. They are themselves as the elevated spirit they were before they incarnated; they are themselves as the earthly personality that they have just lived; and they are themselves as the *multiple* personalities that they have had since they began incarnating on the Earth plane. They are the sum of their experiences, the sum of their personalities and can choose – as one would flick through various channels on a television set – which of those personalities they wish to express at any time. Or, they can come from the standpoint of multiple personalities in order to express something or to consider, understand and resolve something.

Ultimately, as you move up the 'ladder' of spiritual progression before you get to open the 'hatch', you are able to express yourself as a ball of Light-energy (as we have said in previous books), but also you are able to express yourself as one personality expressed as multiple personalities. What I mean by that is that it is quite feasible for you to sit down with a number of people on a high spiritual plane *who are in essence the same person*. As a matter of choice, they can withdraw into *one* personality as an overview of those personalities or they can express themselves through *all* the personalities that they have been and still are.

That may seem very confusing to you at this point but this is, after all, how the universes work and how God works ...in that God is expressed through you and you are part of God and yet seemingly an individual personality. There is no division in a spiritual sense, but you perceive the illusion of division in order to experience and in order to take that experience back to God.

### As above – so below!

You are *one* person – you are *many* people. And, in the group souls that we have talked about in the other books, it would be fascinating from your point of view now to see a conference between members of that group soul that initially might be between five people and then between five-hundred people who are still the same five people – expressed as multiples so that other viewpoints can be applied to a situation and then taken back again into those five people that, ultimately, are not five people at all ...but are God [*laughing*] expressed as five people.

When you move into Infinity, cleansed of that need to view yourself as an 'island' or one earthly personality, you are still one personality but it is the *greater* personality and you are comfortable with it. Then the same process happens in the angelic realm, in that you can begin to express yourself again angelically ...and this brings us *full circle* to the means by which angelic creation takes place, the means by which planets are created and the means by which angelic parents then project part of their personality into the planets that they have created in order to experience, and that part of their personality then takes on a seemingly separate consciousness. It becomes another multiple of that angelic personality and becomes an 'angelic child', in effect, that can then go on to create angelic children of its own but is, nevertheless, part of the angel parent that created it, and those angelic children that it creates are part of the angelic child that it once was. So, all is One and all is an expression from One. The implications of this, of course, are *huge* if you are just venturing into spiritual wisdom.

**The implications are that you are ultimately *all the same thing*.**

**...And, the implication of that is that, if you are all the same thing, how can you harm part of yourself? And also that, if you *do* harm someone else – you harm *yourself*.**

It is the *expansive* viewpoint that I wish to bring to you today and for you to understand that you are not isolated but are part of something greater and that your earthly personality is not a puppet or a tentacle sent out from the greater self. It is a *compression* of the greater self and a *separation in conscious memory* from the greater self because of the effects of the Fall. On other planets and on other planes in other areas of existence, the subject matter of this chapter is known, is a way of life and is the norm. It is only from your skewed viewpoint because of the Fall that you view the multiplicity of existence as something that cannot possibly be.

You are shoehorned into flesh and bone. You are greater than the human frame but are shoehorned into something that cannot hold you so it has to hold a *part* of you. The rest of you, at a spiritual level, is conscious, is accessible and is capable of guidance ...but only when you flick that 'switch' and connect to the greater self.

I hope this also explains the division of souls that was talked about in an earlier book and why you can have two or more aspects of the same soul existing on the Earth plane at the same time and yet there is no division via the greater self.

So, a vast subject for you to consider in today's chapter, particularly if you are used to viewing the world from the point of view of individuality. This book is called *the Spaces Between* for a reason. The space between your conscious memories now and your greater-self memories is there because of the Fall – because in the past you were part of an experiment that you chose but were advised against conducting and, as a result of that experiment, you distanced yourself in *consciousness* from the God-within and from *yourself* within.

There is also a further space between your greater self and your angelic self. When you return to the spiritual realms, you are still only a *portion* of your angelic self. Then, through the experiences that come to you in the cleansing spheres and by the guidance that is given to you, you realise, little by little, that you are part of something greater and that *that* is nothing to fear but is a reason to rejoice. You also gravitate towards members of your group soul, who have also experienced the fact that they are multiple personalities contained within one parcel of spiritual consciousness. As you progress further through the cleansing spheres, you narrow the gap between your greater self and your angelic self and you begin to regain your angelic consciousness that reaches down through that 'hatch' from Infinity the closer you get to it. So, there is a reunification at *every stage* through the cleansing spheres until you become a clear, bright, clean and fully operational angelic being again.

[*Smiling*] I hope I have given you something to think about! But, before I return to my group soul and to *my multiplicity* – those different aspects of me that I love and can sift through as though sifting through a shelf of books (or, I suppose, in this day and age – a selection of DVDs) and can decide: 'I would rather like to express this personality today' – I will leave you with something *vast* to think about as a reader of this book. ...It is possible for me to express that chosen aspect of myself ...and to sit down at a table with *me* at one end and *me* at the other end ...and to have a discussion to examine points of view ...and to reach a conclusion that we are *both* happy with that is absorbed into us ...and then to take back myself into myself.

And, this is what I mean by guidance from the higher self. You are doing the same thing when you reach *in* to your higher self in meditation. You are having a discussion with *yourself*. There is your earthly point of view that is biased because it is impinged upon by the effects of the Fall and by the desires of the Field; and there is your higher self that can bring you a clear view of what should be done in any situation because it is not restricted by that part of itself that is shoehorned into the 'you' that you perceive yourself as being. So, you reach into your greater self to gain spiritual perspective and you are having a conversation with yourself.

Again, there is much speculation in spiritual circles: 'Who is my spirit guide? What is my guide doing? How does my guide *guide* me?' Well, there *are* people who are assigned to you, by their own choice, in order to help you at key moments of your life to, hopefully, make decisions that will move you away from restrictive karma and into areas that will expand your vibration and spiritual consciousness. Those people are with you and can help to an extent, **but the *ultimate* guide is yourself** because that ultimate guide has access to the lives you have lived and to how you have reacted in those lives ...and your higher self is also being advised by your guides.

So, it makes excellent sense to connect to your higher self *daily* and to trust the inspiration that comes from a greater part of you ...that is not restricted by the physical mind and body ...that has access to spiritual wonders ...that has access to the bigger picture ...that can guide you through *any* situation you find yourself in on Earth ...and can prepare you for that *reconnection* more quickly when you return to the spiritual realms.

Questions, please!

**Jane:** Joseph, with all the higher selves that belong to people currently incarnated on Earth, are they all in one sphere that is like a contemplative, 'no-thing' sphere in the spiritual realms? Are they all in the same sphere?

**Joseph:** It is difficult to explain because you are used something being in a certain place so that you can relate to it in terms of *distance* from you ...it is far away ...it is close to you ...it is within your house ...it is in the next town.

It is like a 'cloud'. You have a cloud with the internet at the moment, but this is a *personal* cloud. It is like pouring water into a vase that is too small to hold the volume of water being poured into it so there is an overspill of liquid onto the table or whatever the surrounding area happens to be. *Similarly, there is an overflowing with you.* I have spoken previously about the aura being a far greater envelopment around you than you realise as an individualisation of a reincarnated personality that you appear to be at the moment. The higher self permeates you, surrounds you and is conscious of you when you are conscious of it. It is your *own* consciousness that you give greater voice to at times. As you move through the cleansing spheres, the division between the higher spheres and Infinity becomes more nebulous ...like looking through gauze is the closest analogy I can give to it... and so your higher self and your angelic self become more connected and more interwoven. But, even in the higher cleansing spheres, there is the spilling out of that 'excess of water' around you so that it permeates the surrounding atmosphere but can be drawn into your expression of individualisation at that point to guide you. Does that make sense?

**Jane:** I think so ...it is just that you were saying that the higher self existed in the spirit realms...

**Joseph:** It exists there because it is of the *higher* vibration, but it is yours – just as the memories that I have been talking about are yours. And, many people reading this will say: 'Well, where are my memories? Where are they stored?' They are stored within you and around you as a spiritual entity, but you cannot access them unless you give consciousness to them. Does that make more sense?

**Jane:** Are all the 'overflowings' on the same vibrational level in the spirit realms? Is everyone's over-soul at the same high level?

**Joseph:** No. This is why I mentioned earlier that there is guidance *for* the higher self [*laughing*] but we are then onto the subject of guides and how guides guide on a number of levels. A lot of people might think: 'Why is my guide not guiding me in this situation?' Well, on that lower level there may not be anything that the guide can guide you on. Your guide guides the higher self and the *whole you* – or as much of the whole you as the guide has access to. When you are looking for guidance, if you connect with the higher self then the guidance is there and permeates down but can only be sensed from the lower vibrational viewpoint of your earthly incarnation to the extent that you have freed yourself from the confines of that incarnation through inner seeking. So, this way the guide is guiding you on multiple levels and *you* are guiding you on multiple levels. Does that make sense?

**Jane:** Yes, thank you.

**Tony:** Joseph, staying on that theme – for spiritual-seekers reading this book, are you saying that making a connection with our higher self is basically all we need to do because our guides can then work through that higher self?

**Joseph:** Ultimately, yes! There is this belief on Earth that everything has to come from *outside*, which is a subconscious perversion of the truth because, in spiritual reality, everything comes from *inside*. We sense, as individuals on the Earth plane, that there is something missing – so we seek to supplement that 'missing something' by asking for advice from outside and seeking other people's opinions …when what we should be doing is *seeking our own greater self's opinion*.

We have skewed the perception of guides. The purpose of spiritual guides is to guide us *via our perception as the whole being* that we are that is accessed from a certain level within the cleansing spheres. For example, if you regard the whole being as a 'body', the guide would not seek to put wisdom into the 'big toe' when only the 'mind' can appreciate that wisdom and guidance. This is why many people say: 'Well, my guide doesn't do anything for me.' Of course, they do! What they are attempting to do is to reconnect you to the spiritual wisdom that you have and advise you *at that level* so that, if you go within and connect to your higher self, you are receiving *more* guidance from your higher self and also from your guides, who can connect better to that expression of you that is the higher self than they could ever do to that restricted expression of you that is the seeming individual on Earth.

Does that make sense?

**Tony:** It makes really good sense. Thank you, Joseph.

**David:** Joseph, many spiritual circles talk about a 'guardian angel' and there is always an argument about whether it is the higher self or whether it is a separate being, but I think from what you have said today it is actually a metaphor for a combination of the two.

**Joseph:** That is a wonderful way to end this particular chapter because, to put it in a nutshell (although it is far more complex than this) ...*the guardian angel is you.*

**The guardian angel is *you*.**

So, everyone *has* a guardian angel but the guardian angel is *you* – you as the angelic child that you really are and you as the angelic parent that you really are. That angelic parent has access to *limitless* spiritual knowledge and creative ability via the rest of the angelic host and its shiny, bright connection to God – that is understood far better than you understand the concept of God from this point of view. So, you guide yourself via your higher self and you guide yourself as your own guardian angel.

Now that will, unfortunately for some readers, be an abhorrent concept – so used are they to wishing someone else to take responsibility ...but it is the *ultimate gift*! It is the ultimate gift to say: 'You are your own guide. You are your own freedom (or restriction). You are your own creative agent. You are your own ability to create whatever you want to create. You are your own healer. You are your own advisor. You are your own creator of visions. You are your own link to God.'

That doesn't mean that you are isolated – it means that you are *all* things. It means that, at the point of connection with the higher self and at the point of connection with the angelic self, you have greater connection to the other 'selves' around you ... the other angels around you ...the other higher selves around you ...the other group-soul members around you. And, there is a *wonderful* sense of sharing and of family that far surpasses anything that you can experience from this small point of view of the earthly personality.

So, yes, a wonderful theme to end on...

**Ultimately, you are your *own* guide and your *own* guardian angel.**

Chapter Sixteen
## Super-Powered You

**Joseph:** Chapter sixteen – *Super-Powered You*. At the moment as this book is being delivered, there is a predominance of superhero films, and in the cinema, on television and in literature there is this notion to the fore that there are people with *special abilities* who can solve problems for the world.

**Do you think this is a coincidence?**

At other times in the past, when civilisation has neared its end through its failure to negate the effects of the Fall, there has been a message that we have tried to push through that has centred on the spiritual aspects of mankind. But, before we go into that, let us examine the super-powers that you *already* possess as a spirit. Let us look at the abilities that you have in the spiritual realms – that you also have now but don't realise it.

First of all, let us talk a little about gravity. Gravity in its *purest form* is the pull back from the outermost corners of the universes to the centre ...to the centre of God. Once God has spread Himself outwards into physicality, there is a pull back on His children ...a pull back on His Creation ...a pull back on the planets ...a pull back on the stars. Gravity in its purest form is that pull back to God, to the centre, to the 'beginning', so that you can bring information, experience and illumination back to the Godhead and so that the Godhead can then expand His

Creation again and begin to pull back new experiences. So, gravity is a good thing!

Gravity *here* on Earth, unfortunately, is something that hinders mankind because it has been affected by the effects of the Fall. So, instead of a pull that you feel within your heart, it is a force that is always pulling you *downwards* to this heavy centre that you have created around and through the planet because of the Fall.

In the spiritual realms that pull still exists and, in fact, becomes *stronger* because ...you realise that you wish to return to Infinity ...you realise that you wish to donate your experiences to God ...you realise that you wish to enhance God and *every* expression of Creation by enhancing God; but it is not a pull that hinders you. You are free from gravity as you experience it on Earth in that you can, if you wish to visit another area of a spiritual realm, suddenly take off from the ground, swiftly travel through the air and land lightly at your destination. You are free from the pull of gravity on your body as you experience it here, distorted through the effects of the Fall, and you *can fly* because there is no reason for you to be pulled back to the ground.

**And so, in the spiritual realms, you are a super-being in that *you can fly*.**

On Earth at times, when your mind is not pulled down by so many material concerns, you can experience flashes of precognition and flashes of knowing what another person is thinking or knowing that another person is thinking of you. In the spiritual spheres beyond this one, this is a *natural* state of affairs and you are instantly aware of someone wishing to contact you and are instantly aware of their thoughts and life stories – if they wish to share those thoughts and life stories with you. You have an intimate knowledge of your surroundings and the people within those surroundings. And, *with permission*, you have an ability to tap into the ongoing experiences of the people around you at any time, and to a *lesser extent* (but then to a greater extent as you climb the spiritual spheres) you are also tuned in to the *whole of Creation.*

As you elevate yourself through the cleansing spheres, that ability to know what is happening throughout Creation increases so the circle of your telepathy and knowing extends until a point at which, when you have re-entered Infinity, you can connect *at will* with any part of Creation and experience the thoughts that are going on within that area of Creation and also the thoughts that are emanating from the creation around that Creation. In other words, you can, for example, connect to angelic travellers who are experiencing a certain set of circumstances around a planet, but you can also tune in to the planet *itself.* That ability expands ...and expands ...and expands as you move on and evolve through Infinity. Very quickly you find, when you have left this world behind, you can access the thoughts, the feelings and the intentions of those around you.

**So, when you have passed from this world – you are a super-powered being in that *you are telepathic.***

When you move on from the Earth into the cleansing spheres beyond, you also find that, little by little, you are able to create – *that your thoughts take form if you concentrate and focus them.* Immediately that you depart this Earth, if you have not regained the knowledge of your spiritual personality, you will find that things are much the same as they are here, but gradually you will discover that you are able to influence your surroundings. For example, if you want a vase, initially you will still seek to make that vase from clay (if you have those skills) by shaping and colouring it; but then you will find that you can partially form that vase in front of you simply by thinking about it. Eventually, you will realise that you can manifest that vase as a solid object and also that, when you wish to move it out of your sphere of influence, you can simply deconstruct it and it will disappear.

So, even on the first steps of your spiritual journey through the spiritual cleansing spheres, you are a super-powered being in that *you are a creator.*

The things that you wish to have around you, you can create; and you will find, as you move further through the spiritual spheres, that you will create in conjunction with other people to produce magnificent things ...such as aspects of the landscape and then, eventually as you move out into Infinity ...entire planets, stars and solar systems. So, from the minute you move out into the spiritual cleansing spheres, you are a super-powered being.

You find that when you move into the spiritual spheres *all your senses are enhanced.* You can *hear* at a distance. You can hear the thoughts of others with their permission. You can *see* at a distance, in that you can bring images of areas to you that are outside of what you might think is your normal range of sight, simply by concentrating on them. Your senses are enhanced in that any creation you are involved in brings to you an *emotional response* as well as the experience of simply creating, shaping and deconstructing matter. You find that there is a *perfume* to every object that is around you that you can tune in to or out of at will. All your senses are super-powered.

You find, as you enter the spiritual spheres, you are super-powered in that *you have super-senses* – super-hearing, super-sight and so on.

You must be thinking how wonderful it would be to have such powers – powers that are displayed so frequently at the moment in your films and television programmes. Well, I have to tell you that there is *no difference* between you now and when you first enter the spiritual spheres.

You are a super-powered being *now*.

...The only thing that prevents you from operating as that super-powered being at this moment is your lack of belief in those senses and powers that you possess and the effects of the Fall that you encased yourself in millennia ago.

Am I saying that, if you wished to take off now from one country and land in another, you could? Yes, *if* you believed it and were in full control of your spiritual senses now. Am I saying that you have super-hearing, super-strength and super-sight? Yes, I am saying that! Those things are with you now ...whether you can operate them or not, they are part of you now. You are a super-being. You are an *angelic* being, but you are prevented, shackled and limited by your beliefs and by the effects of the Fall that we are working so hard to bring you out of.

So, what is to be done? It is pointless me saying to you that you are a super-powered being if you do not exhibit any super-powers.

**What has to be done is *work*.**

What has to be done is work in the area of belief, in the area of acceptance and in the area of visualisation. You have to realise that you are more than you appear to be as a flesh and blood and mental being. You are a spiritual being. You have to work against the effects of the Fall. You have to, in effect, take a 'file' and slowly saw through the 'fetters' that are around you because of the Fall. You have to work against that. If you do not, you will always be what you appear to be today – limited, restricted, suffering – and that is not how we want you to be.

So, you have to examine what I have said thus far in this chapter and you have to begin to *trial* what I have said. You have to accept that you are more than you appear to be and, in accepting and pushing away those thoughts from the physical mind that will say: 'No, you are limited. No, you are human. No, you are nothing more than this,' ...you will find that there are flashes of inspiration that happen in your life ...you will find that you will suddenly know when someone is about to call you … you will find that you know what someone is thinking …you will find that you know when someone is in trouble, and you will pick up the phone to ring them and they will say: 'How did you know that I needed you at this time?'

At this stage, you will not manifest objects around you by simply willing them into being; but you will find that, *if you will a concept into being*, you will draw those objects towards you – just as surely as you will create them in the next stages of your spiritual evolution. So, test that theory as well. Look for something that you want and remove all the inhibitions that surround your getting it and prove to yourself, first of all with little things, that you are a creator and that by concentrating on something and then letting it go …by saying, ' I want X or Y,' and then *by letting it go but accepting that it is yours*… it **will come to you.**

Now, the greatest gift that you have as a spiritual being is the ability to bring out *the Light* from within yourself …the Light that changes everything, but there will be more on that in a future chapter [*reference to chapter eighteen*]. I want to speak about that in depth but you are a Light-bearer; you are a Light-bringer. It amuses me to see the terms bandied about in so many areas at the moment, but let us examine in depth what 'Light-bringer' and 'Light-worker' means at a future date – in fact, to conclude this book.

Let us return to the fact that you are surrounded at the moment by what seems, on the surface, to be a trend; and you will say: 'Well, there have been many trends in the media over the years. There have been western films; there have been science fiction films; now there are superhero films.' …There is *more* to it than that. As civilisation pushes itself towards the precipice and refuses to use Light to negate the effects of the Fall and bring itself back from the edge of that precipice, we work very hard to give you some insight into what is happening and to say to you, 'There is another way.' And, if we cannot get through to you

249

individually, we will get through to you *en masse* by attempting to influence writers, producers, directors, film makers and anyone who will disengage for a while from their belief that things are as they are on the Earth, so that we can pour in concepts.

What we are doing at the moment is saying to you: 'This is how you really are. This is what you are capable of. Please don't look at this as fiction – it is an allegory. It is an illustration of what you are capable of.' And, when you watch such films, do you not feel invigorated by what is being displayed on the screen or what you are reading in your books and think: 'Wouldn't this be wonderful! For some reason this excites me.'? ...And, it excites you because it talks to what you really are. It seeks to remind you of what you really are. But, in addition to illustrating to you that you *do* possess what you would regard as 'super-powers' – we are also illustrating in the stories that are around you *a principle that we want you to adopt.* Is it not true that in these films good rises over what you would consider to be 'evil', that order is reinstated over chaos and that, by relying on these super-powers within people, the situation is made better because goodness and order are restored? What you see playing out in your films and in your books at the moment is also a message from us to say: 'Look, what you consider to be 'evil' – appearing on the horizon as the villain in your film or book – represents the effects of the Fall that surround you and threaten to overcome civilisation.'

**What we are saying is that the effects of the Fall are about to swamp you *unless* you use your spiritual abilities.**

**It is as simple as that!**

It is not coincidence or just a trend that these things are popular in the media at the minute, because we will try wherever we can to re-establish a spiritual perspective with you. So, by all means enjoy these films and books but understand that there is *an underlying message* in what you are being shown as entertainment at this time and also understand that *the more popular these things become – the more dire the situation* because they are given to you in contrast. They are given to you to say: 'Here is an entertainment, but here also in allegorical form is a way of living that shows you a comparison between what is happening on Earth at the moment and what could happen.'

**And, believe me, the situation is *dire* at the moment!**

You have several points around the Earth where negativity is growing, where – I wish I didn't have to say 'darkness' – but *darkness* is growing, and by 'darkness' I mean the absence of Light ...the absence of spiritual reason ...the absence of a spiritual viewpoint ...the absence of spiritual reality. Looking at your planet at the moment, there are several grey areas – *literally* grey areas.

As an example, in the case of a corrupt government (and this government has no name, no location and no country – it is just a hypothetical government) if you could see the centre of this fictional government you would see darkness and roiling clouds of greyness and blackness. Then, you would see that roiling greyness and blackness *spreading out* from the centre, which is the ideology by which that government wishes to operate, to the members of that government. Then, you would see the members of that government going home and you would see the greyness spreading from them to the members of their families ...to their wives ...husbands ...brothers ...sisters ...daughters ...sons ... even to their pets and to their houses. And, you would see those members of that fictitious government going about their business attending various meetings, and you would see those meetings being infected by the greyness and the blackness of their thinking. So, like a cancer, that greyness spreads out through a government and, like a blanket, it envelops the goodness of people, the spiritual aspects of people and the morals of people (i.e. 'morals' in the sense of how an angelic being truly operates). And, you would see this fictitious government in this fictitious country smothering the Light ...*slowly but surely smothering the Light.*

Now, just as that blackness spreads out from that skewed central ideology to the members of the government and then to their families and then to the people that they meet – it also spreads out, like a cancer, across the airwaves to other *similar* governments and similar areas of thinking. It doesn't necessarily have to be the same core-thought, but if it is the same twisted vibration then those areas of greyness link up. *It is inevitable because like attracts like.* The areas of greyness link up, the areas of blackness link up and, if you are not extremely careful, then the Earth becomes smothered by that greyness ...the Field of human thinking runs out of energy ...**and civilisation comes to an end.**

**It is as simple as that!**

Because of the effects of the Fall, there is an arrogance on Earth that it will never happen: 'We are years and centuries away from anything happening to the Earth.'

**...Not so!**

Not so! The underlying structure of that end is already in place. What we have to do (and this is, again, down to the last chapter of this book) is to invoke and draw on the Light to change things here. But, make no mistake – as you, perhaps, go to your cinema to watch a superhero film and you come home feeling invigorated – *this action of greyness is happening around you now*. And, the film is there to entertain on one level, but also to say to you that there is a call to action *now*. There is a need for work *now*. There is a need for the Light *now* ...**and that need for Light begins with *you*.**

So, there are reasons to rejoice and there are reasons to be troubled. The reasons to rejoice are that you have with you now in your core *all* those aspects that you will have with you when you move from this Earth into the spiritual spheres. You are, from your earthly point of view, a *super-powered* being now ... you are a person who can make a difference ...you are a person who can effect change …you are a person who can heal …you are a person who can wield Light …you are a person who can transmit ideas, concepts and spiritual values across the globe … you are a person who can link up with others without physically meeting them or ever being with them on a material level …you are immortal …you are eternal …*you are capable of so much*. But, in order for you to exhibit those things that you are capable of, you have to work, you have to open your eyes, you have to do something and, perhaps, more than any other message in my books you need to acknowledge the importance of this one: **THE TIME FOR YOU TO DO SOMETHING IS NOW.**

You have to banish the greyness and, in order to do that, you have to realise that it is there and you have to work to change it. There are no messengers who will approach you on clouds and say: 'This way!' …In order to *go this way* you have to have elevated your vibration, and you haven't done so yet. **There are no easy answers that will come to you from above.** This 'chalice' (to be biblical) will not be taken away from you. You have to change what is in that chalice …YOU! We cannot do it for you. Imagine our frustration in bringing through this information. We desperately want things to change on your behalf, but *you* have to do something *now*.

If you do not, your super-powers will be …not extinguished… but blanketed, covered; and it will be many millions of years before we can get to *this stage* again and warn you that the end is nigh – as the billboards used to say.

**THE END IS NIGH** …*unless change happens now*.

Your questions!

**Tony:** Joseph, at the Sanctuary and as a psychotherapist, I see a lot of people in their twenties, thirties and forties who come to me with psychological and physical issues. In many cases, as children they knew they had super-powers and could tap into other people's thoughts and that ability was at the forefront, but then it was crushed by their parents and by the education system because they were told not to be so silly. Then, by the time they get to twenty-five and thirty-five and I tell them it is actually *psychic ability*, it is such a relief for them – but almost disbelief at first – because it has been drummed into them so much that that is not the way the world is. We see so many casualties along the way of people who knew they had powers in their younger life but whose powers were just crushed.

**Joseph:** Are you looking for a way through that?

**Tony:** Any comment would be appreciated.

**Joseph:** In the illustration that I gave you, the government is fictitious but the effects are *real* and are happening now. Were you to see with *angelic* eyes (i.e. a highly-raised level of vibration), you would see that around people there are these tendrils of greyness and blackness that seek to mummify them, seek to cocoon them and seek to pull them down. And, initially this is instigated by the Field, but the Field is being short-sighted in that it is influencing those who are most easily influenced, who are then feeding the Field with more blackness and the Field will eventually run out of energy.

What is needed is a global realisation by those who are capable of realising that they are spiritual beings, with more and more people sitting in the Light and connecting to each other – which, again, is something that we will consider and detail in the final chapter.

We cannot have ego in this move to change things, and in many instances (not in all instances) I see spiritual people become encased by their own egos where it has to be *their* way and *their* answer; but the minute it becomes *their* answer – not God's answer and the angelic answer – they have no power. What is needed is a true dropping of ego in spiritual work and a true connection of spiritually-minded souls on behalf of the people that you are talking about and on behalf of *all* humanity to counter the greyness and to create a counter-atmosphere within which people are surrounded by sufficient Light to re-establish their spiritual powers ...to know without doubt that what they are experiencing is *real* ...and to know without doubt that anything that is contrary to that is simply an attack by the Field – either through the atmosphere or through the people around them who do not understand what they are capable of.

On a one-to-one level, you can address this and try to get that concept across to those who are suffering, and you can say: 'The truth of the matter is that what you experienced as a child is real. I accept it. The people here accept it. And, we are working in the Light to give you the strength to develop those powers because you are a precious soul and your powers are needed to change things now.'

But, in addition to that, there has to be a greater movement so that you get more and more souls linking together in the Light so that it is not an *attempt* to change things but something that *does actually change things*, because you have created enough illumination to power those souls who have a special mission here and to literally 'push back the darkness' so that spiritual values and spiritual abilities can be re-established.

Does that answer your question?

**Tony:** Thank you, Joseph. Yes.

**Jane:** Joseph, another trend in the media is for films and television to become more violent and more depraved. Is that because those writers and producers are influenced by the spreading greyness that you were talking about?

**Joseph:** That is an excellent question and the short answer is yes. You have a countermovement here to the Light and so depravity spreads. Certain writers are fed by the lower aspects of mankind and by the need to display violence and to display what we are capable of if chaos reigns. From their point of view, it illustrates in fiction what we are capable of, but there is a great danger there by them saying: 'This is what we are capable of!' ...Because the *subliminal message* is: 'Now go and do it!' They are bringing this through and saying: 'No, it is all right – I can depict this because it is a thrill and will boost audience figures.' Unfortunately, the underlying message is: 'Now, go and do it! Now, go and act in this way! Now, go and celebrate this depravity!'

For example, there are many programmes at the moment that depict pain and suffering with graphic violence, harm and torture to the human frame, but the human frame is a sacred thing. **The body is a sacred thing and should not be hurt.** It should not be hurt by mental attacks. It should not be hurt by physical attacks and the depiction of that to us *is the greatest depravity ...the greatest depravity*! You see how the greyness is spreading at the moment in that there is no reaction to this violence that is depicted so graphically. There is *no reaction*. Very, very few souls say: 'Enough!' Very, very few souls turn off the programme. Very, very few souls take to the streets to say: 'We should not be acting in this way!' That, again, is an indication of just how far down the road of acceptance of the Field we have become in our depiction of life.

Fiction should demonstrate the noble qualities of what we are. It should demonstrate what we are capable of. It should illustrate the problems that we have and the ways to solve them – not glorify something that is *contrary* to all spiritual viewpoints. **There is no violence beyond this world.** There is no violence in the spiritual realms. People attempt violence on the lower levels and we have great difficulty with them, but they cannot truly harm anyone. It is abhorrent to us and the important thing is *that it should be abhorrent to you*. If you are reading this and it is not abhorrent to you, please question your values.

Does that answer the question?

**Jane:** Yes, thank you.

**David:** Joseph, it has been said that if you ask, you shall receive. If we are a member of this fictitious country and we want to send Light to the centre of this fictitious government, but we don't feel ourselves quite the 'Superman' that we actually are – I believe you said in the past that we can hand it over to God and then, at that point, the angelic host can intercede to some extent.

**Joseph:** Yes, there is volition (if I understand your question correctly) and that volition opens up the flow of energy so, yes, you can hand it over to God. You are quite right in that, in the early stages of realising what you are, you need added confidence and that added confidence comes by aligning yourself with what you really are. But, remember that that God is also you. You are opening yourself up to a greater expression of yourself. So, in the early stages, whatever your view of the Creative Force is, you can go to that Creative Force – to the God that you may see as outside of yourself that really is within yourself – and say: 'Father/Mother/Source I wish to be strengthened by Your vibration.' The vibration of God is creative. The vibration of God is not destructive – except in the sense (as we have discussed in other books) that at times various scenarios are taken apart so that they can be replaced by higher expressions, and there is an evolution taking place but that evolution is not violent. That taking apart of those scenarios is not violent. It is almost 'constructive' in that those scenarios are taken down in a precise, ordered way so that their molecules can be reused in a higher expression of creativity.

So, yes, it is fine and it is essential to draw on the God-within and the God-without and to appeal to the higher consciousness to intercede and to strengthen. Then, in doing that, you also link up to all those souls on this planet who are trying to change and to evolve things here for the good. You also link up *to us* in the successive spheres, who are attempting (and [*laughing*] this is a terrible thing to say) **to knock some sense into you.** It has to be said at this time, and I do not mean in the sense of *literally* knocking you on the head ...although it would be good if we could tap you on the head with a fist and say: **'Listen! Act! Now!'** That is what we would like to say as time grows shorter.

Does that answer your question?

**David:** It does, thank you.

## Chapter Seventeen
## God Only Counts to One

**Joseph:** Chapter seventeen – *God Only Counts to One*. God does not acknowledge division. In this chapter I will attempt to change your world-view *forever*. I will also attempt [*laughing*] to dispel a few myths, but let us begin with the moment when you are born.

Usually there is a smack ...and a cry ...and a lungful of air ... and you are *here*; and your first experience is of something outside of yourself impacting on yourself – although 'yourself' is something you have only just discovered. Even at that early stage there appears to be division. There appears to be 'you' and 'not you' – you and something that is influencing you and affecting your comfort and security. As you grow from childhood into adulthood, the divisions seem to come thick and fast ...you are divided by race ...you are divided by beliefs ...you are divided by your interests ...you are divided by your work, career and aspirations; and you interact with others that appear to be 'not you'.

**Not so!**

I have to tell you that there is only one number in God's mind. There is only one number in God's Creation and that number is ONE.

**...That number is ONE!**

259

Any other number above One is superfluous to requirements. So, I want to suggest and illustrate to you that *you are part of the same thing*. From that moment of birth to the moment of physical death, you are part of One. You are One – *there is no* division. Yes, you have different attributes to the person next to you. Yes, you have different aspirations and a different viewpoint, but that viewpoint is contained within the One and there is *only* the One.

So, I have to, first of all, suggest to you that there is no division between you and anyone else. And, you will rail against this and say: 'Well, I don't have the same thoughts as the murderer. I don't have the same thoughts as the politician. I don't have the same thoughts as someone who is not of my race ...not of my class ... not of my aspirations ...not of my viewpoint.'

**Yes, you do!**

...Yes, you *do* because those thoughts flow *through* you but are not generated *by* you. And, *you* generate thoughts which flow through everyone else but are not generated by them. *The One interchanges thoughts*. It can only be so, and every thought that exists on this level is a part of you but not necessarily *of* you.

I know that sounds like a mystery, but what I am trying to explain is that there is a pool of thought that belongs to the One and that the thoughts of the murderer, the thoughts of the politician and the thoughts of the person who is seemingly not of your class, background or culture – *all those thoughts* are flowing through you, are part of you and are generated, on a wider scale, by '*you*' because you are One. There is only You. There is the You that is expressed as 'you' and there is the You that is expressed as everyone else on this planet and there is the You that is expressed as God ...only One! This is why, in all the books, I have spoken about the need to create Light to change the present viewpoint, which has been skewed by the effects of the Fall, back to God's viewpoint and the angelic viewpoint of the One that existed before the time of the Fall ...in order to restore the balance so that all thoughts and all viewpoints are *harmonious*.

You cannot escape being part of the One. You will be *forever* part of the One because there is only the One. God has pushed out different aspects of Himself, but He does not regard those aspects of Himself as divisions. He regards them as facets of the One – just as you can have a huge diamond with many facets but it is, nevertheless, *one* diamond and those facets reflect light in different ways but they are part of the *one* diamond.

So, my first statement is that you and every other human being on this planet are one organism ...are part of the One ...are a viewpoint of the One ...are contained within the One ...and are *forever* part of the One. Now, I have to extend that – there is only God, so that One extends *beyond* those other human beings that are part of the One and that are part of you.

It extends, first of all, to the animal kingdom. It extends to every animal and every expression of life on this planet. Am I suggesting that the animals are One with you? Yes, I *am* – they *are* One with you. There is only the One. So, the animals that you are callous towards – that you eat – are part of you. You are exhibiting a type of *cannibalism* because they are part of you. Your pets are part of you. The insects that you find troublesome are part of you. Every form of life ...the poisonous snake ...the kangaroo ...the cow ...every animal you see in a zoo is part of you – is part of the One. And, you will say: 'Well, some of them are savage; some of them are irritating; some of them can harm me; some of them can kill me!' Yes, but only because of the effects of the Fall ...only because you do not acknowledge that Oneness ...only because you do not extend your Love and harmony out to those other life forms.

Let us go a step further. Having established that *you* are One with every other human being and *you* are One with every aspect of life – let us look at the things you create. Let us look at the houses ...and the bottles ...and the cups ...and the cars ...and the light bulbs ...and the steel ...and the glass ...and the tarmac ...and the paving stones. There is only One – there is only One Creation expressed in billions of different ways. So, *you* are a part of the glass, the concrete, the road surfacing, the pavements, the lights, the fabrics and the metals. You are a part of all these things too. They are a part of the One.

**Nothing exists *outside* of the One.**

**God only counts to One.**

So, all the things that you see as inanimate are, in fact, creations of your own thought-patterns but also creations of the One. You flow through everything. Go to your window now, wherever you happen to be reading this book. What do you see? Perhaps other buildings ...perhaps trees ...perhaps roadways ...perhaps vehicles ...perhaps other people – *all those things are you.* All those things are part of you; and the things that you feel are dead and unresponsive and should be treated as 'throwaway' are part of you. The same creative life force flows through every object that you see. Everything you see on your news programmes, everything you see through the car window and everything you see whilst on a walk *is you.*

There is no division and, therefore, you have to treat everything around you as you would wish to be treated yourself. You would expect respect for yourself. You would expect to be comfortable and in a place of harmony and security. All those things are what you want; and all the things around you are *worthy* of that consideration and should be imbued with those vibrations because they are part of you.

**If you want to heal yourself – you also have to heal the world.**

**If you want to be secure – the world has to be secure.**

**If you want to be loved – the world has to be loved.**

**If you want to be in harmony with your surroundings – everything around the globe has to be harmonious and an object of your Love and respect.**

So, each day from morning till night, *everything* that you come across is you. When you realise this ...that every person you meet ...every object you handle ...every animal you come across *is you*, then in your meditations you begin to love those things – to love the things that seem to be right with the world and to love the things that seem to be wrong with the world and to put harmony, Love and Light into the world. Try this with your immediate surroundings and you will see that they respond to you. You will see that the house becomes more loving. You will see that the car becomes more efficient. You will see that there are less mishaps, tumbles and breakages because you are in harmony with the other aspects of yourself.

**I ask you to begin to see the world as One – as God sees it.**

And, there is so much prejudice, so much hatred, so much fear and so much opposition that you will have to battle through in order to see *everyone* as you and in order to see *everything* as you. But, think what a position of power you are in with such knowledge because, *if* everything is you, then you can shape the world to your image. You can shape your surroundings to your image. You can create the world you want to create. Do you want a world of Love ...and harmony ...and peace ...and prosperity ...and security ...and comfort? It is *your* world – it *is* you. You are as important as every other person in contributing to the world that you want to create. You are *vitally* important because there is only *you*.

The world that you create in your heart and mind is not a pipe dream. It is *reality* and you contribute to the reality of the whole by your strength of belief in those surroundings and your ability to put Love into the world. You are a changer of worlds because there is only you ...and here we have to mention the planet. We have talked about the surroundings, the materials and the animal kingdom but what of the planet?

There is only you and **you, *in essence*, are the planet.** You originally created the planet, and you are capable of healing the planet by the same means ...by loving it, by sending out harmony to it, by visualising it as being a green and fertile and harmonious provider. But, it is not only a provider – it is you. So, with this new knowledge, you have to look after the planet, you have to look after the surroundings, you have to look after each person and you have to look after yourself – by sending out Love, by seeing the world as being healed and *by having an ultimate respect for the planet.* Do not deface the planet. Do not denude the planet. Do not skew the planet's ecosystem. Live in harmony with the planet. And, you will say: 'Well, we have gone too far and we need the things around us.' The things around you are you. You can change the things around you because they are you. They are just a vision that you have put out. Put out a different vision and start to respect this world as you would respect your own hand, foot, arm or leg because that, in essence, is what the planet is. That, in essence, is what *every planet* is, which then brings us to a greater exposition and reveal of something...

Is there not a phrase: 'I am in my seventh heaven'? I often sit here on the 'sidelines', as it were, looking in and seeing how you approach spirituality. I see that there is a 'seventh dimension'. I see that there is a 'council of so many people'. I see that there is a 'group of X numbers' waiting to help you. I see there is a 'certain dimension' that you must reach that has a number attached to it.

**There is only ONE.**

**God counts to ONE.**

And, you will say that there has to be a number of dimensions and there has to be a number of souls. Yes, from *your* point of view, but once you elevate yourself to a certain extent beyond the physical world, the need for numbers dissipates and this will (as I love to do) *set the cat amongst the pigeons* because, in much of your spiritual literature, you are used to attributing numbers, divisions and dimensions to spirituality. Beyond a certain level they don't exist. *What you are seeking to do with numbers is actually place into a physical world your concept of there being many and One.* That is all numbers do. And, you will say: 'Well, look at the complexity of mathematics. Look at the way that mathematics can represent Infinity.' No, you are seeking with the physical mind to represent something and place a value on something that is simply an aspect of the One.

And, you will say: 'Well, millions of souls have died and you have talked, Joseph, about soul groups. How many are in a soul group?' A soul group is a 'number' ...(again it is difficult trying to put this into words on this level [*laughing*] without referring to the actual thing that I am trying to dispel)... a soul group contains the aspirations and the harmonies of a certain *portion* of the One. If you were to visit a soul group now and ask: 'How many members do you have?' They would say: 'One. We are a soul group. We are known by the projects that we are undertaking. We are known by our harmony. There is no need for numbers. We are One. The other soul groups are One. We are One with all soul groups. We are One with the Oneness.'

And, [*laughing*] you will talk about sacred geometry and you will say that certain signs and symbols have to be clustered in certain divisions and in certain numbers ...and again... **NO!** You are seeking through the physical mind to compartmentalise and force division on something that is part of the One. It does not involve complexity. It does not involve numbers. It simply involves creation and creation within the One that is God and the One that is you.

'Oh, I don't know whether I agree with that, Joseph.'

...You don't agree with Joseph because you are thinking from your *physical mind*.

I would ask you to look at what I have said today with your *heart-mind*. Get rid of the complexity. Get rid of the division. The greatest division, of course, is the division that you have placed between yourself as the One and God as the One ...and *there* lies your focus on numbers, your focus on dimensions, your focus on mathematics, your focus on aspects of science. At the time that you fractured yourself *in thought* from the One – you then had to look at your landscape and try to make sense of it; and you tried to make sense of it by saying: 'This is me and that is not me.' Whereas, before the Fall, you understood: 'This is me and that is also me – we are One. God and I are One. God and we are One. All aspects of life are One.'

If you take away the need for divisions and the obsession with numbers and dimensions and levels, you are left with *respect for all things*. You are left with the ultimate comfort. You are left with the *bliss* that we experience on the spiritual levels ...and not a 'number' of levels but just a gradual gradation from how you are now to an absolute realisation of your angelic vision again and your Oneness with the One. That bliss is available to you now and needs to be dipped into with some urgency.

That 'sea' of bliss and harmony needs to be dipped into because, as the centuries have gone on, once again you are putting further and further divisions between yourselves. Everything is based on division and *the individual*. Everything is based on you being one thing and everyone else being something else. Even your computer technology is based on division and division and division and division and the clustering of things together into a *number* of things. That is not the way that things work on a universal and creative God-level.

It falls back to the Fall (forgive the pun). Before the Fall, you acted as part of the universes and part of the angelic host. And, the angelic host is not a number of angels – the angelic host is One. The angelic host does not split itself into a hierarchy that is numbered. The angelic host has certain priorities and has certain portions of itself that are engaged in different aspects of creation, but that does not mean that there is a ranking of angelic purpose. That does not mean that there is a division of angelic purpose. Everything contributes to the One.

**The One is examining the One through the facets of the One that the One has created.**

**But the One is always aware that those facets of the One *are One* ...are God ...are Itself.**

And, my plea today is for meditation and periods of silence on your part that allow you to examine what has been suggested in this chapter ...*that all is One, all is singular and there is no need for any other number.*

And, you will say: 'Well, how do we count things down here? How do we look at things and decide how many things there are?' All you are doing in counting things is focussing your attention on an aspect of yourself [*laughing*]. It is so easy for me, I know, to look from my viewpoint and say that everything is One and so difficult for you, because you are used to looking at everything as a division, a quantity and an aspect that must be counted and recorded and 'placed in a box' and must be an absolute. Nevertheless, I have to try to convey to you the ease that can come to you through meditation and contemplation of the One.

There will come a time when you go for a walk and realise that everything around you is One, and there will be perfect harmony. You will be ...not absorbed by the nature around you... but you will feel your soul spreading into the nature around you. For a moment, you will feel yourself becoming the trees ...and the leaves ...and the streams ...and the walls ...and the fields ...and the grass ...and the sky. This is not a daydream. This is something that will happen to you. You will experience Oneness, and in that moment you will find that there is nothing to fear.

You see, your numbers originate from a fear of not being the 'one' that you are. You fear being absorbed by everything else. There is a spiritual core memory that tells you that you are part of the One but, from the point of view of the ego since the time of the Fall, it is terrifying to think that you might flow into everything else and, therefore, *not be you*. However, in meditation when you come to a point, as I said a few moments ago, where you can connect with everything during a walk or wherever you are – you will have that realisation that you are 'you' but you are also everything else. You are not losing yourself ...in fact you are *enhancing* yourself. You are able to look at yourself from so many different viewpoints but still retain 'you' because you are an aspect of the One that is glorious, is precious and forever will be a particular aspect of the One that *adds to itself* day by day, year by year – and then beyond into the spiritual realms through the new expressions of creation and experiences that you go through. But, you also add to everything else and you realise that, in being everything else, you share with everything else ...and also everything else shares with you.

This is why abundance and gratitude are often talked about in spiritual circles. Gratitude is an acknowledgement of all being well ...of all being you ...of all flowing to you ...and all flowing out from you. Perhaps 'gratitude' is too small a word – it is a *harmony* that you should seek. When you seek harmony with everything, you become aware of you *being* everything. So, if you are everything then you can call from aspects of everything that which you perceive yourself as needing at any time. Just as, if you want to raise your hand or want to walk, you do so *automatically* – your provision for yourself is also automatic on a God-level so ...abundance flows to you ...health flows to you because you cannot be unhealthy ...the energies that you need flow to you. And, as you acknowledge that those things are coming to you and are thankful for them – your energies, your perfect health, your perfect abundance and your perfect vision actually go out and mingle with everything else.

I hope that this chapter gives you a new *strength* in being able to care for the world and for everyone in it and in being able to change things, because once you promote harmony, that harmony reaches out to other points of harmony and, if you work hard enough and if enough of you do it, those points of harmony will eventually join up *to re-establish full knowledge of the Oneness of all things*. At that point, the world changes and all those aspects of other personalities that you consider are 'not of you' will have been changed because they will have viewed themselves from the viewpoint of the One and let go of those fears and reactions that are displayed as violence or power-seeking. All those things will disappear.

Once you have experienced the One, you can *only* experience the One and you need nothing else. You don't need to operate from the small viewpoint of the confined ego. You don't need to operate from the small viewpoint of the perceived self. And, you will not have lost yourself – you will still have your interests, still have your pleasures and still have your individual viewpoint, but you will have *enhanced* that viewpoint from the viewpoint of the One.

Once you get away from the cleansing spheres and out into Infinity, then there is, not just knowledge – but the *feeling* and the mechanism of the One flowing through you. The higher you climb through the spiritual spheres, the more you are aware of the One flowing through you – not just the One that you will have left behind by this time of the Earth, its peoples and the aspects of creation on this particular planet – *but the Oneness of all being*. The Oneness of all being is a Love that flows through you to everyone else around you and is put into the projects that you undertake as the angelic beings that you really are, in order to create new experiences for the angelic host to flow through.

And, you will say: 'Well, if I create a new experience and am part of the creation of a new planet, how many angels will then visit that planet?'

**...One!**

The Oneness will flow through those aspects of the Oneness that are represented as angels that choose to go through that sphere of experience in order to add to the experience of each other and to the One.

You are not referred to as numbers once you elevate yourselves to a certain extent beyond this physical plane. You will never see some great shining spirit coming to you on one of spiritual planes saying: 'I want *three* of you to come with me.' There is no need for that. There is a tapping into the Oneness and you will know at any time what is requested of you, what you wish to do and whom you wish to join with. There comes a time, quite early on in spiritual evolution through the cleansing spheres, where it is almost an insult to regard anything as a division or to number things or to look at a certain aspect of creation and say that there are 'X number of souls' joining with what you want to do. It is almost an insult because you are going against yourself by creating a division in your thoughts. There is *no* division, and it is the division on an earthly level that causes the problems.

If I could (and I have said this before) I would tear up many of your spiritual books. I would tear them up! I would tear the ones up that involve you in the head-mind. I would tear the ones up that purportedly come from a number of divisions that attribute numbers and dimensions and councils and levels to Creation. All of these things exist in a sense – in that you have a gradation of the evolution of your personal and group vibration – but there is no division that can be labelled and numbered. We are not looking at division – we are looking at *evolution*. If you regard your spiritual journey as evolution rather than a number of steps, then you are beginning to see things in true focus rather than how you view them at present.

Let me just view my thoughts because this is a complicated subject...

[*There followed a short pause in communication.*]

Yes, before I finish I wish to come back to devas. We have discussed devas in this book and the way that animals (as you see them) are created by the devas and are part of One ...part of the deva mind. When you arrive in the spiritual realms, in the initial spheres you will see that those creations of devas are still manifesting and you will see what you regard as 'human souls' and 'animal souls' existing together and travelling together in Oneness. So, I have to, again, stress *the sanctity of animal life*; and I have to say that the aspect of life that you callously slaughter and eat at the moment – you will, at some short point in your future, be travelling the same road with. How will that make you feel?

## How will that make you feel?

The same is true, of course, of the violence that you inflict on each other. If you attack someone verbally, mentally or physically, *those attacks are against you* and one day you will be travelling the *same road*. No matter what position you are at on the road – whether you are far ahead on the horizon or back here just moving slowing forwards – you will be travelling the same road with the people that you have attacked and have wronged verbally, mentally or physically. How will that make you feel?

## *All that* can be avoided by realising that you are One.

## There is *only* One.

I think I have expressed myself sufficiently. It is difficult because there is only a certain 'slot', as it were, in which I can gather my thoughts, and I have to extract from Michael's mind those images and 'sew' them together into a 'tapestry' that makes sense. I could 'stand', as it were, at a lectern and talk to you for hours – if only the connection was strong enough to allow me to do that, but the Earth closes in and shuts out the communication that I wish to get through. So, I can only push through salient points and pray, as I do before I come here, that those salient points have each been covered as I give my address.

Questions, please!

**Jane:** Joseph, could I ask a question about maths and creativity, please? On this level, if we are creating something such as a chair, we need measurements because of the dense physicality of our reality. In the spirit realms, we can create a chair from the 'no-thing' simply through visualisation so we don't need any measurements. Then, our ultimate creativity when we go back out into Infinity is to make worlds, but isn't there some kind of maths involved in that process because we are creating a kind of division to make an individual world and we might, for example, have a *number* of moons orbiting that planet? You have also said in an earlier chapter that the physical form chosen to house the angelic spirit often has *two* arms and *two* legs – so isn't there is a slight need for maths in creation?

**Joseph:** There is a need for process and a need for creation – not for maths. Your physical mind has surrounded a process with a further process. As an angelic being (which you are now, of course) when you are creating *it is visual*. It is love of creation. It is examination, via a portion of the angelic host, of what you wish to create. It is as though you gather together to share those aspects of the One and you project into the 'centre' (for want of a better word) that which you wish to create and you examine it. You examine its potential – as I said the angelic children did before they decided on the wrong path that created the Fall. Do you see thus far?

**Jane:** Yes.

**Joseph:** So, you are not actually taking out a tape measure or ruler or looking at angles and shapes, but you are looking at prospects and potential and ...(trying to translate it into earthly terms)... that potential is *visual* and is *sensory*. So, you project into the centre of your collective being that which you wish to create, and you examine it to the point where you then bring it forth as a part of creation so that others can examine it and move through it. You don't measure it – *you appreciate that which it can be*. Does that make sense?

**Jane:** I suppose my point is that the physical form visualised for people to travel through a planet usually has *two* arms and *two* legs [*reference to chapter nine*] – so there is still a need for maths in that the limbs are *two* in number.

**Joseph:** [*Laughing*] I see what you mean, but again that is the form. Your form, as you see it, has two arms and two legs but that is only because you have assigned the word 'two' to the appendages that you have. You are a complete being. You put out aspects of that being in order to react in a certain way on this level. Now, those aspects present themselves as what you have described for millennia as 'two arms and two legs' but [*laughing*] they are aspects of that being that allow you to function in the way that you need to function on this planet. They are not measurements – they are projections. You are a complete being.

How can I put this? …You are a projection of that which you need in order to function here. And, that which you need in order to function here after the effects of the Fall manifested itself as the body that you have. Do you see that?

**Jane:** Yes.

**Joseph:** But it is not a division. It is an application [*laughing*] or 'an App' as you say currently. It is a focal point that appears in a certain way, but it is One and is part of the Oneness. Have I made that clear?

**Jane:** Yes, you have. Thank you.

**David:** Joseph, as you were talking then – an image of waves on the sea came to mind and how each wave appears to be individuated from the other waves, but there is only one sea. Perhaps we should stop looking at quantity and think more of quality.

**Joseph:** Yes, everything is part of you so there is no division but simply, as you say, the *one* 'sea' of waves or vibrations. The division comes from the way that you view things. The whole numerical system comes from trying to quantify that which you need and that which you perceive as not being you. It originates from: 'There is an aspect outside of myself that I need to be aware of ...there is another ...there is another ...there is another.' Whereas, if you see yourself as part of that 'sea' and realise that that wave that is you is never-ending, and – just as waves repeat – you repeat in different circumstances, then the need to divide yourself mentally from other aspects of You diminishes. Do you see that?

**David:** Yes.

**Joseph:** They are no longer threats. At present, you see them either as threats or quantities that you feel you need in order to survive. When you realise that you always survive and realise that you are part of everything else, then quantities become irrelevant ...*become irrelevant*!

You see the difficulty we have in explaining to you that the way your mind is used to working is not the way in which it should work. These things are *ingrained* into you and have been ingrained into you for centuries and centuries and centuries, but that doesn't make them right. It doesn't make them spiritual truths – it just makes them a way in which you see the world. What I am suggesting is that there is *another way* to see the world. What I am also suggesting is that God never, ever sees a division. He sees those facets of Himself but not as a division. He sees them as facets that are constantly bringing back information and experience to Him so that the Oneness can become a greater Oneness. Again, is that sufficient?

**David:** Yes, thank you.

**Tony:** Joseph, I understand what you are saying and think I have taken in today's chapter, but when you look at the application of it – we are so divided in our thinking in every aspect of our day-to-day lives. If I think of football matches and the way that people act with an 'us and them' attitude, or how our education system is based on winners and losers, or the way the business model is also based on winners and losers – the re-education that is needed to get this truth over is going to be very difficult and will to have to start in the education process at a very early age. It is a huge task.

**Joseph:** It is 'an unlearning' and it *is* a huge task, and the examples that you have given are excellent. But, nevertheless, if you wish to stop repeating the pattern that brings you to cataclysm ...stasis ...and reincarnation ...cataclysm ...stasis ... and reincarnation – *at some stage* that information has to be understood. In order for it to be understood, what is required of your children and what is required of your business systems is that, built into the schedule of each day is some time – usually at the start of the day – spent in silence, contemplation and a request for inspiration.

All this goes back to themes that I have illustrated before where you have pushed God out. If you substitute the word 'Oneness' for 'God' – you have pushed the Oneness out, and it is the Oneness that needs to be acknowledged in order for you to return to a state of angelic bliss on this planet.

One of the illustrations was particularly excellent where you were talking about football matches, because in a football match you have a 'oneness' operating in a negative way. The people in the crowd that becomes a mob that becomes violent are still operating in oneness but concentrating on those aspects of the oneness that they have decided are 'suitable' for that event and, unfortunately, that very often is violence.

To be a success in business spiritually, you have to remove the word 'need' because the word 'need' comes from perception of there being 'you' and 'not you' and the belief that you need some of the 'not you' to support the 'you'. If businesses wished to succeed spiritually, they would have to acknowledge that there is only the You and that they are creating something that is also of benefit to all the other aspects of the You as well as to themselves. If businesses started in that way, believed that was what they were going to do and meditated on that every day – then the businesses created would benefit *all* the aspects of You and the fear would be taken out of business. Is it not true that much of business is based on fear ...fear of *I have to have so much of the 'not me' otherwise the 'not me' will destroy my business tomorrow*? Much of business is run, not on harmony or a vision of creation – but on seeking to combat those other aspects of the You ...the businesses that are not their business. Does that make sense?

**Tony:** Yes, certainly.

**Joseph:** All would be in harmony, and it is not a fairy tale. It is not a pipe dream. It is not a daydream. I am not being an idealist – I am simply stating how things are beyond your sphere of thinking. And, if your sphere of thinking is to *change*, then you have to recognise the way that things are at your core. In acknowledging and examining the way that things are at your core and bringing out what you find there into your daily lives, you change things *for the better*. There is this ripple that runs through mankind that always wants to change things for the better. If you truly want to change things for the better, you have to acknowledge what you are. You have to acknowledge and draw out what is at your core and apply it to this world.

I almost feel as if I have to apologise and say: 'I am sorry you have to drop so many aspects of what you believe to be true.' I shouldn't be apologising because if you drop those aspects – you discover something far better ...a far better way to live ...the *original* way to live and the original approach you had to those around you.

The mind loves complexity and the Field, of course, loves complexity (as I have said so many times), so anything that involves you in complexity and involves you in seeing yourself as separate, needy, lacking and in ill-health is a wonderful gift to the Field. So, through your physical mind, which you find so hard to let go of for a time each day [*reference to meditation*], the Field anchors onto those aspects of yourself that keep you viewing yourself as separate and *that* feeds the Field. Does that make sense?

**Tony:** Thank you, Joseph.

[*There followed the usual four- or five-minute silence waiting for Michael to come out of trance, but then to our surprise Joseph returned with the following short postscript.*]

**Joseph:** I want to add a paragraph regarding astrology and numerology. I wish to say that these things too – based on numbers, of course – are an attempt by the mind to interpret what is actually happening on a spiritual level through a numerical system. Of course, astrology (as I have said in previous addresses) works because it is a look at the mechanics of the 'great machine' that exists in order to bring out certain karmic conditions and aspects of challenge to the inhabitants of the Earth. Where numerology is concerned, what the person is actually doing by the so-called 'crunching of numbers' is dipping into the intuition, dipping into the soul-view of a person and dipping into the vibration that exists beyond a name or date and interpreting that vibration.

In both cases, the numbers that are used are simply a means of interpreting that which is happening spiritually. So, the ability to understand the movements of the 'great machine' can be done ultimately without numbers, but the numbers on this level are a handy reference that allows that interpretation to be given form.

Similarly, the interpretation of numbers in numerology is a further step away from what is actually happening, which is a dip into the vibration of a person by connecting with them and expressing that vibration as numbers.

In both cases, the numbers are a construct that has actually put a further complexity onto those two aspects of divination. Those aspects of divination exist, as do many others spiritually, but it is the way that they are expressed through numbers that adds a further layer. And, those who are involved in those aspects of divination, through meditation and connection with the core, will find with practice that they are able to express all the aspects that they now express through astrology or numerology but to a *purer* intent by relaxing their numerical hold on the processes that are taking place.

I am sorry that I have had to call Michael back to do this, but I felt that it was important to add this into the section on numbers and Oneness.

## Chapter Eighteen
# The Lighthouse

*...an Inspiration, an Invitation, a Meditation*

**Joseph:** Chapter eighteen – *The Lighthouse ...an Inspiration, an Invitation, a Meditation.* In this book I have tried to illustrate the fact that what you perceive as empty spaces in your life and thin air *are anything but* and that you co-inhabit this Earth with a variety of spiritual beings. Not only that, but you are immersed in a kind of 'psychic soup' ...you are immersed in the thoughts, intentions and dominant vibrations of the Field of mankind at any given moment.

However, having explained that there are no 'spaces between', I have to say that in a sense *there is one very vital 'space between'* ...one very vital gap in your experience that needs to be filled. And, that gap is the space that you created in your heart between yourselves and your God at the time of the Fall. Were I to include the details of the Fall at this point, I would have to insert a complete book, so I would recommend that you also read ***the Fall*** *[reference to Joseph's fourth book]* if you have reached this point and are intrigued by my allusion to this event and my insistence that the Earth and society are not working as they should spiritually 'due to the Fall'.

The gap in your heart is a space that you created at the time of the Fall because, at that point, you decided subconsciously – and later consciously – that you had separated yourselves from your

God and, as civilisations *plural* (because there have been more than one) evolved, you decided that you had separated yourselves from each other ...that you were individual ...that you were not connected ...and that to a certain extent 'survival was the name of the game'. So, survival was the reason that you sought power, the reason that you sought to control other people and the reason why you had to be harsh in your dealings with other people, in your dealings with the animal kingdom and in your dealings with the Earth.

**That gap needs to be filled again.**

That gap needs to be taken away. That gap prevents you and everyone else on this planet from reconnecting to the Divinity-within ...to the Source that brings you healing ...to the Source that brings you abundance ...to the Source that brings you peace of mind ...to the Source that brings you spiritual knowledge ... to the Source that brings you peace ...to the Source that brings you spiritual bliss.

As I have stated at length in all the other books, **the only way to fill that gap is with Light** because Light is the 'tool' that you possess as spiritual beings that enables you to create ...Light is the 'limb' that allows you to reach out to others and to touch their hearts ...Light is the energy and illumination that shines on all the aspects of this world that are skewed and allows you to recognise those aspects and to put them right.

I said at the beginning of this chapter that there was 'an invitation' – and the invitation is to those of you who, having read this book and perhaps some of the others, *feel* that there is something you must do about the state of the Earth, about the state of souls here and about the state of society.

If you feel that you do not want to do anything, then you must move on until such time as you *do* want to do something; but I warn you that eventually you will have to do something because, ultimately, *you are the saviour of your own soul*. So, at some point, you will be moved from within – away from materialism and society as it is – inwards to make a difference, to re-establish your spiritual heritage and to move onwards from this state of affairs.

But, for those of you who *do* wish to do something and are asking at this point: 'Well, Joseph, what can I do?' *You can become a beacon and a channel for the Light.* To this end, I wish to give you a meditation that will help you to channel the Light daily and to send out that Light. Your transformation of society and yourself begins *now*. The minute that you read and practise this meditation, you can begin to change things. And, as you change things, you will become more aware spiritually. You will leave behind your former life by small degrees *and everything will be different.* So, the following meditation and the invitation to become a Light-bearer [*smiling*] carry a 'health warning' ...in that your health will be better ...in that your vision will be changed ...in that your attitude towards yourself, your life, your children, your relatives, your neighbours and everyone on Earth will change from this point ...*and it has to change.*

So, let us presume that, having read this book, you are at a point where you know how to relax and how to go into a state of meditation and self-contemplation. And, we begin this meditation by inviting you to relax ...inviting you to become quiet and to be still ...inviting you to let go of the cares, worries and concerns of the material life around you. Worries about your job, your family and your finances have no place here during this meditation – so let them go! In letting them go, you will create and experience freedom of the spirit.

[*Michael: Please only follow Joseph's meditation below at the point at which you feel suitably prepared for it – whether this preparation takes you a few minutes or half an hour. A quiet, calm, relaxed state of mind will allow you to use your God-given imagination effectively, helping you to more easily visualise the environment detailed in the narrative and allowing you to be of great use as a Light-worker.*]

## The Meditation

Having let go of your cares, *wherever* you are meditating ...perhaps at home in your favourite chair in your favourite room, or at work during your lunch break on a park bench somewhere... I want you to imagine that your spirit self – *the true you* – now stands up and emerges from you. You are not separated (because the material and spiritual manifestations of you are always linked by the silver 'umbilical cord' until such time as you move on into the spiritual realms) but are able, as your spirit self, to be the seat of consciousness of the two of you and to move around independently of the physical self.

So, wherever you are, you walk away from your physical self and you see ahead of you a mist ...a mist that covers all the things you would normally see from this vantage point via your physical self. You walk into the mist and it envelops you. Having enveloped you, it then clears and you find yourself in a completely different place. You are not in your house; you are not in the park... You are on a rocky shore looking out to sea, and you can hear the waves beating softly against the shore. There is a very calming rhythm to the waves, and over to one side you see a cliff towering up from the beach ...and at the top of the cliff you can see a Lighthouse.

Now, there are three means of reaching this Lighthouse ...you can go up the cliff face where, zigzagging their way up from the beach, there are steps cut into the rock ...or there is an elevator within a transparent tube set into the side of the cliff ...or you may simply float up to the Lighthouse if you wish to. The choice is yours! It all depends on your view of daily life (if you are frightened of heights – use the lift, and if you are claustrophobic – use the steps). Let us assume, for the sake of this written meditation, that you use the lift. So, you go over to the foot of the cliff where, set into its base, is a lift with sliding doors which open to admit you. You step in, the doors close and you feel the lift start to move upwards. The lift is illuminated and, as you move higher and higher up the transparent tube at the side of the cliff, you can look out across the shore and across the ocean as the lift travels towards the top of the cliff.

When you reach the top of the cliff, the lift doors open and there is a little path leading from it across to the base of the Lighthouse. You walk calmly over to the base of the Lighthouse and the door of the Lighthouse swings open. Again, you have the choice of either steps that spiral upwards around the curved walls towards the Light or, within the central core of the Lighthouse, there is another elevator. For the sake of this written version of the meditation, let us go for the lift and, again, you are pulled upwards by this mechanism. Out of the windows positioned at intervals in the side of the Lighthouse walls, you can see further across the ocean, across the shoreline and across the land that leads down to the shore. Very quickly the lift doors open and you find yourself in the top section of the Lighthouse. You can see within its framework a powerful lamp that is at the moment extinguished.

You go over to the guard rail surrounding the top of the Lighthouse and you look out to sea, you look across the shore, and you look at the land that slopes down towards the beach. Then, suddenly you are able to see with *psychic eyes* and you can see *people*. You can see people in all countries; you can see people on the oceans; you can see people in aeroplanes. You can see *all* the people around the world ...different countries ...different cultures ...different attitudes ...

different approaches to life. And, in all these people – men, women and children of all ages – you see a *greyness* and *a need*. You cannot describe how you know there is a need, but you can see this thirst, this need, this *gap* within each of these people ...*and they are all turning towards you*. All their heads turn towards you – the men, the women, the children, the babies – all turn towards you as though you can do something about this and you can fill this gap for them.

...And, you have no idea at this point how to do so.

Then, suddenly into your heart-mind comes the *knowing* that you must turn towards the lamp that is behind you in this central top section of the Lighthouse. So, you reach out your hands and touch the surface of the glass surrounding the lens and, as you do so, a spark leaps from your heart and ignites the Light. And, the Light becomes brighter ...and brighter ...and *brighter* but doesn't hurt your eyes because you are in a spiritual body at this time. It begins to revolve ...slowly at first and then faster. And, as it revolves, you can see the Light seeking out every man, every woman and every child across the Earth. It illuminates those people in aeroplanes. It illuminates those people on ships. It illuminates the different countries. It illuminates the different places of worship. It illuminates the seats of power – the parliaments and heads of government. It illuminates the army bases and the people waiting for instructions to launch weapons. It illuminates those people in hospital beds.

**It illuminates *every* soul on Earth.**

And, as it illuminates them, they turn away from you and that great need they have of you *ends*. They turn instead and place their hands on their hearts and begin to smile. They change from grey souls into illuminated, irradiated beings of Light ...**and each of them remembers who they are because of you.** Each of them changes because of you. Each of them sets aside their materiality and their need to try and take from others because of not understanding that what they need is, not the power of others – but the power they have *within* themselves.

And, you see the waves illuminating. You see the land and the countries illuminating. You see the world illuminating. From this vantage point of the Lighthouse, it is as though you are looking out from space and you can see patches of Light beginning to grow around the Earth and starting to link up until the planet is a great shining orb in space.

As it illuminates to this extent, *you see the spaces between* ...the spaces between the Earth, the planets and the stars. You see them for what they really are. You see the wonderful, Divine-potential within each of them. You see the angelic host hard at work creating new spheres of experience. You see the Love that exists in every aspect of the universe – and universes. You see the Love that the angelic host has for every soul on Earth and for you.

The beauty is almost too much for you to bear, so you turn around and face the Light in the Lighthouse. Then something wonderful happens ...the Light condenses and the Lighthouse condenses and, instead of you being in the Lighthouse looking at the Light, *the Lighthouse and the Light are absorbed by you.* You look down at your chest and you can see the *Lighthouse shining out within your heart*, and you can feel that Light from yourself constantly circling ...seeking out every man, every woman, every child, every animal, every aspect of the Earth and the Earth *itself*.

Now, you find yourself back on the shore once more and, with this revolving Light radiating from your chest, you walk back along the shore to the point where everything becomes misty. You move through the mist and find your physical self, sitting, waiting to reintegrate with your spiritual self. You sit down within yourself and gently you let the Light subside, and you reconnect your spiritual self with your earthly self and *feel* that reintegration. You close down your chakras – asking God and asking your Higher Self to do so – so that you are protected from the Field of consciousness of mankind during your normal daily material life; and you come back to earthly consciousness *knowing* that that Light is shining from you all the time.

All it takes to fill the gap for yourself and for other people is a *recognition* of the Light-within. All it takes is a *volition* to shine that Light out. And, I say 'all it takes' but so few people do this **...and this is the *only* way that your world will change.** This is *the only way* that you will reintegrate with the spiritual plan that existed for this world before the time of the Fall. This is *the only way* that you will become aware of your angelic heritage. This is *the only way* that you will stop war ...that you will stop illness ...that you will stop famine ...that you will stop pushing yourselves further from each other rather than reintegrating.

**There is only *one* way and that is to re-establish the Light in this world and in each other.**

Once you do that *then* your endeavours materially to stop war have power. Once you do that *then* your endeavours to stop inhumanity, torture and brutality have power. Once you do that *then* your efforts to eradicate disease have power. Once you do that *then* your efforts to establish a perfect world have power.

### ...But until you do that – *they do not*!

Until you do that – *they do not* because you cannot act from the surface. You have to act from the spiritual centre. I hope in my books I have given you, not just something to think about *but a way to act*. I see quotations bandied about and I see spiritual values being talked about, but I do not see (apart from the few) a lot of action. My books are useless to you unless you act. If you think 'that was a nice read' today and tomorrow are back to the mindset that you had before you read the books, then I have failed. If the books trouble you, stir something within you and make you want to make a difference, then I have succeeded. And, our mission over countless years, as you measure time, has been to bring to you the knowledge that you *and only you* can effect change and that you *and only you* can take yourself out of the situation that you have put yourself in.

So, as a conclusion to this book, I would like to *appeal* to you. I would like to appeal to your conscience, I would like to appeal to your heart, and I would like to say: 'Pick yourself up!' I am so sad for you and so upset for you, and will continue to be sad and upset for you until the day that you decide to change. The day you decide to change, I can turn my back on you (and I am not being harsh by saying that) because you are your own point of Light again from that moment onwards.

Our soul group is ...'anxious' is an understatement but I would not say 'desperate'... is *hugely concerned* for the fate of mankind, for the fate of the planet, for the fate of the devas and for the fate of the animal kingdom. As I have said in other books, you are *perilously close to cutting off that Light within you* to the extent that the planet and civilisation will be entered into stasis, until such time as it can house the human spirit again and the pattern can be repeated.

Please take heed of these words. There are many spiritual books that say that you are fine and that things are getting better ...and it is good if you *are* fine and getting better... but my colleagues and I do not see that! We see a 'tinderbox' that is about to ignite, and you have already lit the 'fuse' that leads to destruction *yet again* if you do not stamp it out through your Light-bringing.

The choice is always yours, and I cannot show you the bliss that awaits you when you make that choice to reconnect with and give out the Light once again. I cannot show you, unfortunately, because you are steeped in the effects of the Fall and I cannot take the scales away from your eyes. Only you can do that. But, if I can give you a glimpse through my words and if I can spur you on to wish to take the scales away from your eyes yourself, then my mission is complete.

I feel that I have covered everything that I wished to cover in this book, but I want to talk for a little while about the nature of the mission with regard to *the Band of Light*.

First of all, I wish to say to *the Band of Light* that we have always been aware that, because of the limitations of the material world, there would come a time when trance was no longer viable for Michael. And, yes, I have put this out of my mind and, yes, I have wished that there would be further books that could be given in a trance state. But, we realise now – particularly with the effects of the world on Michael and on each of you as your physical bodies and minds grow older – that it is no longer viable for that trance state to be entered into because there is too much risk to Michael. We have great plans for you *all* to further *the Communications* and it is of no use to us to have Michael completely unable to function and unable to promote and expand the message to as many people as possible. So, with *huge* Love and with *huge* respect for what you have accomplished thus far, **I am withdrawing my facility to go into trance with Michael.**

...But, having said that, my connection with Michael is by no means over because *our ongoing task together* is to make people aware of the message that we have brought through. So, on occasions when Michael is tired or his mind isn't quick enough in interview situations to come up with the answer that I would like to give, *I will give it.* I will give it through a clairvoyant, clairaudient and clairsentient connection – almost as though he has been taken over in trance but without the injurious effects of that state of body, mind and spirit. So, [*smiling*] I am saying you have not heard the last of Joseph! I am also saying that in quiet times there will be much more that I can bring through and put into words but without the debilitating effect on Michael that has been happening of late.

As a 'reward' (if that is the right word for the work you have done thus far) I also wish to remind you that you are here *through volition* and that *through volition* you each decided to take on board the mission and you each decided ...(and I almost want to say 'against your better judgement')... to reincarnate and to come together to culminate a mission that has taken hundreds of years to set up. There have been generations before you, which ironically you have also been a part of – generations of a small number of souls that came together in successive incarnations with the express intent of providing the means *in this incarnation* for the four of you to actually bring this information through. It has been a huge concern for many years. It is strange because, when you return to the spirit realms and to the soul groups, it will be as though you haven't been away. It will be as though you have sent yourself out on a 'business trip' and have come back at exactly the same point that you set off from but, from the point of the Earth, hundreds of years have passed.

A key person in the expansion of the mission has been Joan* and she is here on the 'sidelines', as it were, this morning listening to the proceedings. And, as Joan is saying, she had no idea during her earthly life that this mission was being undertaken. She had no idea when training Michael to work mediumistically that this was part of a far larger concern to bring *the Joseph Communications* to Earth so that people could choose to look at spirituality in a different way. And, she and Michael reincarnated together at certain points in the past.

Over incarnations in the past you have been drawn towards each other. In some incarnations you did not meet, although you were in a close proximity to each other physically. In other incarnations, you *did* meet. In some incarnations you were totally unaware of the mission that you would undertake, but each step in those incarnations brought you closer together and strengthened the facilities that you now have in order to get the word out and to fulfil the mission.

We also had to select a point in time where your technology would be at a suitable stage to enable you, without persecution and without too much restriction, to spread the word *globally*. And, I hope that answers for you why you appear to be at a certain stage in your lives that is not ideal from the point of view of energy ...in other words, as you have all asked: 'Would it not have been better for us to have done this when we were younger?' The technology and the means to get the message out, as you are doing now, weren't available when you were younger.

So, I want to remind you that you are not who you appear to be and that your daily worries – your worries about health, worries about finance, worries about integration with a society that you feel you don't want to integrate with – *all* these things are surface only and that you are each older souls. I know I have in the past said 'you are *all* old souls', referring to everyone on Earth ...what I should say is that you four are all *'experienced* souls'. You have all taken on this journey from the viewpoint of spiritual experience. What is so sad for us (and, therefore, sad for you) is that, each time you incarnate, you lose that memory and have to work to re-establish it; and you can only re-establish it *partially* within the confines of the Fall and the Field of mankind.

Your mission – and *my* mission – is not over yet. There has to be a change and there has to be a point at which mankind realises that it is not a materially-based life form. We pray ...we are excited about ...we trust that *this time* there will be that change, or certainly the seeds will have been sown for that change.

And, in answer to an unspoken question [*laughing*] ...no, you do not have to come back and do this again *unless you wish to*! There was great debate for quite some 'time', as you measure time here, before you decided to undertake this mission many, many, many years ago. Great debate! ...Who would be best to go into the Field? ...Who would be best to receive the information? ...Who would be best to be reawakened once they were in an earthly body? Because you have to understand that, for each of you, there has been a reawakening and that there have been people and circumstances around you since your birth that have pushed you into a spiritual state of mind; that have reopened your spiritual memories to an extent; that have made you curious about spiritual matters and that have made you want to seek them out. All those connections – all those souls and situations that have done that – have had to be set up and put in place.

The experiences of the reincarnations before this one were to strengthen you for this particular one. It was not as though you could reincarnate and *in one lifetime* come to the point where you could bring out this message and where you could connect to us. And so, it has had to be in gradations and in bursts of energy that have taken you closer to this particular incarnation.

It was decided by Jane that she would incarnate to be the strength that Michael would require because of the sensitivity that he would need in this lifetime in order to connect with me, and that sensitivity makes him particularly vulnerable.

It was decided that Tony would have a 'Road to Damascus' journey in this lifetime and that he would go through a process of self-examination, which at times would seem to baffle him and almost bring him to his knees, in order that he could rise above that and then could be pushed towards Michael, Jane and David – just as they were pushed towards him at *exactly* the right time.

It was decided with David that he would be born with the compulsion to investigate things paranormal and to decide for himself what resonated and what didn't. It is amusing to us that David's vast store of books is hardly ever referred to because he has learnt that lesson and instead goes within and reasons it out for himself. However, the compulsion to store that knowledge is still within him *materially* and so he still seeks out the books.

There have been others around you that have had to be influenced, not that they were vital parts of the journey for you – but were vital parts of pushing you towards the point where you could open up to the soul group and to myself, and we have had to influence them. Through their free will we have had to suggest to them, during the night time when they were asleep or when their minds were switched off, that it would be good for them to do this ...or to open a book ...or to go down a certain street ...or to make a telephone call ...or to go to a certain meeting *so that they could influence you as well.* Nothing is done in isolation.

Also, there are the main instigators of the soul group with regard to communication and they have worked with you for more than one lifetime.

I wanted to remind you of all this because on a physical level you appear to be growing older and, of course, the Field pulls at you. The Field wants to pull you in and say: 'Forget about that spiritual stuff! Forget about the mission and concentrate instead on the aches and pains, the lack of energy and the inability to do today what you could do yesterday.'

So, I wanted to remind you of who you *really are* and that there is purpose in each day and that you touch souls each day. I wanted also to say to you that the books have gone out to so many people and ...have *here* healed someone who was in grief ...have *here* healed someone who has looked at illness in a different way ...have *here* stopped someone being angry ...have *here* stopped someone from resenting someone else ...have *here* touched someone to forgive ...and have *across the world* reignited those Lights that I talked about earlier in the chapter.

So, never doubt what you are doing, and never doubt that there is much more to do and that we will call on you to do *much more* because you agreed to do that! I know that that is a very glib thing to say, but *you agreed to do that* in that you said from your spiritual point of view and spiritual heart: 'Yes, I can cope with this. Yes, I am willing to go back into the challenges and to work until my last breath if I possibly can to bring through this message because, from my standpoint in the group soul, I understand how necessary this is …that everyone has to get out from the effects of the Fall …that the Earth has to be rededicated …that the devas have to be freed …and that things have to be as they were and as they were intended to be angelically from the beginning.'

I won't invite questions on this occasion, but I will say that the latter half of the chapter *should* be included in the book because I think it is important that people understand the *gravity of the mission*. I also think it is important that people should understand that they too are part of soul groups and that certain of them also have a *similar* mission.

I am inextricably linked to you and will be until you come back to the spirit realms and beyond, but there are other points of Light across the world. There is the *same mission* being expressed in different terms, and we pray that that mission will not become bogged down by religion, by dogma and by cultural viewpoints that have no meaning. Only the core truths of the mission have meaning. I want you to include this information because someone today, in reading this book right now, will say: 'Yes, that is what *I* have to do. Yes, I have always thought that I am part of this movement.' Or, someone will say: 'So, that is what it is about. That is my destiny – to be part of a soul group. I have another life beyond this life and that fills me with joy and fills me with new purpose.' **…And, we do need those of you who are dedicated enough to become that 'Lighthouse'.**

No questions please, but are there any comments?

**David:** Thank you! Thank you, Joseph.

**Tony:** Just heartfelt gratitude to be part of the project.

**Joseph:** With my usual sense of humour I would say: 'Wait until the end of your life [*laughing*] before you say *heartfelt gratitude*.' And, we know that there are times when it is very, very difficult for you. We are aware of that, and *our heartfelt gratitude* is to you as our family that has journeyed 'abroad', as our family that is out in hostile territory and as our family that we can protect to some extent but pray for constantly, because we are aware that the hostile territory envelops you, seeks to pull you down and doesn't want this mission to succeed.

**Jane:** Joseph, in the interests of keeping the Joseph message pure, now that you are no longer communicating through Michael, there could conceivably be someone else at some point claiming to be bringing through *your teachings*, so I just wanted a clarification of whether you will be speaking through any other medium in the future.

**Joseph:** Well, first of all, I have to say that I *am* still communicating through Michael. It is like having different channels on a radio, where trance has been one channel but clairvoyance is another – as are clairaudience and clairsentience. But, also, I am an inspiration to Michael in his composing of spiritual material for articles and for social media connections and, as I said in the chapter, I am not going anywhere. None of the soul group is going anywhere except to be connected to you directly for the rest of your lives.

The connection between Michael and myself goes back some considerable time and is to do with aspects of his soul memory that I am not at liberty to reveal, but I have known him in more ways than just what he sees as a connection to a spirit that 'came on the scene', as it were, a number of years ago. There is a greater knowledge of each other than is apparent in what I have told you thus far, but I am not allowed to say what that is. The fine-tuning of that communication between us was reliant on that connection that we already had as souls. And, the references that Michael has made in recent days to being 'hardwired to me', as though there is a permanent connection, *is correct*. The connection between the two of us is a very sophisticated one. It is almost at a molecular level, if you will, which allows the flow of energy backwards and forwards between us.

I am not connected to other mediums and am not connected to any other group because the mission is so grave that I need to connect to the members of the soul group that are out on Earth as part of *this* particular mission.

As I mentioned before, that is not to say that there aren't other *similar missions* taking place across the world, but I am related to you as part of a particular soul group and as part of a particular communication. So, although I can inspire people through the books and will pop in here and there, as I can, to give an inspiration to someone, **I do not directly communicate through any other medium or any other group.** Is that sufficient?

**Jane:** Yes. And, finally, thank you so much on behalf of all the readers. For many years, on almost a daily basis, I have received e-mails and letters from people saying how your books have changed their lives, that the information is what they have been searching for all their lives, and many of them say that they *do* send out the Light ...so, on their behalf, THANK YOU!

**Joseph:** It is with a great sense of *relief* that we feel the Light 'switched on' as people read the books; and it is with great *gratitude* that we send Love, healing and inspiration to all those that have taken the message into themselves and have decided to work on behalf of the soul group and on behalf of Creation to re-establish Light here. We send out Love to *all* souls, but what I am trying to express is that we are moved – not just me but all the members of the soul group – by *each* soul that reconnects to its spiritual heritage as a result of examining the information that we have brought through and acting upon it. We are moved and we are greatly relieved but, having said that, there is also so much *more* work to do.

And, *with permission* we will help those at their time of passing, who have re-discovered the Light through the books, as we are permitted to do. In other words, we will try to assist their passing and try to assist their re-establishment of the spiritual senses, as a result of them taking on board the spiritual truth that is behind the words in the books. We will be able to help to a certain extent and that is a wonderful thing too. So, it is almost like 'an escape committee' – as though, as an analogy, we have souls that are emerging from 'a tunnel they have dug out' back into the Light and we are secretly taking them away when their time comes ...never to return [*smiling*] to the facility that they have been incarcerated in.

Was there anything further?

**Jane:** No, thank you.

**Joseph:** In that case – *and I must stress this is not a goodbye* – I am on hand and am available *instantly* as Michael's energies allow via the established link of clairvoyance, clairaudience and clairsentience. This is not a tearful or sad occasion because I am not going anywhere.

**I am not going anywhere *until we all go somewhere* ...**and we *all* go somewhere at that point when this group and my soul group moves through that 'hatch' into Infinity.

* Joan was Michael's spiritual teacher.

# Revelation

## who you are, why you're here

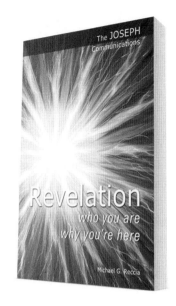

...a book to change your world.

In this first book of the series, Joseph invites you to understand who and what you really are, where you came from, why you are here and the miraculous things you are capable of, revealing the amazing potential of the human spirit and presenting a plan to change the future of this planet before it's too late.

Intelligent, thought-provoking, non-religious. In direct, concise language, **Revelation** will revolutionise your views about life and the nature of reality, empowering you through a new awareness of the active part you play in creation and inspiring you to look at your world in a whole new light.

---

'I've read every metaphysical book I could get my hands on for years but there is information in this book I've not come across anywhere before. I would wholeheartedly recommend this series to anyone seeking answers and the inspiration to finding wisdom within.' *jmj4 (Amazon).*

'Whatever your religion Revelation will inspire and help you to understand why we are here on this planet and make you think about the way you are living your life.' *Joy (Amazon).*

'The most direct and compelling book on spirituality I have ever read.' *G. R. Munro-Hall (Amazon).*

---

£13.95 (ISBN: 978-1-906625-07-8)

From good bookshops, Amazon, and direct from

www.thejosephcommunications.co.uk

e-Book also available for Kindle, iPad and other platforms. Listen to the audiobook.

# Illumination

## change yourself, change the world

...A powerful manual for personal and global transformation.

Time is running out; Earth is heading for cataclysm! **Illumination** reveals how we can literally save this world ...before it's too late.

We need to change and accept personal responsibility now – or Joseph warns there are only three generations left. The Field is so polluted by mankind's negative energy that the planet cannot sustain itself much longer unless radical changes are made to the way we think.

**Illumination** provides all the 'tools' needed to achieve personal and global enlightenment, empowering readers to direct Light and transmute negativity into harmony, joy, love, peace and spiritual progression.

There is great urgency to Joseph's words – we do not have an infinite number of tomorrows in which to put things right.

---

'Read the book, adopt its practices, discover a new life of spiritual harmony and lasting fulfilment.' *Jan Quigley.*

'A masterpiece of spiritual work! What is very clever is the way Joseph builds up his case throughout this book with possibilities to test his meditations as you go – this is not dry theory! I will certainly continue the daily Light-work which I now regard as essential.' *Tony Cross.*

'If you wish to bring peace, joy and abundance to yourself and those you love this book gives you the means.' *Mr. C. Fraser-Malcolm (Amazon).*

---

£12.95 (ISBN: 978-1-906625-09-2)

Available from good bookshops, Amazon, and direct from

www.thejosephcommunications.co.uk

e-Book also available for Kindle, iPad and other platforms. Listen to the audiobook.

# Your Life After Death

## ...your final destination is anything but final!

Countless opportunities and wonders await beyond physical death.

In **Your Life After Death** Joseph delivers arguably the most comprehensive account ever written of what lies ahead when you leave this world behind.

An essential source of comfort and inspiration, **Your Life After Death** is the definitive guide to the afterlife...

... read it and you'll never look at the next life, or, indeed, this one, in quite the same way again.

---

'Packed with very important information, which should have been made available many, many years ago.' *David Feuerstein.*

'The book is outstanding and one of immense value to humanity, particularly in contrast to the mumbo-jumbo we are exposed to in various religions and philosophies.' *Scott Rabalais.*

'Over the years I have read many books on this subject but none have been more informative and in-depth.' *Peggy Sivyer.*

'I have never sat up nearly all night and read a book from cover to cover in one go before and it has had a major impact on me.' *Valerie Ann Riddell.*

---

£14.95 (ISBN: 978-1-906625-03-0)

Available from good bookshops, Amazon, and direct from

www.thejosephcommunications.co.uk

e-Book also available for Kindle, iPad and other platforms. Listen to the audiobook.

# the Fall

## you were there, it's why you're here

...aeons ago everything changed – AND YOU WERE THERE!

You have forgotten the cataclysm that created today's dysfunctional societies and wounded planet...

In **the Fall**, Joseph reactivates that astonishing inner knowledge of your spiritual origins.

By the last page, many, if not *all*, of those elusive answers regarding existence and the great mysteries will be elusive no longer.

From the Big Bang to your role in creation... if you seek meaning to life in general, and your life in particular, you *absolutely, definitely* should read **the Fall**.

...Your views of spirituality, science, and reality are about to change forever.

---

'If I had to be on a desert island with only one book, this would be it.' *James D'Angelo.*

'The Fall is the most important spiritual book ever written.' *Jean Whittle.*

'I have been on this journey for more than 40 years and this book just joins all the dots for me. It is astonishing. It is of vital importance, please read it.' *Katydr (Amazon).*

'Here are the answers to life's impossible contradictions, and what we can do for ourselves and others – brilliant!' *Jan (Amazon).*

'One of the most powerful and influential books in my entire life, completely altering my world view.' *Peter De Ruyter.*

---

£14.95 (ISBN: 978-1-906625-05-4)

Available from good bookshops, Amazon, and direct from:

www.thejosephcommunications.co.uk

e-Book also available for Kindle, iPad and other platforms. Listen to the audiobook.

1st May, 2019

Dear Ellen,

Please find the enclosed copy of *the* Spaces Between.

Thank you for your order.

With kindest wishes,

Jane
jkneen@bandoflight.co.uk

# Band of Light

M E D I A

with compliments

**Tel:** +44 (0)1282 431759 **Website:** www.josephspeaks.com **E-mail:** info@bandoflight.co.uk
**Band of Light Media Ltd,** 10 Sparrable Row, Briercliffe, Burnley, Lancashire. BB10 3QW.

# Trance Mission

## enlightening—informing—a record of Joseph in Public

Over three years Joseph was asked more than 150 questions during 12 remarkable trance demonstrations.

His illuminating, eloquent answers are reproduced in this double-sized, 448-page book, in which Joseph focuses on and expands our understanding of a wide range of spiritual topics, including:

pre-destiny and choice • the nature of time • Indigo children • meditation techniques • God • aliens • reincarnation • angels • past-life baggage • sexual energy • healing • the Bible • animals • infant mortality • ascension ...and many more.

Shot through with Joseph's refreshingly no-nonsense approach to spirituality and presenting practical, illuminating, deeply spiritual information throughout, **Trance Mission** also gives insight into Joseph's background and relationship with Michael, immersing readers in the unique atmosphere of his public appearances.

---

'Rarely do you read any "channeled" material that answers questions directly and sensibly. This book does and I highly recommend it to anyone on their spiritual journey.' *Meria Heller.*

'Wonderful – many of the additional questions I had been asking after reading the other books have been answered.' *Rowen Harris.*

'Anyone seeking to be uplifted from this negative world view should read Trance Mission – much Love and Light and hope on every page.' *Christine Wood.*

'Trance Mission is a magnificent read - so many answers to questions that spiritual truth-seekers yearn to know.' *Joanna Eden.*

---

£16.95 (ISBN: 978-1-906625-06-1)

Available from good bookshops, Amazon, and direct from:

www.thejosephcommunications.co.uk

e-Book also available for Kindle, iPad and other platforms. Listen to the audiobook.

# From Here to Infinity

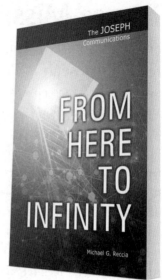

...In his sixth book Joseph clarifies, demystifies and redefines earthly concepts we take for granted and find ourselves immersed in, including: Time, Space, Energy, Perception, Memory and Infinity.

He also offers further insights into the nature of the Divine and reveals advanced ways of transforming and elevating our inner and outer worlds and infusing our lives and this planet with the highest expression of Light.

This 288-page volume is set to expand your ability to live in and give out the Light, empowering you to make a real difference by – literally – illuminating yourself, those around you, and the physical landscape you are a part of.

---

'Joseph REALLY gets into the nuts and bolts of what's NEEDED for us Warriors of the Light! I'm so humbled by this information.' *Jorge Castaneda.*

'I don't mind admitting the last chapter moved me to tears. This book has made me more determined than ever to meditate daily to send Light out to the world.' *Tracy Dewick.*

'I wish it were required reading in every school, library and institution, so important is the message.' *Jeannie Judd.*

---

£14.95 (ISBN: 978-1-906625-08-5)

Available from good bookshops, Amazon, and direct from:

www.thejosephcommunications.co.uk

e-Book also available for Kindle, iPad and other platforms. Listen to the audiobook.

# Many Voices, One Mission

## Group Soul wisdom from the Joseph perspective

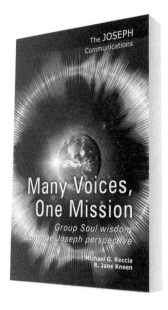

The new Joseph Communications title **Many Voices, One Mission**, giving voice to key members of Joseph's soul group through powerful lectures delivered over many years to medium Michael G. Reccia and life partner Jane, is now available.

Themed sections Life's Journey, Aspects of the Afterlife, The Sacred Earth, Spiritual Science, Connections, Co-Creation and Health and Healing feature wisdom from Joseph's co-workers, and transcripts of Michael's first two public trance demonstrations are also included, plus fascinating insights into how Michael and Jane's lives have been affected by regular interaction with spirit messengers.

---

'Such an inspirational book. Can't put it down. A beacon of Light like all the others. Thank you Michael and your amazing team.' *Deborah Almond.*

'EXCELLENT. Thank you for making it available to the world. Everybody should read it.' *Paul Carter.*

'I cannot keep my eyes/heart out of the book! Thanks to All. I am half way through and more than just once or twice I have cried.' *Margaret Coles.*

'Truly remarkable book and the "Mr Johnson" example really makes me feel at ease with my life, that our home is truly on the spirit side of life and death really should not be feared like it is at this time.' *Karl - Amazon.*

'Fantastic book brimming with wisdom and love.' *A Starkey - Amazon.*

---

£16.95 (ISBN: 978-1-906625-15-3)

Available from good bookshops, Amazon, and direct from:

www.thejosephcommunications.co.uk

e-Book also available for Kindle, iPad and other platforms.